ORGANIZING AND MANAGING THE LANGUAGE ARTS BLOCK

Solving Problems in the Teaching of Literacy

Cathy Collins Block, Series Editor

Organizing and Managing the Language Arts Block

A Professional Development Guide

Lesley Mandel Morrow

THE GUILFORD PRESS
New York   London

© 2003 The Guilford Press
A Division of Guilford Publications, Inc.
72 Spring Street, New York, NY 10012
www.guilford.com

Printed in the United States of America

This book is printed on acid-free paper.

Last digit is print number: 9 8 7 6 5 4 3 2 1

Library of Congress Cataloging-in-Publication Data

Morrow, Lesley Mandel.
     Organizing and managing the language arts block: a professional
development guide / Lesley Mandel Morrow.
         p.   cm. — (Solving problems in the teaching of literacy)
     Includes bibliographical references (p.   ) and index.
     ISBN 1-57230-794-3 (pbk.)
     1. Language arts (Elementary)—United States.   2. Language arts
(Elementary)—United States—Case studies.   3. Curriculum
planning—United States.   I. Title.   II. Series.
LB1576 .M82 2003
372.6—dc21
                                                                    2002005506

*I dedicate this book to the undergraduate and graduate students
I have taught, as well as the teachers I have worked with
in professional development settings.
These outstanding individuals have taught me so much
throughout my career. They are intelligent, hard-working,
dedicated professionals, whose love for teaching children to read
is inspiring.*

ABOUT THE AUTHOR

Lesley Mandel Morrow is a Professor of Literacy in the Graduate School of Education at Rutgers University in New Jersey. She received her PhD from Fordham University in New York City. Dr. Morrow began her career as a teacher in the early childhood grades, became a reading specialist, and now teaches courses in literacy development with an emphasis on early literacy. She works in inner-city schools coordinating staff development programs in literacy. The author of over 200 publications, including books, book chapters, and articles in journals such as *Reading Research Quarterly* and *The Reading Teacher*, Dr. Morrow has been a principal research investigator for the National Reading Research Center, the Center for English Language Arts Achievement and Assessment, and the Center for Instruction in Early Reading Achievement. At Rutgers, she received the Graduate School of Education's Alumni Award for Teaching, Service, and Research, as well as the university-wide Teaching Excellence Award. She was granted the International Reading Association's Teacher Educator of Reading Award, and Fordham University's Alumni Award for Outstanding Achievement. The International Reading Association, an organization with 90,000 members in 99 countries, elected her to the board of directors, as vice president (2001–2002), and as president-elect (2003–2004).

PREFACE

Using the Book for Pre-Service and In-Service Staff Development

This book is prepared for both pre-service and in-service teachers who are interested in creating, revising, or adding new strategies to their teaching of a language arts block (LAB). The book provides information about strategies, but, just as important, recommendations for scheduling, making transitions, and generally organizing language arts instruction in classrooms. In my research and experience with staff development in literacy instruction, I have found that teachers learn new strategies easily. The part that seems more difficult is learning to organize the strategies into a well-choreographed school day. This book seeks to help teachers with the organization of their LAB.

The book begins with a general chapter about organizing the classroom environment and the process of literacy instruction. The discussion in this first chapter addresses these issues for kindergarten through fourth grade. A collage of photographs illustrates the ideas presented. In later chapters, individual cases of exemplary practice by teachers in kindergarten through fourth grade are presented. After each chapter or pair of chapters presenting case material, another chapter provides a series of lesson plans to help the reader organize and carry out a LAB. All of the cases and plans have been written in collaboration with practicing teachers at the different grade levels. Teachers can select those plans they find most useful.

Pre-service teachers will need to be guided through the book by an instructor, while in-service teachers may be guided by a supervisor or each other as they take part in a study group together. When using the book, pre-service teachers should observe or participate in an elementary school classroom to carry out the activities discussed. Practicing teachers who use the book should meet at least once a month to discuss goals and progress. Participants will read the book, set goals, and report back to the group about progress. They will collaborate by sharing ideas, making materials for themselves and others, and offering modeling help when necessary. They will visit each other's classrooms to learn from their peers. The following can be used either in the college classroom or in a school district course outline study group:

1. **Meeting One (read Chapter One in advance of your first meeting)**
   a. Brainstorm major points about organization and direction of the LAB, including elements such as scheduling literacy activities, making transitions between activities, grouping practices for literacy instruction, organizing center work, material storage, design of the classroom environment, and problematic student behavior.
   b. Discuss management systems and other relevant items you already include in your classroom (or those included in the classroom you are observing).
   c. Evaluate your classroom (or the one you are observing) for the characteristics suggested in Chapter One regarding classrooms with good organizational systems and plans.
   d. Select an organization issue, such as the design of the classroom environment to support instruction during the LAB, to focus on until the group meets again. Select from the lesson plans provided to try one or two environmental changes in your room, and observe and describe children's resulting achievement and behavior.
   e. For the next meeting, read the kindergarten case study (Chapter Two) and the accompanying combined kindergarten and first-grade LAB lesson plans (Chapter Four).

2. **Meeting Two**
   a. Describe the changes made in your classroom (or those you would have suggested in the room you are observing) that deal with the design of the physical environment of the classroom to support literacy instruction during the LAB. Discuss the subsequent changes in child and teacher behavior.
   b. Discuss the text you have read, and any of the organization strategies and components you already utilize in your classroom (or describe the organizational strategies and components utilized in the room you are observing).
   c. For the next session, focus on changing the manner in which materials are stored for children and where they are placed to improve the organization of the LAB and literacy instruction. Brainstorm changes you think you will make (or suggest) as a goal for the next meeting. Select lesson plans from the book that are appropriate to help with meeting your goals.
   d. For the next meeting, read the first-grade case study (Chapter Three) and review the combined kindergarten and first-grade LAB lesson plans (Chapter Four).

3. **Meeting Three**
   a. Describe the changes made in your classroom (or those you have suggested in the room you are observing) in the manner in which materials are stored for children and where they are placed to improve the organization of the LAB and literacy instruction. Discuss the changes these caused in child achievement and in child and teacher behavior.

    b. Discuss the text you have read and the organizational strategies and compo-
       nents you already utilize in your classroom (or describe the organizational
       strategies and components utilized in the room you are observing).

    c. For the next session, focus on organizing children in groups for guided
       reading instruction and writing workshops that will help improve the orga-
       nization and management of the LAB and literacy instruction. Brainstorm
       changes you think you will make (or suggest) as a goal for the next meeting.

    d. For the next meeting, read the second-grade case study (Chapter Five) and
       the accompanying block of lesson plans (Chapter Six). Select plans from the
       book that are appropriate to help with meeting your goals.

    e. Before you adjourn, visit two classrooms of colleagues to see changes made
       dealing with organization of the literacy program.

4. **Meeting Four**
    a. Describe the changes made in your classroom (or those you have suggested
       in the room you are observing) in organizing children in groups for guided
       reading. Discuss the changes these caused in child achievement and in child
       and teacher behavior.

    b. Discuss the text you have read, and the organizational strategies and compo-
       nents you already utilize in your classroom (or describe the organizational
       strategies and components utilized in the room you are observing).

    c. For the next session, focus on how you organize center work during guided
       reading instruction and Writing Workshops that will help improve the orga-
       nization of the LAB and literacy instruction. Brainstorm changes you think
       you will make (or suggest) as a goal for the next meeting.

    d. For the next meeting, read the combined third- and fourth-grade case study
       (Chapter Seven) and the accompanying third- and fourth-grade block of les-
       son plans (Chapter Eight).

    e. Before you adjourn, visit two classrooms of colleagues to see changes made
       in dealing with organization of the literacy program.

5. **Meeting Five**
    a. Describe the changes made in your classroom (or those you have suggested
       in the room you are observing) in organizing children in centers during
       guided reading instruction and Writing Workshops. Discuss the changes
       these caused in child achievement and in child and teacher behavior.

    b. Discuss the text you have read, and the organizational strategies and compo-
       nents you already utilize in your classroom (or describe the organizational
       strategies and components utilized in the room you are observing).

    c. For the next session, focus on transitions from one activity to another during
       the LAB that would help improve organization. Brainstorm changes you
       think you will make (or suggest) as a goal for the next meeting.

    d. For the next meeting, refer back to parts of the book that you think you want
       to review. Select lesson plans that are appropriate in helping to make im-
       provements.

    e. Before you adjourn, visit two classrooms of colleagues to see changes made
       dealing with organization of the literacy program.

6. **Meeting Six**
   a. Describe the scenes in your classroom with the changes you have made (or those from the room you are observing) that deal with activities occurring during the LAB.
   b. Discuss where improvements can be made and changes continue to need work in your classroom (or in the room you are observing).
   c. Using the book as a reference, decide which areas dealing with organization of the LAB need more work, such as creating more word study materials. Discuss assignments and goals to continue to work on. If possible, divide responsibilities so that each teacher in the group has an assignment. For example, if word study materials are needed, one teacher could choose to make "Word Wheels" for several classrooms. This type of cooperation cuts down on the work any one teacher has to to and builds a sense of community in the school.
   d. Visit two classrooms of colleagues to note changes they have made.

7. **Continuing the Staff Development**
   a. Continue to meet and share ideas about organization of the LAB in your classroom (or the one you are observing). Discuss time allotments for activities, transitions, storing materials, and placing materials in the room. Discuss the physical design of the classroom to support language arts instruction, organizing center work, guided reading instruction, and the selection of groups for instruction.
   b. Continue to share materials and ideas.
   c. Continue to visit each other's classrooms.
   d. Read additional material about the topic and select plans to carry out.
   e. Visit teachers in other school districts.
   f. Attend professional conferences that address the topic.
   g. When the group members feel they no longer need to discuss this topic, select another issue of mutual concern, select reading materials, select goals, and continue to meet.

It is apparent that staff development is critical to achieve exemplary practice. The National Reading Panel report (2002) found that particular strategies promote success in literacy development, such as the systematic study of phonics, phonemic awareness, vocabulary, comprehension, and fluency. The report also stated that teachers who have ongoing staff development are the most successful at helping children achieve. This book was written for teachers to participate in ongoing staff development in study groups. It is hoped that sections will be read, goals set, and the sharing of concerns and success will take place. To ensure successful reading instruction, continuous professional development is necessary.

ACKNOWLEDGMENTS

This book could not have been written without the encouragement and patience of Christopher Jennison, Senior Editor at The Guilford Press. I also want to thank Marie Sprayberry, copyeditor, for her meticulous editing of the manuscript. In addition, I had the help of wonderful classroom teachers who have been my students at Rutgers University in the Graduate Programs in Teacher Education and the Reading Specialist Certification. Their insight and ideas overflow in this book and prove how professional, intelligent, and knowledgeable teachers are. They are Ellen G. Abere, Jacki Abrams, Stephanie M. Bushell, Heather Casey, Melissa Collucci, Kim Duhammel, Kristen Fahey, Angela Feola, Nancy Fittipaldi Bonham, Sue Gallagher, Lara Lynn Heyer, Taylor Holt, Joanne Jacobson, Karen Lombardy, Danielle Lynch, Margaret Niemiec, Allison Porro, Michelle Rosen, Amy Sass, Stephanie Schraeder, Jill Stuckwisch, Jessica Temlock-Fields, Donna Turso, and Gregg Wammer. Their pictures appear on the following pages.

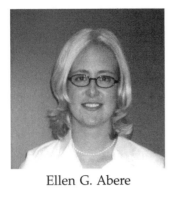

Ellen G. Abere

Jacki Abrams

Stephanie M. Bushell

Heather Casey

Melissa Collucci

Kim Duhammel

Kristen Fahey

Angela Feola

Nancy Fittipaldi Bonham

Sue Gallagher

Lara Lynn Heyer

Taylor Holt

Joanne Jacobson

Karen Lombardy

Danielle Lynch

Margaret Niemiec

Allison Porro

Michelle Rosen

Amy Sass

Stephanie Schraeder

Jill Stuckwisch

Jessica Temlock-Fields

Donna Turso

Gregg Wammer

CONTENTS

ONE

A General Look at Organizing
a Language Arts Program

Investigations into exemplary practices in early literacy attempt to capture as many dimensions of teaching excellence as possible. In this type of research, investigators examine real-life situations in which many variables are successfully integrated. The results of this research show many similarities among the classroom practices of effective and exemplary teachers. A partial list of these characteristics would include the following (Morrow, Tracey, Woo, & Pressley, 1999; Pressley, Rankin, & Yokoi, 1996; Ruddell & Ruddell, 1995):

- Multiple and varied teaching strategies and learning experiences are used to meet individual needs and styles.
- Skills are taught through modeling strategies in structured lessons.
- Opportunities are provided for children to practice their new skills both independently and with other students.
- Classrooms are carefully organized to support learning with literacy-rich environments and accessible materials.
- Varied structures for instruction are utilized to meet individual needs, including whole-group, small-group, and one-on-one settings with the teacher and peers.
- Emphasis is placed upon careful organization and direction of strategies and structures for optimal literacy development to occur.

These characteristics point to the purpose of the present book, which is to describe the organization of the language arts block (LAB) through various aspects of the classroom environment and through careful selection of structures and strategies for learning. These environmental and other organizational factors are often overlooked, while the *content* of strategies for instruction is frequently emphasized. And yet, without the support of the classroom's physical environment and thoughtful attention to the *process* of instruction, early literacy instruction is not likely to be effective or exemplary.

With this background, let us take a general look in this first chapter at an early childhood classroom. As I discuss the teacher in action, keep in mind that the story is based on a collective profile of several teachers identified as exemplary. I observed these teachers for a year as part of a study on exemplary literacy instruction in first and fourth grades. This investigation took place in five states where supervisors nominated exemplary teachers. These teachers were chosen not only because if their supervisors' observations, but also because of their students' achievement and their reputation among colleagues, parents, and children. By synthesizing my findings on these "expert" teachers, I present a composite sketch of an exemplary classroom that highlights

(1) the classroom's physical environment; and (2) the structure of the LAB, with an emphasis on the assignment of independent work in "centers," and on small-group instruction for meeting students' individual needs. Although this is a composite of several teachers, for the purposes of this chapter I will call this teacher Amy Holt. The design of her classroom, most of the activities and strategies discussed, and the organization of her LAB could be implemented in almost any kindergarten through fourth-grade classroom. The biggest differences would be at kindergarten and in the fourth grade; these would mostly be in the content and difficulty of the materials being read and written about, and in the time allotted for various activities.

THE PHYSICAL ENVIRONMENT IN THE CLASSROOM

Teachers must provide appropriate materials and a classroom arrangement that will set the stage for learning to take place. As Plato said, "What is honored in a country will be cultivated there." Teachers who honor the development of literacy demonstrate that attitude by providing within their classrooms a rich environment where the use of books can be cultivated. Their students honor literacy development by assimilating the attitudes and atmosphere presented by the teacher.

Arrangements for Whole-Group Work, Morning Meetings, and Guided Instruction

Amy Holt's room exemplifies her own philosophies regarding the physical design of a classroom. Amy arranges her room so that it is "student-friendly." She stores materials for easy access. Amy finds that a rich supply of materials enables her to meet the different abilities and interests of her children. Although her room is in the basement of an old inner-city school, Amy's classroom has adequate space for her 23 children, is well lit, and is kept clean. The children's desks are arranged in groups of four to encourage social interaction. This arrangement also saves spaces for other materials. The room has provisions for whole-group instruction as well, with students sitting at their desks and/or on a rug in the Literacy Center. In the area for whole-group meetings, there is a chalkboard, a pocket chart, and an easel with an experience chart. Amy has a rocking chair that she uses when teaching mini-lessons or reading stories to the children.

Amy's morning meeting area includes functional print, such as a calendar, a weather chart, a helper chart, and rules for the Classroom. Signs communicate information, such as "Quiet Please" and "Please Put Materials Away after Using Them." A notice board is used to talk with the children through print. In addition, there is a Word Wall that features high-frequency "words of the week." There are additional Word Walls for other skills and strategies being taught or ones that a child feels he or she would like to learn. There is a bulletin board labeled "People around the World," which represents the thematic unit currently being studied.

There is a table situated at one side of the room. At this table, Amy meets with small groups and individual children for explicit guided instruction in reading and writing based on need. Amy keeps all the materials she uses for guided instruction on this table. These include leveled books selected for the children's different reading needs, a pocket chart, an experience chart, individual writing slates for work with word

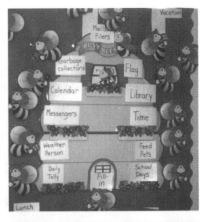

Print-rich environments at all grade levels will include a large book collection, print about functional activities, print about themes being studied, and print about literacy instruction.

study and writing, and folders for students to assess their success and needs. On the windowsill are corrugated cardboard book bins labeled with children's names, where they store individual work (such as their writing journals, books they are reading, homework assignments, etc.). These materials are packaged in zip-lock-style plastic bags.

Learning Centers

To accommodate small-group and independent work, there are Learning Centers —each labeled according to content area. The centers integrate literacy learning into content areas by featuring reading and writing activities linked to those areas; Amy believes that these linkages give literacy activities more meaning. She uses themes for de-

A table for small-group work geared toward individual needs is set aside for guided reading instruction.

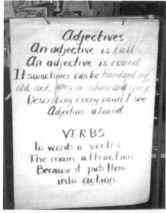

Materials for guided reading are accessible, such as an experience chart, a pocket chart, a Word Wall, and book bins where students store their writing journals and books for reading instruction.

veloping new vocabulary, new ideas, and purposes for reading and writing. Each of her Learning Centers has general materials that are typical of the center's content (such as scissors, paste, crayons, and paper in the Art Center), but also includes special materials that are linked to the current thematic topic of study. For example, the unit dealing with "People around the World: Multicultural Education" is quite evident in the different centers:

- The Social Studies Center features *National Geographic* magazines, maps of countries around the world, and foreign stamps. There are also musical instruments from different countries, such as maracas from Mexico and a Caribbean steel drum.
- The Science Center offers cookbooks from other lands and the ingredients for making multicultural dishes.
- The Math Center has an abacus, samples of foreign currency, and both English and metric rulers.
- The Art Center has blank flags for children to decorate to represent different countries, as well as special paper and directions for folding Japanese origami figures.

The Literacy Center: Basic Equipment

The Literacy Center is the largest of the Learning Centers. It consists of a number of different centers, areas, and stations for various literacy activities. These are called by slightly different names in different teachers' classrooms, and in fact some teachers—such as Danielle Lynch, described in Chapter Two—refer to "Literacy Centers" in the plural. The similarities among the functions of the different centers, however, far outweigh the occasional differences in their names. The Literacy Center includes space

Special materials that are linked to current thematic topics of study are added to existing centers. This photo shows the Science Center during a unit about dinosaurs (its sign has been changed to "Dinosaur Mania" for the occasion).

The Library Corner of the Literacy Center includes baskets of books representing different themes and genres. Books at different levels of difficulty are labeled from A (most difficult) to F (easiest), so children can select easy material for fun or difficult material for a reading challenge.

and materials for writing, reading, oral language, listening, comprehension, and word analysis skill development. In one area, there are a rocking chair and a rug, since many literacy activities take place on the floor. This is where Amy holds group meetings, teaches some lessons, and reads aloud to children. There are pillows and stuffed animals to add an element of softness.

In the Literacy Center's Library Corner, books are stored in open-faced shelving for displaying titles about themes being studied. These books are changed when the themes change and when special selections are featured. Amy stores some books in baskets, which she labels by genre (such as books about animals, books about the seasons, poetry, biographies, etc.). To aid selection, other books are labeled with the letters A, B, C, D, E, and F, to represent the difficulty of each book (A is most difficult and F is easiest), therefore, children can read something easy for fun or difficult for a challenge. Books and other materials selected for the Library Corner should appeal to a variety of interests, and it is advisable to stock multiple copies of popular books. Children sometimes enjoy reading a book because a friend is reading it (Morrow, 1985).

In her classroom, Amy has five to eight book selections per child at about five different reading levels. She has picture storybooks, poetry, informational books, magazines, biographies, cookbooks, joke books, novels, fairy tales, and many other genres. She has acquired these over the years by purchasing them at flea markets, using points gained from book club sales, soliciting donations from parents, using her allotted classroom budget, and buying some herself. She rotates her books regularly to maintain children's interest in them, and children can check books out to read at home. The Library Corner also includes foreign dictionaries, as well as many books related to the current multicultural theme, such as *Chinese Mother Goose Rhymes* (Wyndham, 1968).

Other Materials in the Literacy Center

The literacy center needs to contain language arts materials for skill development, as well as manipulative materials that help children reinforce the word study elements being focused upon. These manipulatives come in the form of magnetic letters and boards, puzzles, bingo games, and concentration and board games, to name a few. Teacher-made materials can be used as well. Manipulative materials to enhance comprehension, such as puppets, taped stories with headsets, and felt boards with story characters, must also be available in the Literacy Center. For example, using a felt board and its characters for storytelling (see Figure 1, bottom) engage children in demonstrating knowledge of story sequence and structure, classifying details, predicting outcomes, and interpreting text—all skills that enhance comprehension of text.

A "roll movie" (see Figure 1, top) can also be used to enhance comprehension skills. A roll movie can be constructed from a box with a picture window cut out that makes it look like a television. Dowels are inserted at the top and bottom of the box. Shelving paper is written on and illustrated, and is attached to the dowels for presentation. The Literacy Center should include materials from which children can make their own books, felt board stories, and roll movies. (See Appendices B and E for more manipulative materials.)

In addition, attractive posters that encourage reading are available from the Children's Book Council (568 Broadway, Suite 404, New York, NY 10012; http://www.cbc-books.org) and the American Library Association (50 East Huron Street, Chicago, IL 60611; http://www.ala.org).

The Author's Spot (which may be called the Writing Center in other classrooms) is a portion of the Literacy Center that is set aside especially for writing. This area includes a table, chairs, and writing materials (such as colored markers, crayons, pencils, paper, chalk, a chalkboard, and various types of paper). Index cards are used for re-

Children use manipulative word study materials to practice skills taught.

Roll Movies

Making a roll movie is an excellent method for recording an original story. A roll movie box is an important piece of equipment for the classroom. With this device the child can write and illustrate his or her story and present the finished work to the class.

Directions:

1. Select a strong cardboard box about 18" high by 14" wide by 10" deep (45 cm x 35 cm x 25 cm).
2. Remove the cover or flaps of the box, leaving the sides and bottom.
3. Cut a rectangular shape out of the bottom of the box, leaving about 2" (5 cm) as a border on all sides.
4. Cut two holes on both sides of the box, close to the opening, yet far enough away to fit the roll of paper that will contain the illustrations (see diagram).
5. Obtain two wooden dowels about 20" (50 cm) long and place them through the holes in the box.
6. Cover the outside of the box with self-adhesive vinyl.
7. Draw each picture for the story on white shelving paper the right size to fit and show through the opening in the box. Write the text of the story under each illustration.
8. Turn the roll movie box to its back side, and attach the beginning of the roll to the top wooden dowel with masking tape. Roll up the pictures onto the top dowel and then attach the other end of the paper roll to the bottom dowel. Now roll the strip to its beginning position, and it is ready to be rolled and told.

Note: The movie box may be used horizontally, with the strip rolling onto the right-hand dowel. However, this may be more difficult, since the box cannot sit flat but must be held by someone or be placed on the edge of the table or desk.

Another idea: If you are lucky enough to have an old wooden TV frame, bore some holes and use it to show movie strips.

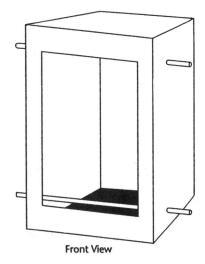

Front View

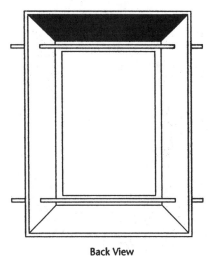

Back View

Felt Board Story

FIGURE 1. When children create their own roll movies and felt board stories, they enhance their comprehension skills as they sequence events, include details, and interpret ideas.

cording "Very Own Vocabulary Words," which are stored in index card boxes. Folders, one for each child, are used to collect writing samples. The Author's Spot includes a Computer Center as well: Amy has two computers with excellent software for writing and reading activities.

In the Author's Spot, Amy also has materials for making books, which include many sizes of writing paper, a stapler, construction paper, and a hole punch. Amy prepares blank books keyed to themes, such as a booklet in the shape of a country studied. There is a place for children to display their written work, as well as a mailbox, stationery, envelopes, and stamps for children to write to each other and to pen pals. Through the Internet, Amy has found a class in Mexico interested in corresponding with her class via e-mail.

In short, everything in the Library Center has a function, a purpose, and a place where it is stored (see Figure 2). Amy introduces new materials by modeling what their purposes are, how they are used, and where they belong. Early in the school year, she has fewer items in the different centers and stations; she adds to them slowly as the class studies different themes and learns new skills.

The Literacy Center is a cozy place to read alone or with friends.

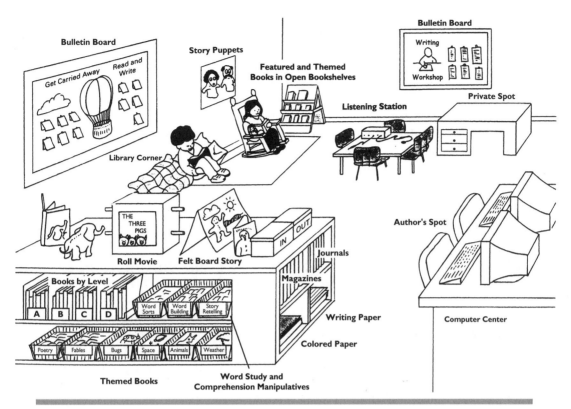

FIGURE 2. Diagram of the Literacy Center in an exemplary primary classroom.
(Adapted from Morrow [2001]. Copyright 2001 by Pearson Education. Reprinted by permission.)

The Philosophical Basis of Classroom Design

Amy's own philosophies and practices regarding classroom design and organization echo findings from historical perspectives and research concerning the manipulation of the environment and its effects on learning. Amy's performance is also very consistent with the research findings on both effective instruction and exemplary teaching practices.

Historically, theorists and philosophers emphasized the importance of the physical environment in early learning and literacy development. Pestalozzi (see Rusk & Scotland, 1979) and Froebel (1974) described the preparation of manipulative materials that would foster literacy development in real-life environments. Montessori (1965) advocated a carefully prepared classroom environment to promote independent learning, and recommended that each kind of material in the environment have a specific learning objective. She prepared her own classroom with materials that were accessible for children.

Research has shown ways in which the physical design of the classroom affects children's behavior (Loughlin & Martin, 1987; Morrow, 1990; Rivlin & Weinstein, 1984). Rooms partitioned into smaller spaces, such as centers, have facilitated verbal interaction among peers and have enhanced cooperative and associative learning. When rooms are carefully designed for specific types of instruction, such as a table for meeting with a small group of children, there is more productivity and greater use of language than in rooms where no attention is given to setting (Moore, 1986).

Literacy-rich environments stimulate activities that enhance literacy skill development (Morrow, 1996; Neuman & Roskos, 1992). As noted above, manipulatives such as puppets or a felt board with story characters improve story production and comprehension, including recall of details and the ability to interpret text (Morrow, 1996). Researchers have found that children like cozy corners with pillows and rugs to retreat to when things get hectic, and that opportunities for privacy are especially important for children who are distractible and for those who have difficulty relating to peers (Weinstein & Mignano, 1997). Young children work best in rooms with variation—that is, rooms with both warm and cool colors, with some open areas and some cozy spots, and with both hard and soft surfaces (Olds, 1987).

ORGANIZING INSTRUCTION TO MEET INDIVIDUAL NEEDS: GUIDED READING AND CENTER ACTIVITIES

There are a variety of strategies for organizing language arts instruction. Children can be taught as a whole class, in small groups, and individually. Children can be grouped homogeneously or heterogeneously by abilities, needs, or interests, or they can be divided into peer groups for cooperative learning. The use of diverse organizational strategies is important, because some children benefit more in one setting than in another. The use of several different grouping schemes within the same classroom also tends to eliminate the stigmas attached to a single grouping system. Finally, variable grouping makes it more likely that children will interact with all others in one group or another.

Whole-Group, Small-Group, and One-to-One Learning Settings

Whole-group instruction is not appropriate until children are almost 3 years old. Younger children lack the ability to concentrate or sit in a large-group setting and listen for any period of time. Whole-group lessons, sometimes referred to as "shared experiences," are appropriate when information needs to be introduced to all the children and the presentation can be understood by all. In early childhood literacy development, storybook readings by an adult, group singing, class discussions, and brainstorming sessions are appropriate whole-group activities.

Small groups are effective when close interaction with children is necessary for explicit instruction and assessment, as with guided reading and writing instruction. Small groups are also used for cooperative projects, with children working independently of the teacher. Teachers should use many types of small-group formations, such as guided reading or writing groups for explicit instruction of skills, groups based on friendships or interests, and independent reading and writing groups. The various group configurations permit children to have experiences with many others, and to avoid the stigma attached to being associated with only one group, as noted above.

Working with children on a one-to-one basis and allowing them to work independently are both forms of individualized instruction. Although children need to

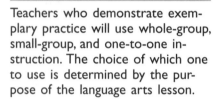

Teachers who demonstrate exemplary practice will use whole-group, small-group, and one-to-one instruction. The choice of which one to use is determined by the purpose of the language arts lesson.

work cooperatively with peers and adults, they also need to solve problems and accomplish tasks on their own. One-to-one instruction provides an opportunity for the teacher to offer personal attention to a child and to learn much about the child. When a teacher works with a child alone, he or she can take running records for assessment and do story-retelling instruction and assessment. Children can get help on specific skills they are having difficulty with, and/or can discuss a new piece they are writing.

The two classroom diagrams shown in Figure 3 will accommodate the kind of teaching that Amy utilizes. They are designed to handle whole-class, small-group, and one-to-one instruction, and to provide materials and space for independent activities as well.

Selecting Children For Grouping

With such a variety of group formations, many teachers ask, "How do I select children for each type of group?" Children can make decisions about participating in some groups, such as those based on friendship and interest. Guided reading and writing groups are selected by the teacher, because the instruction in these groups is based on need and instructional level, or ability.

Many pieces of information should be used to determine students' needs and abilities for guided reading and writing group selection. In this book I discuss several types of assessment that should form a composite picture of the child to help determine group placement. One of the most important types of information is teacher judgment. Other types of assessment that will help in group placement include the following:

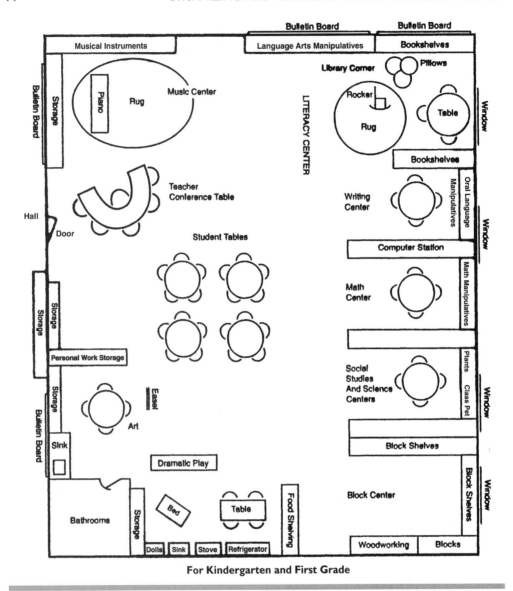

For Kindergarten and First Grade

FIGURE 3. Diagrams for a kindergarten or first-grade classroom (left) and a second- to fourth-grade classroom (right).
(Reprinted from Morrow [2001]. Copyright 2001 by Pearson Education. Reprinted by permission.)

- Running records to determine text reading level, types of strengths and weaknesses in word analysis, fluency, and self-monitoring.
- High-frequency word tests.
- Comprehension evaluation.
- Standardized test scores.

Alternate rank ordering is another way to assign children to groups. This method is mainly based on teacher judgment. List all the children in your class, placing the

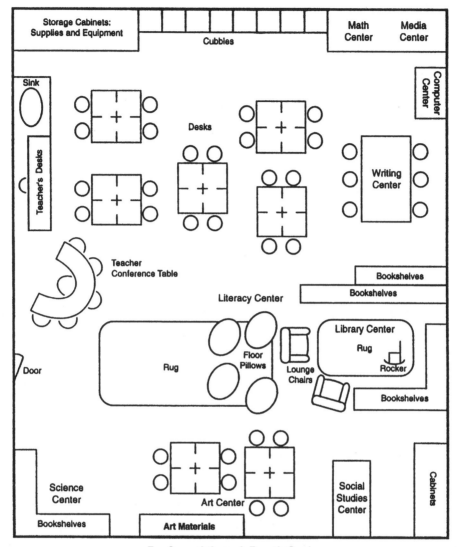

For Second through Fourth Grades

child you rank as having the highest literacy ability at the top, and giving the others in order down to the last child (the one you rank as having the lowest ability). To assign groups, select the top and the bottom child to start two different groups. Place the next child from the top into the group with the top child, and place the next child from the bottom into the group with the lowest ability. Continue this procedure, each time asking yourself whether these children are similar enough in their abilities to be in the same group. When the answer to that question is no, then start a new group. You should end up with four to six groups for your class, with about five children per group. After several meetings, if groups do not seem to be right for certain children, change their placement. As children are evaluated on a regular basis, their grouping placement may change.

The teacher administers a running record to help determine group placement for small-group guided reading lessons.

Directing Independent Work during Guided Instruction

The purpose of much small-group work is for children to learn to work independently of the teacher and in cooperative social settings with peers. During time in the various portions of the Literacy Center and in the content-area-related Learning Centers, children engage in self-selected independent reading and writing activities and can participate in active, hands-on activities. The teacher acts as a facilitator by answering questions and keeping children on task if necessary. During guided reading and writing, the teacher is occupied with these forms of instruction and cannot be disturbed; therefore, the children who are not in the guided lessons need to know exactly what to do, when to do it, and where.

The activities that Amy models for her class for independent work are those involving skills that have been taught before and need to be practiced. Some of the activities are related to the theme being studied. In the beginning of the school year, she spends time introducing children to the various centers in the room and the types of activities they include. She has her class practice working on the different activities. At this time, Amy does not work with small groups during independent work; rather, she helps the children so that they eventually will be able to work independently.

It is important for a teacher to be clear when introducing independent work to a class. When the teacher presents a new assignment by describing and modeling, more students will understand better what is expected of them. Also, the teacher can use activity cards or post the assignment. This will help eliminate further confusion; especially for those students who were absent the day a new assignment was modeled (Grossman, 1995).

The children are assigned some tasks and can select others to do. The tasks engage the children in reading and writing that will help with skill development. For example, when her class was doing a thematic unit on animals, Amy assigned activities 1, 2, 3, and 4 listed below for all children. They could choose to do activities 5 or 6 (also listed below) after they finished the required tasks.

1. For partner reading, children paired off and read the same book together. They could also read separate books and then tell each other about the stories they had read. Because the class was studying animals, children were to select books from the open-faced bookshelves that included stories and expository texts about animals. Discussion about what was read was encouraged. Each child had to fill out an index card with the name of the book read and one sentence about the story.
2. The writing activity required the children to create a fable or illustrate a fable read. Amy featured fables because so many of them include animals and the class was studying animals. The elements of a fable were discussed, and a brainstorming session was held as to how to create a fable. In their rewritings, children were to include the story elements discussed, such as setting, theme, plot episodes, and the resolution.
3. For an activity that involved working with words, the children were to find animal-related words that had the *sh* and *ch* digraphs in them. They were to classify these words by writing them on a sheet of paper under appropriate digraph headings. Children could also look through books to find these digraphs and include those found on the recording sheet provided.
4. The Listening Station in the Literacy Center had taped stories about animals. For each story, there was a recording sheet of paper with a question to answer about the story.
5. The Art Center had magazines with many photos of animals that children could use to create animal collages. Each child was to create a written set of directions for creating an animal collage when he or she finished this activity.
6. The Computer Center included software with animal-related math and literacy activities. Students printed out the activities they participated in.

Amy has an organizational chart that she uses for assigning children to the various centers. The rotations occur in coordination with the groups that she meets with for small-group instruction. If children finish a required activity before group rotations, they can start one of the optional activities or go on to the next task if there is space at a center. There is a basket for completed work, and every center has sign-in sheets and requires a finished product to be handed in. The teacher can monitor work in progress by circulating the room before calling a new small group for guided instruction. This can help to ensure that students are completing their work and that they understand what is required of them. All activities require some type of work to be handed in, to demonstrate that children are accountable for their time and actions (Weinstein & Mignano, 1997).

In the beginning of the school year, some teachers, like Amy, start center time in a structured fashion. They assign the groups and tasks. As children learn to function independently, they are given opportunities for decision making and select groups to work with or tasks to accomplish.

The organization of center time is crucial for its success. Students must know what their choices are, which activities they are to participate in, what rules guide participation concerning the selection of materials, and what is to happen in groups or when they are working alone. Children can help generate the guidelines and rules for working independently. Two sets of rules that are important for independent work during

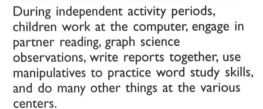

During independent activity periods, children work at the computer, engage in partner reading, graph science observations, write reports together, use manipulatives to practice word study skills, and do many other things at the various centers.

guided instruction are (1) rules for using materials and completing work, and (2) rules for cooperating and collaborating. These rules are listed in Figures 4 and 5, respectively.

Your students need to be taught the particular rules and procedures for your classroom. Telling students the rules is not the most effective way to communicate what you will be expecting of them. Rather, first demonstrate the rules and procedures, and then spend time rehearsing them with the students. This will help children to learn the appropriate behaviors. You should also use positive reinforcement and feedback to let students know whether they followed a procedure correctly. Feedback lets the students know what they did and whether or not that behavior is deemed acceptable. Remember to be consistent with your expectations. Students will misbehave when they know a teacher will not follow through with a penalty. In order to be consistent, you must con-

- Do all required jobs before you do the optional jobs.

- Speak in soft voices; people are working.

- Put materials back in their place.

- Take care of the materials so they are in good condition for others.

- Put your completed work in the assigned place.

- Record your completed work on a record sheet or in a log.

- If you have any questions, use the "Ask three and then me" rule. That is, seek help from up to three other students designated as helpers before asking the teacher when he or she is in a guided reading group.

FIGURE 4. Rules for using materials and completing work.

tinually expect the students to behave appropriately, and rewards/penalties should be implemented on the same consistent basis to reinforce desirable behaviors (Sanford & Emmer, 1988).

Some teachers provide a list of independent activities to do during guided instruction, such as Amy's list above. This list may indicate that the first few activities are mandatory and the others are optional, if the children have time. Some teachers allow children to go from one activity to the next listed on the chart. They can use a center only if there is an empty chair for them, which avoids crowding. When a child finishes an activity, he or she places the product in a designated spot. As emphasized above, accountability for independent work is a necessity (in the form of a record sheet, a performance, a completed project, etc.).

Another way to designate independent work is through the use of a center/activity chart. There are many variations on this type of system. The chart in Figure 6 is an adaptation of the Work Board described by Fountas and Pinnell (1996). (Icons for creating a center/activity chart are provided in Appendix A of the present book). It designates several choices for three or four heterogeneous groups of children. The chart is made of tagboard and has a row of figures representing various centers or activities. At

- Share materials when you are doing activities with others.

- Take turns.

- Listen to your friends when they talk.

- Offer help to others you are working with if they need it.

- When you complete an activity, ask yourself: "Was I helpful to others?" and "Did I share materials?"

FIGURE 5. Rules for cooperating and collaborating.

the top of each row is a place to attach names of children. The figures are movable, as are the name cards. They can be attached to the chart with Velcro, or the chart can have several pockets.

Some teachers prefer a more structured approach to assigning independent work, especially early in the school year. A teacher may assign children to different centers, and then have them rotate from one to the next as the teacher rotates guided reading/ writing groups he or she works with. For example, Amy's students sit in groups of four desks pushed together, which she calls "pods." These children are heterogeneously grouped and move together from one center or activity to another as listed on the chart. From time to time, Amy will change the pod groups so children have the opportunity to work with many different people. When Amy meets with her first guided reading group, the other children have designated center assignments. When the first guided reading lesson ends, all children move to the next center with their group to work on a new project. Later in the school year, the children are able to select their activities; as they complete one activity, they immediately move to the next. At the end of an independent work period, each student fills out a form like the one shown in Figure 7 to indicate which centers were used and which activities were completed during this time.

Transitions between Activities

When students move from one activity to the next, organizational problems can occur. These problems can delay the new activity and create some chaos in the classroom. Common transition problems include (1) students' talking too much between activities and (2) too much movement in the room. Regardless of which transition problem may be occurring in your classroom, all can be frustrating and waste a great deal of time.

Using a designated signal, such as ringing a bell or raising two fingers, can be one way to alert students that it is time to move on to the next activity. Establishing a routine schedule for each day of the week can also help students become more aware of what will occur next in the sequence of the day. Many teachers have found that transitions run more smoothly when they give the students some notice before they end the current activity. This alerts students that a transition is about to occur and that they need to finish the assignment they are doing.

Remember to recognize appropriate student behavior during transitions. This will prompt other students to behave in a positive manner. Most students seek a teacher's approval and enjoy receiving personal attention and verbal praise. Being consistent with your expectations is an effective and clear way to communicate them to your students (Good & Brophy, 1994).

CONCLUSION

The organization of the LAB is a contributing factor to how well children achieve. Teaching that is carefully planned and organized will look like a beautifully choreographed ballet, as it flows seamlessly from one activity to the next throughout the school day. The remainder of this book provides more specific guidance for doing this at different grade levels.

Janine, Jen, Keith, Kelly, Rumon	Holly, Michael, Ben, Mat, Alexis	Darren, Tisha, Ivory, Sam, Matt	Sarah, Tim, Yassin, Josh, Kyle
Buddy Reading	Listening Station	Oral Language	Journal Writing
Journal Writing	Computer Center	Word-Study Manipulatives	Buddy Reading
Oral Language	Word-Study Manipulatives	Buddy Reading	Listening Station
Word-Study Manipulatives	Buddy Reading	Journal Writing	Computer Center
Listening Station	Oral Language	Computer Center	Word-Study Manipulatives
Computer Center	Journal Writing	Listening Station	Oral Language

All figures and name cards are removable and can be changed around.

FIGURE 6. Sample chart for designating centers or activities for students, or helping students select their own. Adapted from Fountas and Pinnell (1996). Copyright 1996 by Heinemann, a division of Reed Elsevier, Inc. Adapted by permission.

Center/Activity Recording Form

Today's date: _____

Center: _____

Students: _____

_____

_____

What did you do? _____

_____

_____

_____

_____

_____

_____

What did you learn? _____

_____

_____

_____

_____

_____

_____

_____

_____

FIGURE 7. Sheet for recording centers used and activities completed during an independent work period.

TWO

Kindergarten Case Study

INTRODUCTION TO THE TEACHER, DANIELLE LYNCH

Danielle Lynch (a composite of several teachers) has been teaching kindergarten in a suburban, middle-class community that has been experiencing rapid growth. During her 6 years of teaching in this school, Danielle has attained a master's degree with reading certification and is currently working toward her second master's degree. Her kindergarten class consists of 23 children from the following ethnic background: 11 European American, 4 Asian American, 3 African American, 2 Native American, and 3 Hispanic. There are 12 girls and 11 boys. A collaborative atmosphere is apparent among teachers, administrators, and parents. Professional colleagues are found sharing ideas and best practices with one another throughout the day. For various portions of the kindergarten day, parent volunteers are present assisting with classroom routines.

TEACHING PHILOSOPHY

When asked to talk about her philosophy of literacy instruction, Danielle responds with the following:

> "From the first day of school, a supportive and accepting environment is created and nurtured by myself, parents, administrators, and the children themselves. The resulting classroom community allows all of the children to feel secure as they develop socially, emotionally, physically, and intellectually. As the children develop, I support their individual developmental needs through thematic instruction, which integrates content areas and presents skills in a meaningful context and in an explicit manner when necessary. It is through small-group and individual lessons that I am able to address the skills in a differentiated manner. In an effort to foster a positive attitude toward the language arts and an appreciation for the role that they play in our lives, I strive to provide my students with authentic literacy choices. These opportunities enable my students to develop as responsible and accountable individuals. At the same time, these opportunities enable the children to become collaborative problem solvers. As a teacher, I believe that it is important for me to grow as a professional, just as my students grow as independent learners. As a result, I will always be looking for new and innovative practices, which will aid me in helping my students to attain their highest potential."

THE PHYSICAL ENVIRONMENT IN THE CLASSROOM

Upon entering Danielle's classroom, one is greeted with the sounds of children's voices and classical music. As the children engage in their varied activities, the value of literacy is quickly apparent. The literacy-rich environment is adorned with children's work and a host of environmental print. An interactive Word Wall serves as a child-accessible reference for approximately 70 high-frequency words, including the children's names. The district designates that by the end of kindergarten 100 words are taught.

Within the Reader's Corner are blankets, stuffed animals, a large wicker chair, a child's rocking chair, and a child-size table and chairs. The wicker chair serves as the "special chair" where Danielle or a parent volunteer reads stories to the class, or where children share their writing. One wall of the Reader's Corner contains a large bulletin board. This board holds materials for various components of the morning meeting, such as a calendar, a weather/seasons chart, a days-of-school chart, a daily schedule, daily news, and a monthly countdown. A smaller bulletin board displays materials that individual children use when teaching their classmates a lesson of their choice during their turn as "Tomorrow's Teacher."

There are shelves filled with general interest books and magazines of all levels and genres. There is also a series of shelves containing books separated by themes, such as "Dinosaurs," "Bears," "Weather," "My Family and I," "Friends," "School," "Famous People," "Farm," "ABC's," "And "123's." Some of the books are also grouped by authors' names, such as Eric Carle and Ezra Jack Keats. Next to the wicker chair is a basket labeled "Old Favorites." Books such as *Somebody and the Three Blairs* (Tolhurst, 1990), *Chicka, Chicka, Boom, Boom* (Martin & Archambault, 1989), *We Share Everything* (Munsch, 1999), *Piggies* (Wood & Wood, 1991) and *Brown Bear, Brown Bear, What Do You See?* (Martin & Carle, 1967) fill the basket. A large tote entitled "Books by Us" contains books written and illustrated by the children in the class, either independently or with a small group of peers in the Writing Workshop.

Additional books written by the children are found in the Writing Center in the children's "Best Pieces Portfolios." The Writing Center is located by the interactive Word Wall and has a table for the children to write at. The shelf in the Writing Center contains many materials; some of which include various kinds of paper (lined and unlined), pre-made

Baskets of themed books are accessible for children.

miniature blank books, various kinds of writing implements, envelopes, rubber stamps, picture dictionaries, sight word lists, tape dispensers, and stickers. One of the two easels in the room is located here. A chart used during a mini-lesson to teach children how to use an upper-case letter at the beginning of a name has been left displayed.

There are four tables in the center of the classroom labeled with the children's names. These tables are named by the vowels *A*, *E*, *I*, and *O*. Danielle tells me that by the end of the year, she is able to call each table not only by its letter name, but also by letter sound and words beginning with each of the letters. A U-shaped table used for guided literacy instruction is located at one side of the room, but its position allows Danielle to see all areas of the classroom. By this table is a rolling cart with four draw-ers. Materials for guided literacy instruction are separated into the drawers. The draw-ers contain slates, wipeboards and corresponding materials, general materials (sen-tence strips, writing implements, scissors, highlighting tape, plastic bags, index cards), and books to be used in upcoming guided literacy lessons, as well as teacher reference materials and various kinds of literacy manipulatives (magnetic letters, teacher-made games to reinforce skills, letter- and sound-sorting cards).

A pocket chart labeled "Literacy Centers" is clearly visible and child-accessible. (Note Danielle's use of "Literacy Centers" in the plural, in contrast to Amy Holt's "Lit-eracy Center" as one large center containing smaller centers and stations; see Chapter One.) A separate section of this chart depicts the four content-area-related Learning Centers—the Art, Math, Science, and Social Studies Centers. Children use photographs of themselves labeled with their names to denote their center choices. During guided literacy instruction, children are able to move freely in and out of the various centers. The Literacy Centers include Reader's Corner, as well as areas for listening, computers, letter study, the Word Wall, storytelling, and writing. The theme being focused on is ev-ident in the activities provided in each of the centers. Charts, posters, poems, book dis-plays, and children's work around the room also clearly convey the current theme of study. When leaving a particular center, the children fill out an accountability sheet lo-cated in the center. When it is time for a new guided reading group to form, Danielle announces the children's names, and those children remove their pictures from their center choices and place them in the pocket labeled "Reading Place."

CLASSROOM GUIDANCE AND DIRECTION

Good classroom organization is the foundation to effective instruction. And key to any organizational system are the guidance and direction of children, through the establish-ment of clear expectations and consequences. Danielle states that her approach to this can be summarized by the words "If you want them to do it, you must teach them to do it." Danielle explains that she uses the first month of school to focus on themes such as "Manners," "School Routines," and "Cooperation." Throughout these themes and then for the remainder of the year, Danielle continually reinforces the positive behaviors she is looking for the children to embody. By the second week of school, she finds that the children start to become familiar with these expectations and are able to express them in their words and in their actions. As a result, at the close of the second week, Danielle has the children state what manners they feel are important. As they do this, Danielle transcribes what is said onto a bulletin board entitled "A Bunch of Magnificent Manners." All statements are recorded in positive terms—for example, "We can listen when someone is talking."

The children in Danielle's class each have their own daily behavior-tracking system called their "Classroom Stoplight." A library pocket with three cards—green, yellow, and red—is located in each child's cubbyhole. The green card has a happy face on it, the yellow a straight face, and the red a sad face. Next to this pocket is another pocket with a "Happy Gram"—a Post-it Note that reads, "Today, I had a really great day at school. I used my manners all day long. I am so proud of my day that I would like to tell you all about it." The children, with Danielle's guidance, monitor their behavior throughout the day. If all goes well, a child's card remains green, and the child can then choose to sign and take home the Happy Gram (one Happy Gram is provided per week). A yellow card is a signal to the child to slow down and think about his or her behavior. Red results in a "Think Time," where the child takes a few minutes to reflect on his or her behavior and what can be done to improve it. Danielle and the child then discuss what happened and how the child can do better.

Transitions are a major component of the instructional day. When done efficiently, transitions can take only a few moments and help to set the stage for the next activity. Danielle uses a variety of strategies to get the children's attention, all of which are effective. Her strategies include clapping out a pattern and having the children clap it back, saying, "1, 2, 3, eyes on me"; counting to a stated number; or singing a series of directions to a familiar tune, such as "Twinkle, Twinkle, Little Star."

The environment of Danielle's classroom also contributes to her effective guidance of children, as indicated above. All materials that students need are easily child-accessible. Furthermore, all materials are assigned "A home." Various containers with labels are used to organize materials the children used. In addition, Danielle arranges her room in a way that enables her to see all areas clearly, no matter where she is in the room.

Careful planning of lessons and materials contributes to the success of this classroom as well. Danielle's plan book is organized in a user-friendly manner; it gives her room to jot down notes concerning the success of a lesson, the need to revise the lesson for future use, or the new direction that a lesson may have taken due to "teachable moments." In order to keep herself on track and to inform the children about their day, the day's upcoming events and lessons are posted during the "daily schedule" portion of the class's morning meetings. A small shelf located by Danielle's desk houses all materials that will be needed for the week's lessons.

In order to keep children who finish activities earlier than their peers actively engaged, Danielle uses a system entitled "Pick a Pocket." Twelve library pockets, each labeled with a specific literacy activity, are taped to the front of Danielle's desk. When children finish early, they can take a craft stick with their name on it and put it in one of the pockets. Only two children's names are permitted in each pocket at a time.

TYPES OF READING EXPERIENCES AND SKILL DEVELOPMENT

Danielle uses multiple strategies for teaching reading. One day, for instance, a shared reading experience was observed following the morning meeting. The big book *Mrs. Wishy-Washy* (Cowley, 1999) was being used and reflected the theme of the week—"Farm Animals." It was obvious from the start of the reading that the children had enjoyed this story in the days past. The reading was filled with the excitement of the children's voices, actions to match some of the wording in the story, and Danielle's tracking the print from left to right with a pointer as the children read. After the reading, Danielle began skill instruction on the use of upper- and lower-case letters. She used text from the story to highlight how upper-case letters were generally used to denote the beginning of someone's name, the beginning of a sentence, or the need for the reader to read with inflection. This skill was then applied to a follow-up activity, which had the class developing an alternative text for the story just read. During that week, other shared reading experiences focused on vocabulary development, the retelling of the story using a felt board, and the identification of story elements (including main character, problem, solution, and setting).

During the course of each day, Danielle allows her students independent reading time. She states,

> "This independent reading time is so valuable for the children and myself. It is a time for the children to practice their developing reading strategies. More importantly, it is a time for them to independently foster their own love of reading. For me, it is an optimum time to observe my students' literacy development. It's also a time for one of my greatest pleasures—seeing and hearing children become excited about literature and themselves as readers."

During independent reading, the children self-select books to read either independently or with a buddy. As the children settle into their comfortable spots, their voices can be heard reading their selections. Some children use pictures to guide their storybook readings, while others attempt to use their developing reading strategies to decode a simple text. Other children select patterned text books, which they have heard read many times before; as a result, they are able to "chant" the book. A group of three children have selected *Brown Bear, Brown Bear, What Do You See* (Martin & Carle, 1967) from the "Old Favorites" basket. Two other children pride themselves in sharing their personal publications with each other. Just as the children settle into their places on the floor or in cozy chairs with stuffed animals, Danielle does the same. She uses this time not only to be a part of this reading community, but also to observe the children's development as readers. At the end of independent reading, the children use pictures and invented spelling to record which books they have read in their journals. As they do this, Danielle goes to her anecdotal record-keeping binder to make a few brief notations concerning her observations.

Another form of reading that the class engages in is a read-aloud. One day while the class was still engaged in the "Farm Animals" theme, Danielle chose to read *Piggie Pie* (Palatini, 1997). A sense of excitement was evoked in the class when Danielle explained to the children that she had learned of this book through the school's media specialist and that she had met the author herself.

DANIELLE: Two years ago, I was looking for a funny book to read about farm animals. Our librarian told me all about this book, *Piggie Pie*. Well, after reading the book, I went right back to the librarian and told her that she was absolutely right—I loved

Children read alone or with a buddy during independent reading time.

it. Then she surprised me and told me that I was going to be lucky enough to meet the author. Ms. Palatini came to our school about a year ago. She shared with teachers and students how she came up with the idea for *Piggie Pie,* and she even autographed this very book. (*Danielle shared the inscription with the class.*)

Following this, Danielle allowed the class a few moments to simply look at the cover. She then told the children to turn to a buddy and share what they thought the story was going to be about. After approximately 1 minute, Danielle asked a few children to share with the class their buddies' predictions.

STUDENT 1: My buddy thinks it's going to be about piggies who want to go out for pizza. But the witch is going to try to eat their pizza.

STUDENT 2: My buddy thinks it's going to be about a witch who wants to make a pie, but none of the piggies will help. Like in *The Little Red Hen.*

STUDENT 3: Me and my buddy think it's going to be about a witch who wants to eat all the pies the piggies make.

Excitement for the story grew as the children shared predictions. Then Danielle read the story, using varied character voices and inflection. The children laughed heartily. Danielle stopped at various points for predictions. Following the story, the children were asked to share their story reviews with the class. One child simply asked, "Can we put *Piggie Pie* in our 'Old Favorites' basket?" Many others in the class quickly matched the child's request. To close, Danielle had the children make connections between the story just read and other stories they had heard in the past.

Explicit skill development occurs during another kind of reading experience called guided literacy instruction. This instruction occurs in small groups, while other children are engaged in activities at the Literacy and Learning Centers. Just as she does with all other reading experiences, Danielle evokes a sense of excitement in the children as she makes the guided instruction highly interactive. The two examples of such lessons that follow illustrate how guided instruction is differentiated to match the needs of the children in a particular flexible group.

In one group in just the first 3 minutes, Danielle had the children use their voices and hands to recreate a rainstorm. They discussed feelings that a storm evoked and the kinds of things that they might see, hear, and smell after the rain. An excerpt from their discussion follows:

STUDENT 1: Lightning and thunder make me feel scared.

OTHER STUDENTS: Me too!

DANIELLE: What do you do when there's thunder and lightning?

STUDENT 1: I go to my mommy or daddy.

DANIELLE: How does that make you feel?

STUDENT 1: Better!

DANIELLE: What do you and your mommy or daddy do while it's storming out?

STUDENT 1: We read stories and play games.

STUDENT 2: Me and my mommy sing songs.

DANIELLE: What kinds of things do you do after a rainstorm?

STUDENT 3: Stay inside.

STUDENT 4: I make mud pies!

STUDENT 5: I jump in puddles!

STUDENT 6: I look for a rainbow!

DANIELLE: Wow! You do keep busy during and after rainstorms, and believe it or not, the little boy in this story does some of the same things you do after a rainstorm. Let's take a picture walk through this book called *After the Rain*.

Following the picture walk through *After the Rain* (Meadows, 1997), which was strongly guided by picture cues, the group read the story. Danielle followed up with a skill-based sound sort that had the children discriminating between two initial consonant sounds heard in the story.

Immediately following this group, Danielle met with another group for guided literacy instruction. This second group focused on the skill of matching upper- and lower-case alphabet letters. As a set to the lesson, Danielle showed the group a card with a single alphabet letter on it. If it was upper-case, they were to "stretch real high," and if it was lower-case, they were to "get real low to the ground." Danielle then took the same cards and spread them out across the top of the table face down. The group then proceeded to play a letter-matching game that resembled "Memory." To close the lesson, Danielle had the children sort the cards into two piles—upper- and lower-case letters.

TYPES OF WRITING EXPERIENCES AND SKILL DEVELOPMENT

The writing experiences in Danielle's classroom are as varied as the reading experiences. The children begin each day with independent journal writing in their "Important to Me Journals." Children can be found at all stages of writing development writing about things, people, or events that are important to them. The topics are as varied as the children themselves. One child may draw a picture of a playground, because that is where he spent his afternoon the day before. Another child may be using invented spelling to write about a vacation that she took the summer before. Danielle uses this time not only to greet children as they arrive, but also to take advantage of the individual teachable moments that arise as the children write. For instance, she may guide one child through her invented spelling; with another child, she may reinforce the concept of leaving spaces between words in sentences; with yet another, she may discuss how to create multiple sentences using periods, rather than linking all thoughts with the word "And."

Interactive writing is a form of writing that the children experience numerous times throughout the day. As part of the morning meeting, Danielle has the class create a daily news report. She pulls a child's name from a cup, and then that child reports news that is important to him or her. The child whose name was pulled one morning reported, "I got a new baseball bat yesterday." Danielle then began to share the pen with the children as they recorded the news. Following this, another child said, "*Cat* rhymes with *bat*." Danielle took advantage of this teachable moment and had the children brainstorm a list of other rhyming words for *bat*. The class then sang "The *-at* Family Song" to the tune of *The Addams Family* theme song.

Interactive writing was used again during a lesson where the children were creat-

During the morning meeting, the daily news is reported and written down.

ing a "T-chart"—a two-column chart with the headings "Farm Animal Parents" and "Farm Animal Babies."

DANIELLE: Let's name a farm animal.

STUDENT 1: Pony.

DANIELLE: Okay. Let's get *pony* on our T-chart. Which column should we write that under—"Parents" or "Babies"?

CLASS: "Parents."

DANIELLE: What letter does *pony* begin with?

CLASS: *P*.

DANIELLE: How do we make a lower-case *p*?

STUDENT: (*tracing out the letter in the air*) Top to bottom, bounce up and around.

DANIELLE: You've got it. Now when you write it on the chart paper, remember the lower-case *p* begins at the middle line. As Sabine writes the *p* on the chart paper, let's sky-write the letter with her. (*This student came up and recorded the letter on chart paper, and the students remaining on the carpet traced the letter out in the air.*)

Interactions continued in a similar format for the remainder of the brainstorming session.

Danielle also has a Writing Workshop, in which (among other things) students have a mini-lesson in a writing procedure, skill or strategy and then are given time to write using what has been taught. The skill being focused on during one mini-lesson I observed was invented spelling. Danielle informed me that similar lessons had been done in the past; however, this particular skill was one that was continually developing in her young learners. The following is an excerpt from this mini-lesson.

DANIELLE: Just like stories, words have beginnings, middles, and ends. Let's listen to the word *farmer*. What letter do you hear at the beginning?

CLASS: *F*.

DANIELLE: Right! Now since I want to write the word *farmer*, I am going to write the letter *f* on my paper. Am I finished with this word?

CLASS: No!

DANIELLE: Right again! I still need the middle of the word. What letters do you hear in the middle?

STUDENT 1: *R* and *M*.

DANIELLE: So now I should write those letters on my paper, but I forget . . . how do I make an *r*? I know there's places I can check, but where are they?

STUDENT 2: The ABC line.

STUDENT 3: *Picture Dictionary*.

STUDENT 4: My name tag.

STUDENT 5: The *Little Red Hen* book.

DANIELLE: Wow! I have a lot of resources. I'm going to check Brandon's name tag. (*She walked to the name tag on the table.*) Oh, here it is. That's right. It goes top to bottom, bounce up and over just a little. Let me go write an *r* down next to my *f.*

Exchanges similar to these occurred for the remainder of the word *farmer* and then for the word *barn.* The children then were asked to make a list of things that they would find on a farm.

Once the children were settled into their activity, Danielle called a small group of students together for a guided writing session. Guided writing is another part of the Writing Workshop, which provides direct, explicit instruction.

During this guided writing session, Danielle worked with four children who were recording only the initial and/or the final letter of a word when they were using their invented spelling. Danielle asked a child to name something she wanted to write on her list, and she replied, "Turkey." Danielle then took out a rubber band and stretched it out slowly, just as she verbally stretched out the word in a similar fashion. As an aside, Danielle stated that segmenting a word both physically and verbally provided her students with a concrete experience. She then handed out rubber bands to the four children. She asked them to stretch out the rubber band and the word *turkey* as she had just done. Then she asked them to stretch them out again, this time only making the sound of the first letter. She recorded it on the chart paper. She followed up by asking them to stretch the word out three more times, until all of the sounds were represented on the chart paper. The group repeated the exercise with the word *tractor.* Danielle kept the group with her for a few minutes following this discrete skill instruction, and monitored and instructed them as they used the rubber band to aid with stretching out and recording the words of their choice.

As usual, Danielle closed her Writing Workshop with the Author's Chair activity. Four children were given the opportunity to share their assigned writing or free writing from the Writing Workshop. All students who shared received one specific compliment from Danielle focusing on their writing, and one compliment from one of their peers.

CROSS-CURRICULAR CONNECTIONS

All curriculum areas are tied together through thematic instruction in Danielle's classroom. During the thematic unit "Farm Animals," described earlier, the literature used during language arts lessons acted as a springboard for cross-curricular lessons. For example, in the story *Mrs. Wishy-Washy* (Cowley, 1999), a tub and sponge are used to clean the animals. This provided a springboard for one of Danielle's math lessons for that week. The class used pan balances to compare the weights of similar items that were dry and wet. For another thematic tie-in, Danielle located 18 farm picture books. She created a recording page consisting of pictures and labels of farm animals, with a line next to each animal. Each child received a book and recording page. His or her job was to count and record the number of times each animal appeared in the book. After this independent work, the class came together, reported their findings, and compared the numbers.

The book *Mrs. Wishy-Washy* also lead to a science lesson where the students compared the absorbency of items and made general conclusions about what kinds of materials could absorb water. In addition, the class explored the displacement of water. In the above-mentioned story, Mrs. Wishy-Washy places three different-sized farm animals in a tub of water. Using clear cups and various-sized objects, the class discovered that larger items make the water in a container rise higher than do smaller items.

Social studies was brought into the theme through the use of a nonfiction book entitled *Milk Makers* (Gibbons, 1987). After the read-aloud, the class engaged in interactive writing and generated a human-sized flow chart that highlighted the farm-to-table milk-producing process. The book also engaged the class in discussions focusing on other items that come from the farm.

TEACHABLE MOMENTS

Teachable moments are abundant with young learners. Their minds are continually making connections between what is being presented and what they have experienced in their lives. For the children, these connections can raise questions or they can spark curiosity in those around. During one daily news writing session, a student in Danielle's class stated, "Look! The little word *to* is in *today*." This simple statement made another child realize that the little word *day* was also in the word *today*. What happened next follows:

DANIELLE: Great observation! Look at this. Ryan, come up and highlight the word *to* for us. (*The child used highlighting tape on the word.*) Now, Sophie, you highlight the word *day*. (*This child used a different-colored highlighting tape.*) We know *today* is one word, because there is no space in between the two little words. A word that has two little words in it is called a "compound word." Another example is *baseball*. Let me use my hands to show you how this works. I'm going to say the word *base* to one hand, and then I'm going to say the word *ball* to the other. When I move my hands together, I get one word—a compound word—*baseball*. Can you think of other compound words?

STUDENT 1: *Football*. *Foot* is one word and *ball* is the other. Watch. (*The child used his hands, just as Danielle did.*)

DANIELLE: You've got it! Anyone else?

STUDENT 2: Butterfly!

For the remainder of the day, students pointed out compound words both in writing and in Danielle's speech. For Danielle, this teachable moment helped to reinforce how powerful the reading strategy of finding little words inside of bigger words can really be, and it also opened the door to a brand-new concept for many of her students.

Danielle describes one of her favorite teachable moments from the year as follows: During a thematic unit on "Sea Creatures," the class enjoyed a read-aloud about various sea creatures, one of which was the blue whale. In the book, it stated that a blue whale could average 100 feet long. The children began to estimate how long 100 feet would be. Some thought it would be the size of the classroom; others thought it would be as tall as the school. Danielle recalls:

"It was the perfect cross-curricular teachable moment. We gathered up all of our rulers and yardsticks, and we went out to the blacktop. We reviewed how a ruler was 1 foot long and that it would take 100 rulers to show us 100 feet. Then we discovered that a yardstick was equivalent to three rulers. One ruler and yardstick at a time, we laid them out on the blacktop. When we ran out of measuring tools, we decided that we could mark the beginning of the line with chalk and begin placing the rulers at the other end. When we finally reached 100 feet, the children began to cheer. They asked if they could use sidewalk chalk to draw around the rulers and make it look like a real blue whale. The teachable moment turned into a priceless cross-curricular lesson."

THE DAILY SCHEDULE AND A TYPICAL DAY IN KINDERGARTEN

A typical day in Danielle's kindergarten demonstrates the need to spread a LAB throughout a school day. The description of such a day below illustrates how certain components of the block can only be used once or twice a week. Danielle believes strongly in providing her students with a developmentally appropriate program, which includes age-appropriate content, materials, and lesson time allotments, as well as time for the children to freely explore the world around them.

Following is a schedule for a full day of kindergarten:

8:45–9:05: **Children arrive**
Attendance/Lunch Station
Folder check-in and Note Basket
Helper chart
Journal writing
Buddy and independent reading

9:05–9:35: **Morning meeting**
Morning message
Daily schedule
Daily news
Word Wall
Calendar
Weather report
Large motor control

9:35–10:15: **Math**

10:15–10:30: **Dramatic play**
Pretend play using thematic props and clothes
Pretend play using play areas established for year-long use (kitchen/ restaurant, post office, and store)
Blocks

10:30–10:40: **Read-aloud**

10:45–11:15: **Lunch**

11:15–11:35: Outside recess (weather permitting)

11:35–12:00: Shared reading
Shared reading of literature
Skill based lesson in a meaningful context

12:00–12:30: Related arts class

12:30–1:15:   Guided literacy instruction/Literacy and Learning Centers activities

1:15–1:45:   Snack/inside free time/rest

1:45–2:20:   Science/social studies/health

2:20–2:30:   Independent reading

2:30–2:50:   Afternoon meeting
Review activities from the day
Allow for additional Author's Chair time
Coming attractions for tomorrow
Goodbye song

The following description demonstrates how Danielle integrated literacy instruction into a typical kindergarten day.

As noted above, the children arrived over a 15-minute span in the morning. As the children entered, they checked themselves in at the Attendance/Lunch Station, proceeded to their cubbies, and unpacked. The children placed their folders in designated "Folder Holders," and their notes were placed in a basket labeled "Note Basket" on Danielle's desk. Following these routines, the children then completed any "Class Helper" jobs that they had been assigned.

As arrival routines were completed, the children got their "Important to Me Journals" and recorded an entry for the day. The date was recorded on the chalkboard and served as a reference for the children so that they could record the date on their entry. Children selected anything that was important to them that day to write about. (For those children who may have trouble selecting a topic, a page entitled "Journal Ideas" is stapled into the cover of each child's journal. Four times a year, the children bring home a blank copy of this page and work with their families to brainstorm five things to write about in their journals. The resulting pages are stapled in the cover of the journal, so children have a variety of personally relevant topics to choose from.)

As the children wrote in their journals, Danielle greeted children who were arriving, addressed notes that had been placed in her "Note Basket," and facilitated journal writing. As the children finished their journal entries, they shared them with Danielle, who provided every child with specific positive feedback. For example, she stated to one child, "I like how you tried to hear the beginning, middle, and ending sounds in all your words."

Once all children had arrived, attendance and lunch count were recorded. Two "Class Helpers" then delivered the slips to the office, and two others initiated the flag salute. The morning meeting came next. During this time, the morning message, the daily schedule, the daily news, Word Wall work, the calendar, and the weather report were all completed. These literacy-rich activities were then followed up by a large mo-

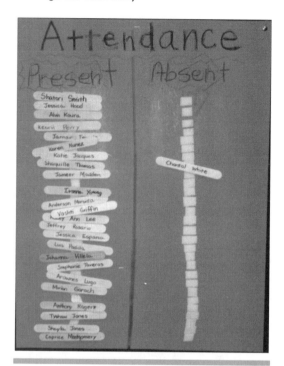

When children arrive at school, they check in at the Attendance Station.

tor control activity. Danielle chose to have the children do "Phonercise" (Feldman, 2000), an exercise that reinforced their phonic knowledge. The children were to say a letter of the alphabet as they stretched to the sky, make the letter's sound as they touched their hips, and say a word that began with that letter as they touched the ground. Danielle provided closure to this brief activity by asking children to share new words that they were able to come up with during the exercise.

Math was next on the class's daily schedule. A shared reading experience of the story *Ten in a Bed* (Rees, 1988) opened the lesson. At the end of the story, the children were asked to identify how the numbers were being counted in the story. After agreeing that the numbers were being counted backward, Danielle asked the children to go to their cubbies and bring out their stuffed animals that they had brought in to go along with their "Bedtime" theme. Once the children had returned with their animals, she showed the children a number line that she had taped to the edge of the bookshelf. One by one, the children brought their animals to the counter and seated them above the numbers. With all the animals on the counter, the children counted the number of animals aloud, as Danielle pointed to the numbers on the number line. She went on to tell the students that they were going to use their animals to tell the story again. The class proceeded to use the bears to reenact the story, this time counting backward from 18 to 0. After all the bears had rolled over, the class practiced counting backward, as individual children were called upon to use a pointer to point to the numbers as they were said. To close the lesson, Danielle handed out sentence strips with number lines written on them; she modeled for the children how they were to use their fingers to follow the numbers as they counted backward.

The children then enjoyed a 15-minute dramatic playtime. During this time, many of the children chose to create a farm and in turn to become farmers or farm animals, using the various farm-related clothes, masks, and puppets that were made available to them. They used blocks to create pens and corrals. Some children chose to play "house" using the dress-up clothes and kitchen area. Two children worked cooperatively to create a menu for their restaurant.

A read-aloud was next on the schedule. Danielle had the children collect their animals and snuggle in on the carpet for the story. She held the book—*Wynken, Blynken and Nod* (Fields, 1985)—so that all the children could see it and read the title, the author's name, and the illustrator's name. She asked the children to share their predictions for the story based upon the cover's picture and title. Before beginning to read, she asked, "Who do you think Wynken, Blynken, and Nod are?"

As the story was read, a child quickly made note of the rhyming words in the text. Danielle praised the child for this observation and encouraged the others to listen for the rhyming words. Danielle stopped occasionally to think aloud: "Is this little girl dreaming?", "Could a little girl really fly in the starry sky?", "I'm still wondering . . . who are Wynken, Blynken, and Nod?", "Who is the author talking about when he says 'the fishermen three'?" As Danielle thought aloud, the children would call out possible answers. At the end of the story, Danielle invited the children to share their reactions to the story. The students began a discussion focusing on their dreams. Danielle made this reading an interactive experience during which she modeled for the children effective comprehension strategies.

It was time for the children to line up for lunch and outside recess. Danielle began the transition by calling the children up one at a time to place their bears back on the number line and to line up by the classroom door. Once all children were in line, Danielle handed a pointer to the line leader and clapped out a pattern to get the class's attention. The line leader then used the pointer to point to the words of the poem "Ready for the Hall" as he led the class in a choral reading.

Upon the class's return from recess, they reassembled in the Reader's Corner for a shared reading experience using *Goodnight Moon* (Brown, 1947/1991). Danielle guided the reading through the use of a pointer. The class began with the cover, reading the title and author's name. They proceeded to the title page, where they reviewed publisher and copyright. Following the reading, the class used highlighting tape to highlight the pairs of rhyming words found in the text. An interactive writing experience, in which the class generated a T-chart of rhyming words, was next. Students made observations concerning the similarities in the spelling of some rhyming words and the differences in the spelling of others; Danielle encouraged and praised these student observations. After generating the list, the class chose one pair of rhyming words to work with at a time as students made a sentence with each pair. The class then lined up for the related art class and followed the same routine as earlier.

Activities in the various centers and guided literacy instruction followed. After reviewing each of the centers that was open and the activities that went along with them, the children were called two at a time to make their personal center selections. Once all children were in their centers and actively engaged, Danielle called her first guided literacy instruction group. When the group assembled, Danielle put on a colorful beaded necklace. There were 24 beads on the necklace—one bead to represent each person in the class, including the teacher. (Danielle refers to this as her "Cooperation Necklace." When she is wearing it, the children are not to disturb her or the group/individual she is working with, unless it is an emergency. The necklace is a constant reminder to the children that they need to work together to solve problems and to respect the learning time of others.)

There were four children in this group. They were going to be working with a book entitled *The Birthday Cake* (Van der Meer, 1992). Danielle began the lesson by having the children sing the song "Happy Birthday to You." After singing, the group members discussed what the song made them think of. After accepting numerous answers from each child, Danielle handed out a copy of the book to each child and asked them to make predictions. She then guided them through a picture walk of the text.

After the picture walk, Danielle provided each child with a rubber fingertip with a long rubber fingernail. The children slipped these on their pointer fingers and then proceeded to chorally read and point to the words in the title. They continued in this fashion as they read the book, which contained only two words per page. After the choral reading, Danielle invited each child to do an independent reading of the story, practicing the one-to-one correspondence. She made a note that her objective for this group was to aid them in developing a one-to-one correspondence between words read and words on the page.

Once all the children finished, Danielle provided each child with a plastic bag containing every word from the story written on index cards. After modeling how to build a sentence from the story using their word cards, and how to read the sentence by moving the words to the left as they were read, Danielle allowed the children time to do the same. To close, each child conducted another independent reading of the story, and then was given another plastic bag labeled "My Reading Place Book—due back in 2 days!" Each child placed the book, finger pointer, and word cards in the bag. The children then put their bags in their cubbies, so that they could share their book and materials with their families.

Danielle then met with two other groups. The materials and activities used varied for each group. To signal that center time was over, Danielle sang a cleanup song. The children returned to their tables after cleaning up. As part of their routine, Danielle and the children then proceeded to share compliments with one another focusing on behaviors observed during center time. Student compliments included: "I like how Ivory helped me retell the story *Lunch* [Fleming, 1993]," "Me, Whitney, and Josh played Alphabet Bingo together nicely," "I like how I worked with somebody new in the Writing Center." These brief exchanges brought about a positive closure to this important instructional time.

A snack and indoor free time followed. Children were given the option of taking a rest time; however, none of the children in the class opted for it. During the indoor free time, children were permitted to use any of the materials in the classroom. Eight of the children chose to write in the Writing Center, and three chose to read in the Reader's Corner. The board games *Candyland* and *Pizza Party* occupied six children. The rest of the class was either engaged in dramatic play or the construction of a forest using Legos.

The final lesson for the day was a social studies/health lesson. Danielle had the student brainstorm things that they do before going to sleep. As the class brainstormed, Danielle recorded their ideas with a simple picture sketched next to each on chart paper. Ideas offered by the children included "Brush my teeth," "Say good night," "Give hugs and kisses," "Drink water," "Go to the bathroom," "Take a bath," "Brush my hair." After the brainstorming, Danielle informed the children that they had become songwriters without even knowing it. She then led the class in singing "This is the way . . . " to the tune of "Here We Go Round the Mulberry Bush." A sample follows: "This is the way I brush my teeth, brush my teeth, brush my teeth. This is the way I brush my teeth at bedtime." They continued in this fashion for each idea brainstormed. After singing once, the children were inspired to add ideas to the list. Finally, the students sang their song again, this time using hand motions to act it out. The day came to an end with an independent reading time and end-of-the-day routines.

SUMMARY

The children in this kindergarten classroom experience literacy in many different forms. The terminology used to describe these literacy experiences remains consistent with that used at other grade levels; however, the content, strategies, and time allotments provide for a developmentally appropriate social, emotional, physical, and intellectual experience.

The children are involved in an environment that made literacy a part of all that they do. The literacy experiences value the developmental nature of the young learners and address the varied learning styles of all children. An enthusiasm for literacy and learning is apparent in all that Danielle does. Her excitement is contagious. As a result, her students embody a positive attitude toward literacy, learning, one another, and themselves as individuals.

THREE

First-Grade Case Study

INTRODUCTION TO THE TEACHER, CATHERINE KEEFE

Catherine Keefe (a composite of several teachers) has been teaching for 9 years. She has a master's degree in education and became certified in an undergraduate teacher education program. Prior to teaching first grade, she was a kindergarten teacher.

Cathy teaches in a school district that provides strong staff development for its teachers. The in-service sessions are usually presented by someone from within the district who has received the necessary training. The principal takes a major role concerning instruction in the school. He visits classrooms regularly and is respected by teachers. Teachers are given a great deal of responsibility in making decisions about instruction. The climate in the building is professional and friendly. Collaboration among administrators, teachers, and parents creates a positive and productive atmosphere in the school.

The school in which Cathy teaches houses kindergarten through second grade, in a small, middle-class, urban/suburban setting. The population in the school is diverse. Fifty percent of the children are of European origin, 20% are of African descent, 10% are Hispanic, 10% are Asian, and 10% are from various other backgrounds. The town is next to a large university, and many of the students are children of college professors.

There are 23 children of diverse ability in Cathy's class. According to school policy, each classroom must contain children of all ability levels. Cathy reports that although most of her students were emergent readers at the beginning of the school year, some children did not know all of the letters of the alphabet, while others were reading at the second- or third-grade level.

There is a teacher's aide in Cathy's classroom for about 1 hour each morning. The aide helps students work independently at centers while Cathy works with guided reading groups. Parents are encouraged to work in the classroom, especially during center time. Cathy has also requested student teachers.

TEACHING PHILOSOPHY

Cathy believes in the importance of using extended periods of time to develop language arts skills. Her program is designed around literacy themes, such as studying poetry, reading the words of a particular author, or learning the elements of story struc-

Portions of this chapter are adapted from the following sources: (1) Morrow, Tracey, Woo, and Pressley (1999). Copyright 1999 by the International Reading Association. All rights reserved. Adapted by permission. (2) Loden, Morrow, and Asbury (2001). Copyright 2001 by The Guilford Press. Adapted by permission.

ture. Along with the literacy themes, she also integrates content area units into all aspects of her curriculum, including reading, writing, math, and social studies. Cathy uses children's literature to teach skills, and she reinforces skills whenever opportunities arise. She feels strongly that the way to meet individual needs is to work with children frequently, in small homogeneous groups, using guided reading instruction. Within these groups, she is very attentive to individual needs. She utilizes strategies from an integrated language arts perspective, has a strong program for skill development, and employs a carefully thought-out design for delivering instruction.

Cathy's classroom style is exemplary. Her outstanding characteristics include knowledge of multiple literacy strategies, an ability to integrate different elements of the curriculum, and strong guidance/direction skills. Above all, Cathy talks and works with children in a supportive manner. Cathy's support and the positive atmosphere in her room motivate the children to work for themselves and for her as the teacher.

Familiar scenes in Cathy's classroom involve mini-lessons and guided reading. During a mini-lesson, children sit on the rug in the front of the room and are thoroughly engaged in what Cathy shares with them. During guided reading lessons, Cathy works with a small group of students while the rest of the class is productively involved in independent work. Cathy has modeled each independent activity for them. Reading and writing are always in progress. Children work both alone and in collaboration with others. Students know exactly what to do and where to do it. The children are self-directed and constantly engaged in activities that will enhance literacy development. The children smile and are pleasant to each other; they are also extremely helpful to each other and seek guidance from peers when necessary. The day is seamless, as one activity flows into the next.

THE PHYSICAL ENVIRONMENT IN THE CLASSROOM

Cathy's classroom is a literacy-rich environment. The room is average in size and rectangular in shape. Children's desks are arranged in groups of four to encourage social interaction, as in Amy Holt's room (see Chapter One). Bulletin boards exhibit children's work, and charts containing print about work children are doing are hung around the room. Each theme being studied is quite evident from the artwork, written work, artifacts, charts, and posters displayed around the room. Open-faced bookshelves display theme books, and there are also books in baskets arranged by different reading levels, genres, and topics. There is a system for checking books out of the classroom to take home. Children are encouraged to use all the materials, which are all easily accessible.

Group meetings and mini-lessons take place on the rug in the front of the room. The wall near the rug is adorned with a calendar, weather chart, helper chart, classroom rules, and other functional charts that help the class work. In this area there is also an experience chart on an easel, and a special chair from which Cathy or the students can address the class during storytelling and sharing times.

Centers are organized along the walls. Also as in Amy Holt's classroom (see Chapter One), these include Art, Math, Social Studies, Science, and Literacy Centers, and the Literacy Center includes a number of different centers and stations. Each of the centers has materials relating to the content area, as well as special materials for daily activities linked to current topics. Space is available to store manipulatives and toys (such as blocks, building toys, and puzzle materials). Children sign in at each center they use to record their participation.

Guided reading lessons take place at a circular table. At this table, Cathy has a pocket chart for sentence strips, individual white boards for word analysis work, leveled reading materials, record-keeping folders, and a flip chart stand for writing charts. Children store their books in a bag on the windowsill in this area, one compartment per student. This area also contains plastic baskets for each child's markers, scissors, and various materials needed to carry out work during the day.

CLASSROOM GUIDANCE AND DIRECTION

One of the first steps in effective classroom organization is setting up the classroom. As noted above, Cathy's classroom is designed to be student-friendly. It is rich in materials that support instruction. The materials are housed in such a way that children have easy access. The room is arranged for whole-group, small-group, and one-on-one instruction. Early in the school year, children are introduced to the physical design of the classroom and how the different areas are used.

The management of children is well coordinated. For example, during snack time, a child who is in charge puts on a tape of classical music; this signals all students to set aside what they are doing, take out their snacks, and enjoy eating and socializing. After 15 minutes, the child in charge turns the tape off, and the students go back to what they were doing.

Starting with the first day of school, Cathy teaches her children to be self-directed learners. She believes that children must be taught to think and do for themselves. The first few weeks of school are used to familiarize children with the morning routine. During this time there are whole-class mini-lessons; then Cathy models activities for the children to do independently while she works with reading teams. Children are taught to do buddy reading, and to care for their guided reading materials by storing them in a special spot on the windowsill. They know where the centers are and how to fill out the sign-in sheet for each center activity they have completed. The children have helped create the class rules, and Cathy is consistent in making sure that both she and the children follow these rules. For example, one rule states that if a child misbehaves three times, the student must return to his or her seat or leave the rest of the group, and work on assignments from his or her folder. Cathy enforced this rule one day with Jeremy. After Cathy had talked to him twice about misbehaving, she said "Jeremy, you have one more chance, and then you will have to go back to your desk." When Jeremy interrupted the morning discussion a third time, Cathy looked over at him and said, "That's three times, Jeremy. I'm sorry, but you'll have to go back to your desk now." Cathy did not raise her voice, was very matter-of-fact, and almost sounded as if she was giving Jeremy positive reinforcement. Jeremy, although not happy about having to leave the group, understood the reason why he had to go and what he was to do when he got to his seat.

In preparation for independent work, Cathy carefully models each of the new tasks at each center in the classroom. Students then know what to do and where to do it. Children have to accomplish all tasks described for their self-directed learning, but

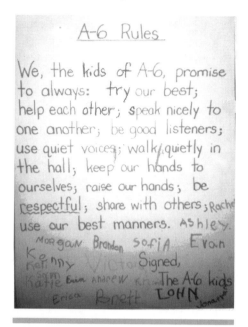

A-6 Rules

We, the kids of A-6, promise to always: try our best; help each other; speak nicely to one another; be good listeners; use quiet voices; walk quietly in the hall; keep our hands to ourselves; raise our hands; be respectful; share with others; use our best manners.

Rules are taught early in the school year, and an emphasis on following them is always evident.

in no particular order. Children may use a center when there is an open seat there; about four children can work comfortably at each center.

Cathy is very aware of what is happening in her class at all times. Like Danielle Lynch (see Chapter Two), she is always in a position where she can see everyone in the room. When she is involved in a guided reading lesson, she is in a corner of the room where she can glance at all the children.

Cathy realizes that planning interesting activities, allowing movement from one area of the room to the next, and providing different settings for learning (from whole-group contexts to meeting students on a one-on-one basis) will keep children engaged and act as preventative measures for misbehavior. According to Cathy, if children are actively involved in interesting experiences that are challenging but can bring success, they are likely to remain engaged in their work. At all times, students respect her and understand the rules, and this nurturing and sensitive atmosphere works to maintain discipline and on task involvement. In general, children are rarely in need of disciplinary action, since their rules, their routine, and the respectful atmosphere created by the teacher provide a productive environment.

Cathy always speaks in a soft, warm, pleasant voice. When she needs to speak to a child about being on task, it is in the same tone of voice that she uses when teaching a lesson or giving positive reinforcement. Cathy has a large vocabulary of encouraging, positive, and reinforcing phrases, such as "Good job," "Wow, you really do understand that," "I bet you'll get that right if you try," "Let me give you some clues about that," "I love the way you are doing your work today," and "I think you'll really like this new job I have planned for you." Cathy's expectations for her students are high but not unrealistic. Students experience success often. She constantly encourages them to go forward, but not in a way that will cause anxiety. The positive reinforcement she offers is for real accomplishment. She offers constructive criticism when necessary, but it is done with respect and concern for children's self-esteem.

TYPES OF READING EXPERIENCES

Cathy involves her children in many types of reading on a daily basis. She begins the day with a choice of independent reading or buddy reading. During the morning gathering on the rug, Cathy reads aloud from a high-quality piece of children's literature to the whole class. The story is always tied to the theme being studied, or to some other special event. Cathy reads from the comfortable chair while the children sit on the rug in front of her. Cathy always has a purpose for the reading, which is reinforced with discussion before, during, and after reading the story. One day, for instance, to emphasize the skill of story retelling, Cathy reviewed the elements within a narrative piece: the setting, the problem faced by the main character, the events to help the main character solve his or her problem, and the resolution to the problem. She told the class that after the story was read, different children would have a chance to retell it. She asked them to really listen for the parts of the story so that these could be included in their retelling. Comprehension skills are emphasized in the whole-class readings, and opportunities for reinforcing word analysis skills are taken when they arise.

Children engage in partner reading on a daily basis. They select a book of their choice from a special basket that has books by authors they are studying, or content area themes they are learning about. The partners share the reading. They help each other if they need it and are very engaged in social interactions during the reading of their stories.

Poetry charts are hung around the room, and poems are often chanted together. These have usually been selected to match the current class theme or to emphasize a word analysis skill.

Reading also occurs during the meetings of teams. Teams consist of children of similar reading ability and meet daily for guided reading. There are five teams in Cathy's room. Each child brings a "book in a bag" to the guided reading lesson. This is a plastic bag containing not only a book, but all of the materials the child needs for the lesson. During guided reading, the children first get to read a familiar book, one they have read before. A new book is then introduced. All books are from a group of leveled materials. Cathy reads through with the children and writes down notes about their reading, such as "Reads slowly," "Reads word by word," "Self-corrected errors," "Uses skills taught to figure out new words." The book and the bag are then taken home with a reading homework assignment written out for the parent, which has a place for the parent's signature. Cathy evaluates the students in each team on a monthly basis, and teams are changed as skill needs change. (The guided reading lessons are discussed further below under "Skill Development.")

As described earlier, Cathy has a large collection of children's literature sorted into separate baskets that are labeled by topics, genres, and levels of reading. This makes for easy selection when children read independently.

Children bring their work for guided reading in their individual "book in a bag."

TYPES OF WRITING EXPERIENCES

Students write every day in Cathy's class in many different capacities. She emphasizes how important writing is to the development of reading, and how closely connected she feels reading and writing are. Cathy says, "I can often tell a child's reading level when I review a piece of the child's writing."

Children have journals in which they write short daily personal entries at the beginning of the school day and as an independent activity. They also use their journals for spelling words and other special words they learn and wish to record. Three times a week, Cathy has a Writing Workshop. Children generate their own topics for writing. They choose things that are of interest to them, such as a movie they have seen or a person they admire. Before writing, Cathy conducts a mini-lesson about some element of writing, such as punctuation or creating well-formed stories. The lessons are selected based on needs that Cathy observes in her children. Children then write their stories and have conferences with Cathy about revisions they can make. When each story is finished, it is read to another child in the class for feedback. Children are guided in how to offer feedback, such as "I like the first part of your story, but the second part is hard to understand. You need to explain things more clearly." When stories are completed, which may take a week or even 4 weeks, they are bound and placed in the classroom library for others to read.

Cathy's students also observe Cathy writing on a daily basis. Cathy writes the morning message, which is dictated to her by the children. She writes in a fine model of manuscript for the children to observe.

The story read aloud by Cathy during the morning gathering always includes a discussion about the book and a written response of some type from the children. This response is done during center time with a partner. The partners are encouraged to talk about what they would write: for example, after Cathy read *Arthur's Tooth* (Brown, 1985) during American Dental Week. After hearing this story about a child losing a tooth, the children were to write about an experience they themselves had had with losing teeth. Cathy checked to see that everyone either had a loose tooth to talk about or a tooth that had already fallen out. The children first discussed what they were going to write about with their partners. Then each child did a draft of his or her story. Next, each child read the draft to his or her partner, who gave some suggestions for revisions. The children did their revisions and then read the pieces again to each other for final editing.

The children therefore have the opportunity to observe writing by the teacher, as well as to participate in free writing in journals, story writing with a purpose, content-related writing, and writing with a partner.

Writing occurs all day long and in all content areas. Records of scientific experiments are kept in journals. Some math projects require expository or narrative writing. For example, one day students had to measure objects in the room that appeared to be either 6 inches or 12 inches long. Strips of paper cut to these sizes helped children to determine items of the appropriate length. When they found them, they classified them as 6-inch or 12-inch items and had to write them on a piece of paper. They sought the help of peers and used the dictionary when hunting for unknown spellings.

SKILL DEVELOPMENT

Skill development is evident throughout the school day. It happens purposefully and is planned, but spontaneous lessons occur as well. When children share with the group things they've brought from home, for example, they are reinforcing their language skills. They must speak clearly in a voice that everyone can hear, use complete sentences, and pronounce words to the best of their ability.

At the bottom of each morning message, Cathy will print initial consonants or word chunks for children to find in the message. These consonants and word chunks are those being emphasized at the time a given chart is written. Sometimes none of the print elements will be found in the morning message, so children may be asked to generate a list of words that have the elements in question.

A mini-lesson follows the morning message. The lesson emphasizes development of such skills as learning digraphs, silent consonants, or vowel sounds. Cathy will connect the mini-lesson to the content of a story whenever possible. For example, when teaching the children about the vowel digraph or chunk *ou*, and the sound that it has as in the word *mouse*, Cathy read the book *Mouse Soup* by Arnold Lobel (1977). She put the two words *mouse* and *soup* on a chart and said, "Remember these words from the story we just read? Can someone read them for me?" Tisha raised her hand and read the two words. Cathy pointed out the *ou* chunk and reminded the children that they had been learning about its sound in words. She asked, "Which of these words has the sound of *ou* together as we learned it?" One of the children said, "*Mouse*." Cathy offered positive reinforcement for the response and asked someone to read the other word. Chris volunteered and read "*soup*." Cathy asked whether both words had the same sound. Everyone responded, "Nooo!" Then Cathy asked, "Which one sounds like the *ou* we learned?" Everyone said that *mouse* did and *soup* did not. They then proceeded to make a list of words that had *ou* in them and sounded like *mouse*, and those that had the *ou* sound as in the word *soup*.

Most skill development takes place during guided reading. As noted earlier, children are placed in teams for guided reading. Cathy has five teams in her classroom. The teams meet daily and are grouped by ability. There is a 5-day plan for the meetings, emphasizing different skills each day. The basic format for the lessons includes reviewing words from a story already read and writing them in a journal, reading a familiar story, and building a comprehension strategy into the discussion of the story. After the story is read, children arrange cut-up words from the story into sentences and have sentence strips from the story to order and read. They then mix up their words and sentence strips and have to reorganize them to make sense. A word analysis skill embedded in the books they are reading is taught. Each child has his or her own white board to work with words. They do some work with sound–symbol relationships and some practice in phonemic awareness if necessary. Next, a new book is introduced with new vocabulary; the book is discussed first to build background knowledge, and then children take turns reading. As described earlier, Cathy takes notes as the children read to remember special needs they may have. They then work with cut-up words from the new story, sorting them into sentences as well as sentence strips. Each child is to write the new words in his or her journal, and a journal entry as well. Finally, Cathy discusses homework; this often includes reading the familiar book to a family member, practicing word cards associated with the book, and reading the new book together. Parents are to sign the homework card.

To accommodate individual differences, the teacher meets the children for guided reading instruction in small groups.

During guided reading, Cathy pays close attention to the individual accomplishments and needs of each child. She writes a personal note to each family, telling the parent about the success and needs of the child, and work that is to be done together. The child follows along as the note is written.

Each day in a guided reading lesson, Cathy will focus her attention on one child to discover his or her strengths and weaknesses. This child will be asked to participate in more tasks than others on that given day. Other children in the group will participate in activities; however, the focus child will get more attention. In this way, not only is each child participating in a small-group setting, but simultaneously once a week he or she is the focus child in a one-to-one setting as well.

Cathy has a very systematic method for teaching skills. Comprehension skill development is embedded in storybook readings and guided reading lessons, and many strategies are introduced to students—from engaging children in story retelling, to repeated readings of stories to instill revisiting the text. She also works with having her students make predictions, draw conclusions, and demonstrate knowledge of structural elements of stories. Students study the styles of authors and illustrators, and respond to literature in writing as well as in oral discussions.

Cathy also has a very strong skill word analysis program. She works with vowels and consonants, and she does a lot of work with word chunks or patterns. Cathy includes activities in an area of word analysis that she has taught in a mini-lesson. She reinforces the concepts through planned experiences during independent work at centers, as well as in guided reading lessons. She uses poems to emphasize specific skills, lists of words demonstrating patterns in print, and rhyming games when these are available.

Cathy states that while she emphasizes skill development in the classroom, the manner in which these skills are taught is also very important. She teaches phonics within the context of literature, in teachable moments, and more explicitly with worksheets she creates for practice. She also has manipulative materials that help children develop skills in an active manner.

CROSS-CURRICULAR CONNECTIONS

Cathy's teaching is filled with cross-curricular connections. Her class is always engaged in the study of a theme, which may be an author study, a science or social studies topic, a holiday, or a special event. The stories she reads are always theme-related. Books for silent reading, partner reading, and even guided reading are theme-related when possible. Assigned writing and independent activities are tied to the theme as well.

On Halloween, for example, Cathy read the story *Charlie and the Chocolate Factory* (Roald Dahl, 1964/2001), which was related to the surprise snack she had brought for the children for their Halloween party that afternoon. She had also selected that book since it was filled with rhymes, and the literacy theme being emphasized was rhyming words. In addition to rhyming words, Cathy asked children to look at double vowels, such as those in the words *Halloween, green,* and *tree.* For guided reading, Cathy got some little Halloween books that were very predictable and easy to read for the lesson. She also had Halloween poems to read and used Halloween words for rhyming.

The Math Center had different types of chocolate bars in a basket (this was Cathy's surprise). Children were to poll members of the class as to which type of chocolate they would like for their treat—for example, plain milk chocolate, a chocolate bar with almonds, or a dark chocolate bar. They then had to tally how many people wanted each type of bar. In the Art Center, the children were making masks for their Halloween costumes.

Themes are integrated into every day in Cathy's activities. This is one of the outstanding characteristics of her classroom. Cathy notes:

Children use manipulative materials to practice skills.

"It is difficult to pull together theme-related materials regularly, but I believe it to be very important to make learning meaningful. Every year I teach, I add to my repertoire of stories, songs, poems, art activities, math, science, social studies, and vocabulary for units of study . . . and now it isn't difficult to accomplish. I have the materials and ideas."

TEACHABLE MOMENTS

It is apparent that Cathy plans her teaching carefully and takes advantage of teachable moments. For example, on the day the children talked about the *oa* sound, Danny brought in a miniature boat that he had put together with his dad for sharing time. Cathy immediately drew the children's attention to the sheet of paper where they had written words that had the *oa* sound earlier, to see whether the word boat had been included. It was on the chart, so they didn't have to write it in.

Very often in the course of conversation, Cathy gives the children reminders such as: "Remember when we were learning about the chunk *and*? Well, the word *brand* that we just talked about uses that chunk."

THE DAILY SCHEDULE IN CATHY KEEFE'S CLASSROOM

When children walk into Cathy's room, they are immediately engaged in writing journal entries of their choice about their family, friends, or experiences. If there is extra time before the morning meeting, they can take a book and read.

The day formally begins with a morning meeting held on the rug. During this meeting, the calendar and weather are discussed. A morning message follows, which is associated with the content area theme being studied and with plans for the day. After the message is written and read, the class talks about and looks for print within the message related to word analysis that they are studying. Next, five children have the opportunity to share things brought from home. They are encouraged to bring in materials that relate to the theme at hand.

At this time Cathy reads a theme-related piece of children's literature, beginning with a discussion that focuses on the development of comprehension or word analysis skills.

After the story, Cathy reviews independent activities for children to pursue at the centers while she meets with other children for guided reading in small groups. The independent activities include partner reading, a writing assignment relating a storybook read, and one task selected from either the art, math, or science centers. Cathy models each independent activity before they begin. While children engage in these self-directed activities, Cathy meets with teams of children as they are called for guided reading lessons. Everyone breaks for a snack at about 10:00 A.M. After the snack, independent activities at centers and guided reading groups continue. Lunch comes after the guided reading group lessons and lasts from 11:30 to 12:10. The afternoon begins with a math lesson. Depending on the day there could be writing workshop, spelling, art, or social studies.

Children can participate in quiet book reading when they enter school in the morning, after they have completed their journal entries.

A TYPICAL DAY IN FIRST GRADE

Upon entering the room, the children immediately took out their journals and began writing about something of interest to them. Rosangela wrote about her birthday party, and Damien wrote about his pair of new sneakers. Janet finished her entry and was reading a book about nutrition, which was related to the content area theme being studied: "Healthy Bodies and Healthy Minds."

After opening exercises at 9:00, the day began with a discussion about the calendar and the weather. The children counted how many days had already passed in November and how many days were left. Cathy then began the morning message, which had some news about a visitor they were having who would help them with an exercise program, which was also linked to the current theme.

For the morning message, children dictated sentences about healthy food they had eaten over the weekend and healthy activities they had done. Jim talked about the salad he ate, and Jovanna talked about how much exercise she had done. Others talked about bike riding or long walks they had taken with their families.

After the message was written and read, Cathy asked the class to look for print within the message related to word analysis. The *th* chunk was a digraph they had discussed. They noticed that the word *healthy* used the *th* chunk, as well as *the*, and then they added others.

Today it was Jon's, Adasha's, Andra's, and George's turn to share things brought from home. They had brought some things that related to the theme. For example, Adasha had her mom's grocery list and read all the healthy foods on it. George had a cookbook and had marked some healthy recipes.

Next, Cathy prepared to read a theme-related piece of children's literature. The story was about a Hispanic child and her grandmother who speaks only Spanish. Since her grandchild could speak English, she'd bring her along shopping for food, so she could act as her helper in asking for things she was unable to ask for in English. The name of the book was *Grandma's Helper* (Meyer, 1993).

Before beginning the reading, Cathy started a discussion about good foods we need to keep our bodies healthy. Then the discussion turned to helping others, which is another way to make us feel good about ourselves. One child talked about helping her grandma walk, since she had to use a cane.

Cathy told the children they would hear a story called *Grandma's Helper*. She asked the children to listen while she read, and to find out how many times and in what ways the little girl helped her grandmother. She also said that during independent activities, she would like the class to write about when they helped someone and how. After the story was read, the class talked about different ways in which the little girl in the story helped her grandma. Then Cathy asked the children how they had helped others. Cathy wrote on the big chart how she herself had helped her mother prepare Thanksgiving dinner, as a model for what the children would be doing.

Following this discussion, Cathy reviewed independent activities for children to participate in at the centers while she met with teams for guided reading in small groups. She modeled each of the activities.

In the Math Center, she posted a sheet that said, "Find a partner. Have someone use a timer, and count how many jumping jacks you can do in 1 minute and how many hops. Write it down in the box on the paper provided. Now you do the same for your partner."

In the Science Center, there was a figure of a child on a felt board and figures with felt backings of a brain, heart, lungs, and stomach. Children in the Science Center were to place the body organs in the right part of the body. There was a sheet with the figure and the body parts, on which each child was to draw the organs in the right place on the body.

In the Art Center, children were to cut and paste from magazines healthy food collages. They were also to classify the foods in the basic four food groups.

For word analysis in the Literacy Center, children were to write all the foods they could think of from A to Z. There was a sheet with a box for each letter. The children were to write the word in each box, and draw a picture of it as well. This they could do with a partner, since it was a big job.

Before the self-directed activities began, the children chanted the following poem, which was on a chart. It was taken from the book *Potatoes on Tuesday* (Lillegard, 1993).

Potatoes on Tuesday

On Monday, cabbage, on Tuesday, potatoes,
On Wednesday, carrots, on Thursday, tomatoes,
On Friday, peas and green beans too—
On Saturday, a great big pot of stew, MMMM.

Cathy asked the children to look for the initial consonant *T* and the *th* chunk in any of the words.

Now the self-directed activities began, with students selecting a book to read with a partner. Some of the books included *Grandma's Helper* and *Potatoes on Tuesday*, as well as *Potluck* (Corbitt, 1962), *Cookies* (Pappas, 1980), *This Is the Plate* (Trussell-Cullen, 1995), and *Engelbert's Exercise* (Paxton, 1993). These books all reflected the "Healthy Bodies and Healthy Minds" theme.

Partners read together, and when they finished, they started on their writing activity about someone they had helped and how. They continued their partnership in this writing assignment by doing a prewriting discussion, and having a conference about what was written after the first draft. In addition to these activities, children then selected one of the modeled center activities to complete, as described above. While children engaged in these self-directed activities, Cathy was meeting with teams of other children as they were called for guided reading lessons.

Everyone stopped working at 10:00 A.M. and had a snack. After the snack, the independent activities at centers and guided reading groups resumed. In the guided reading groups, children first read familiar books, some relating to the "Healthy Bodies and Healthy Minds" theme. They worked with sequencing sentence strips, identifying words from the cut-up sentence strips, and putting them into order. The story read was discussed. A new book was then introduced, with background information provided. Cathy kept records on the children's performance, and sent notes home with homework and the book-in-the-bag materials.

Lunch came after the guided reading group lessons (from 11:30 to 12:10). In the afternoon, Cathy had a Writing Workshop. Children were working on writing books about good nutrition and exercise. She did a mini-lesson about capital letters at the beginning of sentences, and periods, exclamation marks, or question marks at the end. Then the children continued writing. Some had conferences with Cathy and were at the final editing stages with their stories. Others were still revising.

The rest of the afternoon included math and a special whole-class activity. They started with a written recipe for making fruit salad, then discussed the types and amounts of fruit they would be using. A parent volunteer came in to help the children make the fruit salad, which they all got to eat before going home.

SUMMARY

Cathy's classroom is happy, productive, and a wonderful place for any first-grade child. She has built a community of learners in her classroom, filled with cooperation, respect, and a strong expectation for hard work and achievement. Those who work along with her, such as parents, aides, children, and student teachers, continue to foster the goals Cathy has set forth and the atmosphere she has created in her class.

Cathy's classroom is rich with materials, so that children have choices, challenging activities, social interaction, and success. The classroom also has space and provisions for whole-group lessons, small-group instruction, and one-on-one interactions. Her school day is structured to include various experiences that are developmentally appropriate, yet with an emphasis on the acquisition of skills. Children have been taught routines and rules, and know how to use the room when they are in self-directed roles. In particular, children working independently have learned to respect the teacher and their peers when these others are engaged in a group lesson. Cathy is consistent in her guidance and direction; therefore, children know what is expected of them, and carry out work that needs to be done.

The affective quality in the room is exemplary. Part of this comes naturally to Cathy, who is a warm, relaxed, and gentle person. However, a great deal of it is purposeful. She speaks to children with respect and in an adult manner. She does not raise her voice; nor does she use punitive remarks, facial expressions, or intonations in her voice that would suggest disapproval. Yet children learn to understand appropriate classroom behavior.

The day flows smoothly from one activity to the next. The routine is consistent and therefore easy for the children to follow. The activities are varied to keep children engaged. Some activities are done alone, and others with groups of children. There is a lot to do, but it can be accomplished.

Children have the benefit of experiencing literacy in many different forms. There is extensive exposure to literature in the forms of shared read-alouds with the teacher, independent reading alone, buddy reading with a peer, and guided reading for skill development with the teacher. Writing experiences are similar, with journal writing, Writing Workshops, and observation of writing by the teacher.

Reading and writing are done with a purpose. Whatever the literacy theme or the content area unit, it is integrated into reading and writing experiences to bring meaning to skill development.

This very fine classroom is directed by a person who has a natural talent for teaching. However, the classroom is as it is because of a lot of hard work and experience. It is

Rules for good writing—some of which have just been covered in a Writing Workshop mini-lesson—help students check their work.

also exemplary because Cathy is in a school that supports and expects outstanding performance by teachers. The atmosphere in the building is professional, collaborative, and committed to excellence. There are frequent staff development sessions; teachers meet regularly at grade levels to share and plan. The principal plays an important role in supporting curriculum development. In addition to this supportive environment, Cathy takes advantage of what her school has to offer. She has expanded her knowledge by receiving a master's degree in education; she also attends professional conferences and reads professional literature. As a result, Cathy demonstrates a well-balanced approach to literacy development, with strategies that utilize an integrated language arts approach—explicit direct instructional settings for skill development, as well as settings that encourage social collaboration and development of problem solving. Cathy has developed her own strong philosophy for teaching literacy, and creates a program that illustrates this philosophy. What we see in her room are the results of careful thought, planning, experience, and expertise.

FOUR

Kindergarten and First-Grade Activities and Plans

GETTING STARTED

Language Arts Block Time Schedules

These suggested schedules should be rotated for a balanced program. Note that each schedule covers the LAB *only* and not the entire instructional day.

Schedule 1: Suggested for Kindergarten

8:30–8:50:   **Things to do when the students arrive**
                   Attendance/Lunch Station
                   Folder check-in and Note Basket
                   Helper chart
                   Journal writing
                   Buddy reading
                   Independent reading

8:50–9:20:   **Morning meeting**
                   Morning message
                   Daily schedule
                   Daily news
                   Word Wall
                   Calendar
                   Weather report
                   Gross motor development

9:20–10:00:   **Guided reading instruction/independent work at centers**
                   Meeting with guided groups
                   Using a center/activity chart
                   Buddy and Independent Reading Center
                   Listening Center

Writing Center
Letter Study Center
Story Props Center
Technology Center
Rhyming Center
Science Center

10:00–10:30: Shared reading and reading aloud
Shared reading of literature

Schedule 2: Suggested for Kindergarten

8:30–8:50: Things to do when the students arrive
Attendance/Lunch Station
Folder check-in and Note Basket
Helper chart
Journal writing
Buddy reading
Independent reading

8:50–9:20: Morning meeting
Morning message
Daily schedule
Daily news
Word Wall
Calendar
Weather report

9:20–9:50: Shared reading
Shared reading of literature

9:50–10:30: Writing workshop
Mini-lesson
Guided writing
Independent writing
Sharing

10:30–10:40: Independent reading

Schedule 3: Suggested for First Grade

8:30–8:55: Things to do when the students arrive
Attendance Station
Lunch Station
Class Helper chart
Journal writing
Buddy reading
Independent reading

8:55–9:20: Morning meeting
Morning news

> Calendar
> Weather
> Morning message
> Mini-lesson: Word Wall
> Mini-lesson: Comprehension

9:20–10:20: Guided reading groups/independent work at centers
> Word Study Center
> Writing Center
> Listening Center
> Buddy and Independent Reading Center
> Math Center
> Reading the Room
> Science Center
> Overhead Projection Center
> Word Wall Scavenger Hunt Activity

10:20–11:05: Writing workshop
> Mini-lesson
> Buddy writing/independent writing
> Teacher-guided writing
> Conferences with the teacher
> Sharing

Tools for Teaching Language Arts

Classrooms contain many materials—some supplied by the demands of the curriculum and the school district and some supplied by your own preference and personal ingenuity. You may have a fully stocked classroom, or you may have one with only a minimum of materials. Be creative with what you have. And be creative when your needs go beyond what is readily available to you. Don't be afraid to ask students to bring in anything from crayons to fabric to glitter and beyond! The following list is intended to help you get started. Then it's up to you!

- Big books.
- Pointers.
- Highlighting tape.
- Framing devices (e.g., a fly swatter with the center cut out).
- Chart paper.
- Easel.
- Index cards.
- Markers.
- Crayons.
- Presharpened pencils.
- For the Listening Center: cassette player, headsets, books on tape, and books.
- Classroom rich with environmental print.
- Classroom library (which contains varied genres of children's literature).
- Wide variety of other reading materials (magazines, newspapers, etc.).
- Baskets for organizing books and materials.

- Beanbag chairs and pillows for the Reading Corner.
- Stuffed animals.
- Stick puppets; other types of puppets.
- Felt board and felt board storytelling pieces.
- Roll movie box for storytelling.
- Clothes, hats, and props for "dress-up" corner.
- Magnetic board.
- Magnetic letters and numbers.
- Chalk.
- Overhead projector.
- Leveled books.
- File folder games.
- Journals.
- Envelopes.
- Classroom mailbox.
- Dry-erase boards and erasers.
- Varied kinds of writing paper.
- Sentence strips.
- Art supplies (paint, markers, crayons, pencils, scissors, glue, construction paper).
- Computer, printer, programs.
- Pocket charts and stands.
- Book bins/book boxes.
- Small chalkboards and erasers.
- Magnetic or cardboard word chunks.
- Blank books.

Ideas for Classroom Organization and Management

Purposes:

- Use time effectively and efficiently.
- Provide a structure to the classroom setting.
- Make smooth transitions from one activity to the next.
- Gain the attention of the children

Keeping Disruptions to a Minimum While You Are Working with a Small Group:

It is essential for the children to understand that when you are working with a small group, they are not to disturb you. This must be established at the beginning of the year and followed through consistently throughout the year.

- Wear a "Do Not Disturb" or "Stop" hat. The children know that when you are wearing this hat, they must not interrupt your lesson.
- Provide a "Sign Up for Service" paper. If the children need help while you are engaged in small-group instruction, they sign their names on the "Sign Up for Service" paper. You will attend to their needs when you are finished with the small groups.
- Establish a "Teaching Table" or "Teaching Area" for small-group instruction.

The class members know that when you are at the "Teaching Table," they must try to solve their problem alone or ask a friend for help.

- Create a portable "Stop" and "Go" sign (one side says "Stop," the other side says "Go"). Carry the sign to different areas of the room. When you are working with a group, use the "Stop" side of the sign. When you are available to help students, use the "Go" side.
- Assign one or two reliable children to be the others' "helpers." When other children need help, they may ask the "helpers."

Methods for Gathering Attention:

It is helpful to have one or two routines that you regularly use to call the children's attention. The routine must be established in the beginning of the year. The expectations for the students' behavior when they hear the "call to attention" must be specific and clear. You must be consistent.

- **Listening Ears:** When you say, "Give me your listening ears," the children are to cup their hands around their ears, get quiet, and look at you.
- **Freeze:** When you say, "Freeze," the children are to stop what they are doing, get quiet, and look at her.
- **Hands Up, Ears Open:** When you say, "Hands up, ears open," the children are to put their hands in the air, get quiet, and look at you. You then say, "Hands down, ears still open."
- **Knock, Knock:** When you knock two times and raise your hand, the children stop what they are doing, raise their hands, get quiet, and look at you.
- **The Cleanup Chant:** When you say, "It's time for our cleanup song," the children are to clean up and return quietly to their seats after singing:

> Clean up, clean up,
> Everybody, everywhere!
> Clean up, clean up,
> Everybody do your share.

- **Clap Back:** Clap out a rhythm. The children are to clap back the same rhythm.
- **ABC Song:** If children need to move (e.g., to their tables, the Reading Corner, etc.) tell them where to go and have them sing the ABC song with you. By the end of the song, everyone should be in the designated area.
- **Finger Spelling:** Tell the children where to go; then finger-spell alphabet, using the signs for each letter in American Sign Language. By the end of the alphabet, the children should be in the designated area. This keeps the children focused, and it introduces them to another form of communication.
- **Counting:** Tell the children where to go; then have them count with you to a predetermined number. They should be in the designated area by the time they reach the number.
- **Tickets, Please:** After a lesson or activity, tell the children that their ticket to the next activity is an answer to a question related to what they were just learning. For example, after you have read a story aloud and discussed characters from the story, the ticket could be to name one of the characters from the story. Or you can ask for an open-ended response by asking the children to name their favorite character, the funniest character, the character they liked the least/most, and so

on. If a child is unsure of an answer, allow him or her to think about it, and return to this child after "tickets" have been collected from a few other students.

- **The "If" Game:** Make a statement beginning with "if." If a student or students can say "yes" to the statement, then they may move on to the next activity/place. For example, if it is just about snack time and the children need to go sit at their tables for snack, say, "If your name begins with *D*, please go sit down at our table for a snack." Continue with other letters.
- **All Good Listeners:** Say, "All good listeners point to your ears. All good listeners touch your shoulders. All good listeners look at the teacher." When children are following along, give the directions.
- **Follow the Leader:** Start by clapping your hands, and then change to patting your head, touching your nose, and the like.
- **If You're Ready and You Know It:** Begin singing,

> If you're ready and you know it, clap your hands.
> If you're ready and you know it clap your hands;
> If you're ready and you know it, then you'll sit right down and show it.
> If you're ready and you know it, clap your hands.

The words can be changed to fit various tasks. Let the lyrics flow for each situation at hand. For example, if the children are engaged in an art project and it is time to clean up, sing something like this:

> If you're ready and you know it, put your glue stick away.
> If you're ready and you know it, put your scissors away.
> If you're ready and you know it, then your face will really show it.
> If you're ready and you know it, put your project in the Work Basket.

THINGS TO DO WHEN THE STUDENTS ARRIVE

This section includes meaningful literacy activities for children to do when they enter school. Sometimes there is more than one activity for each area. Select one or more to use, and vary them throughout the school year. These activities should be planned to cover a period of 20–25 minutes.

Folder Check-In and Note Basket

Purposes:

- Build children's independence, responsibility, and accountability.
- Help children discover that written forms of communication are functional and meaningful.

Materials:

- One folder per child.
- Basket to hold folders.
- Basket for notes.

Activity:

1. Children go to their cubbies, hang up their belongings, and take out their folders they took home.
2. Any notes from home that are in their folders are placed in the Note Basket for you.
3. Homework in the folders is placed in the Folder Holder.

Management Tip:

→ You can check folders in the Folder Holder to ensure that all children have done their homework.
→ At the beginning of the year, to help foster home–school communication let the parents know that you will check the children's folders daily for homework and the Note Basket for notes from home. Encourage them to use this form of communication often.

Attendance Station

Purposes:

- Help children recognize their names in print.
- Use nontextual visual information to take attendance.

Materials:

- Laminated poster board chart divided into two columns labeled "Absent" and "Present."
- Two vertical strips of Velcro attached under the column headings.
- Name cards labeled with each child's name and Velcro tabs on the back.

Activity:

1. Place the chart near the door.
2. Place all the name cards on the "Absent" side of the chart.
3. In the morning when the children arrive, they remove their name cards and place them on the chart in the "Present" column.
4. At the end of the day, children put their name cards back on the "Absent" side of the chart.

Variations:

→ A picture of a tree and name tags in the shape of owls can be used.
→ Two coffee cans labeled "Absent" and "Present," and children's names labeled on sticks, can be used.

Management Tip:

→ Have "Check Attendance Station" as one of the classroom jobs. Each morning, the student with this job verifies present and absent students. In the afternoon, the student monitors replacing the name cards in the "Absent" column.

Attendance Chart Diagram

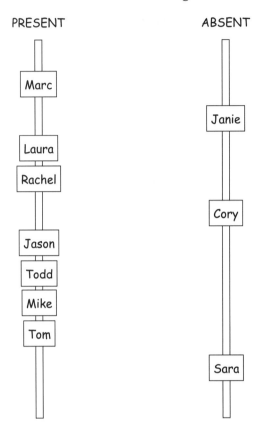

Lunch Station 1: Suggested for Kindergarten

Purposes:

- Engage children in a meaningful literacy activity.
- Build children's independence, responsibility, and accountability.

Materials:

- Pocket chart.
- Tongue depressors.
- Optional: Picture of each child.
- Sturdy plastic containers labeled with the lunch choices being offered (write a selection on each container and include a simple picture).

Activity:

1. As children enter the classroom, each child goes to the pocket chart and locates the tongue depressor with his or her name on it.
2. Children place their sticks in the cups corresponding to their lunch selections.

Variations:

> → The Attendance Station and the Lunch Station can be separate stations.
> → The Attendance Station can be created using a magnetic chart or laminated poster board.
> → The Attendance Station can be a journal where children sign in.

Management Tips:

> → Materials should be located in an accessible area near the entry door or cubby area.
> → Only two children may be at the stations at a time. Children are instructed to form a line and wait their turn.
> → Place the children's pictures beside their sticks. As children develop the skill of recognizing their name in a group of names, pictures may be removed.
> → Two helpers can reset the Attendance Station at the end of the day, or children can move their sticks back to the pocket chart as they leave.

Lunch Station 2: Suggested for First Grade

Purposes:

- Help children build their sight word vocabularies.
- Create an organizational system for taking lunch count.
- Help children learn to respect each other and wait patiently for their turn.

Materials:

- Coffee cans labeled with the lunch choices being offered.
- Children's names labeled on clothespins.

Activity:

1. As the children enter the room, each child locates the clothespin with his or her name on it.
2. Children place their clothespins on the cans corresponding to their selections.

Variations:

> → Popsicle sticks labeled with each child's name may be used instead of clothespins.
> → Poster board with library pockets labeled with each child's name, and color-coded cards marked with the different lunch selections, may be used.

Class Helper Chart

Purposes:

- Encourage children to follow directions.
- Help children build their sight word vocabulary.

Materials:

- Name cards.
- Class Helper chart.
- Velcro.
- Daily classroom jobs.

Activity:

1. Affix Velcro on the back of each name card and next to each job on the chart.
2. Children check the Class Helper chart to see whether they have a job to complete.
3. The jobs may include:
   - Paper Passer.
   - Line Leader.
   - Messenger.
   - Zookeeper (cares for classroom pets).
   - Gardener (waters the plants).
   - Lunch Record Keeper (tallies the lunch count for the day).
   - Inspector (makes sure centers are clean after center time).
   - Pledge Leader (leads the class in reciting the Pledge of Allegiance).
   - Board Cleaner.

Variation:

- ➜ Poster board with library card pockets labeled with each child's name, and separate cards labeled with different jobs, may be used as the chart.

Management Tips:

- ➜ At the beginning of the year, or if a new job is added, model how each job is performed.
- ➜ The jobs should change each week.
- ➜ Children should get an equal opportunity to have a variety of classroom jobs.

Class Helper Chart 1: Suggested for Kindergarten

Purposes:

- Encourage children to develop a sense of community and shared responsibility.
- Help children use pictures and print to read words.

Materials:

- Bulletin board listing all jobs.
- Velcro.
- Name tags.

Activity:

1. All responsibilities are listed on the Class Helper chart.
2. Next to each job, two student's names should appear. At the beginning of a new week, rotate the children's names.

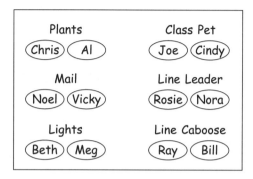

3. If a child's name is next to a job, he or she is to complete the job immediately after unpacking notes and homework. *Note*: Some jobs are on an "As-needed" basis. Not all children will have a job to complete in the morning.
4. Appropriate jobs:

   - Lunch Reporters—Count and report the number of sticks in each cup.
   - Class Pet Checkers—Perform a number of jobs related to the class pet (feeding it, giving it water, replenishing cedar chips, etc.). After feeding the class pet, the child can turn a sign from "I'm hungry" to "I'm full."
   - Plant Waterers—Water the plants and then place a sign in front of them that says, "Thank you."
   - Mail Deliverers—Pass out notices to the cubbies.

Variations:

→ A pocket chart with sentence strips can be used.
→ Other jobs that children can be responsible for at specific times of the day include:

   - Line Leader.
   - Line Caboose.
   - Letter Carriers—Deliver notes/messages to other parts of the school.
   - Electricity Savers—Turn lights off when the class leaves the room.
   - Supply Helpers—Assist with passing out needed supplies.
   - Center Checkers—Check centers after they are used.

Management Tips:

→ Model jobs for the students.
→ Weekly job assignments provide the children with a routine.

Class Helper Chart 2: Suggested for First Grade

CLASS HELPERS

Paper Collector		Michelle
Board Cleaner		Steve
Pledge Helper		Tyrone
Zookeeper		Dana
Gardener		Tina
Line Leader		David
Line Caboose		Shanique

Journal Writing

Purposes:

- Allow children to practice writing skills independently.
- Encourage children to write from experience and feelings.

Materials:

- Journals or blank notebooks.
- Pencils.
- Crayons.
- Markers.

Activity:

1. Give each student a journal to decorate.
2. Introduce students to journal writing. Define them as "A good place to write about how you feel and what you think."
3. Model journal writing for students, including putting the date at the top of each entry. Explain that they're allowed to scribble-write, write one letter, write a word they know, or make pictures if they feel they can't write.

> 12/2/01
>
> On Saturday, I adopted a kitten. His name is Jasper. He's very frisky and loves to play with straws. I love spending time with him.

4. Students will write in their journals at their desks when they arrive.
5. Students should be allowed to share their journal entries occasionally.
6. Share some of your own journal entries with the class.

Thematic Ties:

→ Children's journal writings can be theme-related.
→ You can provide a theme-related written prompt or picture prompt.

Buddy and Independent Reading

Purposes:

- Allow children to read a variety of literature independently.
- Help children to read with comprehension.

Materials:

- Magazines.
- Newspapers.
- Books of various genres.
- Leveled books previously read during guided reading.
- Library books to which you have assigned a level rating.
- Student-made books.
- Class-made books.

Activity:

1. Children select material to read.
2. Children find a comfortable spot to read. They may go to the Buddy and Independent Reading Center (described later) or read at their own desks/tables.
3. Children read with a buddy or by themselves.

4. After each reading session, students fill out a Book Record (see the first form following this section) to keep track of titles read.

5. To monitor comprehension, once a week have students select one title to use for a literacy activity involving manipulative materials. Such activities may include the following:

   - Roll movies (see Chapter One).
   - Felt board stories (see Chapter One).
   - Drawing a picture with a sentence.
   - Retelling a story into a tape recorder.

Variation:

➜ It is helpful to have multiple copies of books on hand for children to read with a friend.

Management Tips:

➜ When children buddy-read, they are to use "whisper voices."

➜ Teach children the "five-finger" rule for choosing books to read independently. They are to read a page of the book and put up a finger each time they come to a word they don't know. If they put up five fingers, the book is too hard for them, and they should choose another book.

➜ It is important to model buddy and independent reading on a regular basis by engaging in uninterrupted reading yourself.

➜ Use the second form following this section to keep track of children's literacy activity with manipulatives. Encourage students to try a variety of such activities.

_____'s Book Record

Week of _____

1. _____

2. _____

3. _____

4. _____

5. _____

Chart for Literacy Activities with Manipulatives

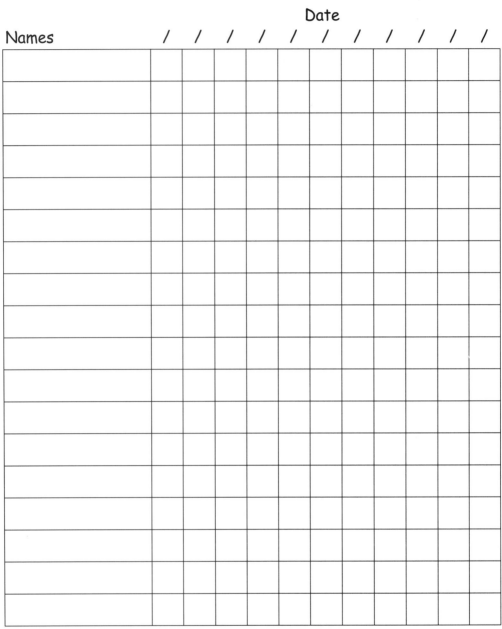

Date

Names / / / / / / / / / / /

Key: F = felt board story   P = puppet   R = roll movie   S = picture and sentence
T = tape recording

Others:

MORNING MEETING

The morning meeting is meant to help you include meaningful activities in the LAB. It should last for 25–30 minutes.

Morning News

Purposes:

- Encourage children both to listen and to understand what is heard.

Materials:

- Newspaper.
- Chart paper.

Activity:

1. The class gathers on the carpet in the meeting area.
2. Write important news on chart paper (students' personal news, as well as school and world news).
3. Read the news for the day.
4. Students may volunteer other news that is added to the chart.

Variations:

→ Read an article from a newspaper or magazine, and the class can discuss the article.
→ Check the Internet for the latest news.
→ Bring news articles from home and share them.

Thematic Ties:

→ The news that you share can relate to the current theme.
→ Students can be requested to bring in a news article or something from home related to the current theme.

Calendar

Purposes:

- Help children learn the days of the week and the months of the year.
- Encourage children to speak about events using calendar vocabulary.

Materials:

- Calendar.
- Velcro pieces.
- Laminated chart paper.

Activity:

1. The class gathers in the meeting area.
2. Students fill in specific parts of the calendar (date, month, year, season, and day of the week).
3. Review the months, days of the week, etc.
4. Students fill in sentences on a laminated piece of paper you have prepared. Examples:

   _____ comes after Wednesday.

   Today is _____.

5. You reread each sentence, and the class decides whether the information is correct.

Variations:

→ A pocket chart with written sentences that need to be filled in with correct words can be used. Examples:

   Karen's birthday is on _____.

   _____ was Jeff's birthday.

→ The sentences can become more challenging to answer. Example:

   There are _____ days of school in the month of December.

→ Students can write their own sentences and ask the class to answer.
→ Keep a chart of how many days have gone by in the current month.

OUR CALENDAR

Day:	Date:
Tuesday	16

Month:	Year:
February	2002

The season is:

winter

The season is:

Outside it is:

snowy

Weather Report

Weather Report 1: Suggested for Kindergarten

Purposes:

- Show children how to use visual aids.
- Encourage children to speak for a variety of purposes.
- Teach children to make oral predictions and draw conclusions.

Materials:

- Two pieces of paper.
- Markers.
- Thermometer.
- A sign that says, "We think tomorrow will be . . . ".

Activity:

1. Have one child be the weather reporter and report the current weather (sunny, partly sunny, cloudy, foggy, snowy, windy, rainy).
2. Place a tally mark next to the corresponding weather word. See diagram.

Sunny	
Cloudy	
Foggy	
Snowy	
Windy	
Partly sunny	
Rainy	

3. Lead the class in a song about weather.
4. As the weather word is spelled, point to the letters on the chart.
5. After reporting the weather, make a prediction about the next day's weather and post it.
6. Have a child help to read and report the temperature.

Variations:

→ Read the weather report and forecast from the newspaper to the children.
→ At the end of the month, have children make observations about the weather for the whole month. Record their observations on the bottom of the paper. Post these in the classroom and discuss trends in the results. Results can be recorded in the form of a bar graph.

Weather Report 2: Suggested for First Grade

Purposes:

- Help children use simple charts, graphs, and diagrams to report data.
- Encourage children to make predictions.

Materials:

- Newspaper.
- Weather graph.

Activity:

1. The class discusses the weather and the weather person fills in the weather graph.

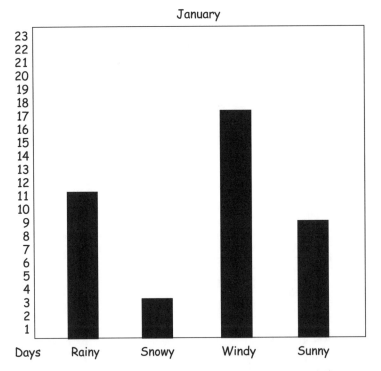

2. The children predict what the weather will be tomorrow.

Variations:

→ Students can write sentences to predict the weather forecast.
→ Create a Word Wall titled "Weather Words."
→ A pocket chart with written sentences that need to be filled in with correct words can be used. Examples:

   Yesterday it was _____ outside.
   Today is _____.

→ Look up the weather on the Internet.

Morning Message

Purpose:

- Show children how to revise content, organization, and other aspects of writing.

Materials:

- Chart paper.
- Markers.

Activity

1. The children gather in the meeting area.
2. A message is written on chart paper.
3. Read the message together aloud.
4. The message contains grammar mistakes. Have the class correct the message.
5. Use the message to teach a skill or to review a skill.
6. Discuss the skill located within the message. Example:

   Today I found a bug in my coffee mug. As I went to pour the coffee out,
   I tripped on a plug and fell on my rug. Thanks, little bug!

   Your teacher, _____

7. This message is intended to teach children about phonemic awareness and word families.
8. Have the class listen to and chant the words that sound alike.
9. Discuss word families. Have the students find the phonogram (-*ug*) within the message. List -*ug* words on chart paper.
10. Name other words having the -*ug* phonogram and list.

Variations:

→ The message can contain any skills or strategies that you are concentrating on. Examples:

   - Contractions.
   - Compound words.
   - Blends.
   - Digraphs.
   - Vowel patterns.
   - Vivid verbs.
   - Similes.
   - Metaphors.
   - Analogies.

→ The message can have missing words or mistakes in spelling or punctuation for the children to find and fill in.

→ You may cover up the rime (word family) or the onset (initial sound) of some words, for the children to predict the missing word. Encourage the children to use meaning and structure to make predictions.

Thematic Tie:

➡ The message may be theme-related.

Creating a Word Wall

Purposes:

- Demonstrate how to use a reference for reading and writing.
- Aid in the composition of texts that are diverse in content.

Materials:

- Large poster board or bulletin board.
- Colored note cards or construction paper.
- Scissors.
- Stapler.

Activity:

1. Post the letters of the alphabet across a large bulletin board that is centrally located in the classroom. The Word Wall should be prominently placed, so students can refer to it during daily reading and writing.
2. Select three to five new words each week and add them to the Word Wall. Words should be harvested from the message time, shared reading, shared writing, or other whole-class activities. They should include high-frequency words and the best exemplars of word chunks (e.g., *cat*, *car*, *see*).
3. Choose different-colored note cards or construction paper for different-purpose words. For example, key words for word chunks may be red, names may be green, and high-frequency words may be white.
4. Arrange the words alphabetically by first letter.
5. Do daily practice and review activities, so that words are read and spelled automatically. An effective Word Wall grows throughout the year, is neat and uncluttered, is an active part of daily instruction, and is visible to all of the students.

Variations:

➡ Choose a "mystery word of the week": Write a clue every day, and fill a letter in the blank until the word Wall Word is discovered.
➡ Construct Word Walls for rhyming words, word chunks, vowel sounds, and so on.
➡ Have a scavenger hunt for Word Wall words each morning when the children arrive, or each afternoon after they return from lunch.

- "Hide" the Word Wall words in plain sight around the room.
- When the children enter the room, they are responsible for finding three Word Wall words that they can read.
- The children share their words with their cooperative groups.
- Make sure the children are finding different words each day.
- The children may write a sentence for one or all of their words.

Thematic Tie:

→ Construct a theme-related Word Wall. Add words to it as they are discovered throughout the theme.

Sample Word Wall:

Aa	Bb	Cc	Dd	Ee	Ff
after	but	cat	dog	eat	for
always	ball	candy		every	from
and	bear	can		end	first

Daily Word Practice with the Word Wall

Purposes:

- Reinforce reading and writing of high-frequency words.
- Teach word chunks.

Materials:
- Jar.
- Paper.
- Five words from the Word Wall.

Activity:

1. This daily activity can begin when there are a week's worth of words on the Word Wall.
2. When five new Word Wall words are introduced, write them on a slip of paper and add to the word jar.
3. Choose five students to pick a word from the word jar.
4. One student at a time reads a word and finds it on the Word Wall. The class chants the spelling.
5. Have each student write the five words on paper and draw around the shapes of the words.
6. Practice looking at the spelling and writing the same five words every day for 1 week.
7. Add five words next week.

Variation:

→ Add five new words on Monday and practice them Monday and Tuesday. The rest of the week can be used to practice other words and review.

Thematic Tie:

→ A theme-related Word Wall can be constructed, containing vocabulary words related to the current theme. Children can refer to this wall to assist them with reading and writing connected to the theme.

Management Tips:

→ In order for the Word Wall to be a valuable teaching tool, it must be referred to often.
→ Place Word Wall words in library pocket cards at the bottom of the Word Wall, for children's easy access during independent writing.

Reading Aloud

Purposes:

- Expose children to a variety of literature, including literature written by authors of different genres, cultures, ethnicities, and genders.
- Have children listen to an experienced, fluent reader.

Materials:

- Access to a library (classroom, school, town, county) that shelves high-quality children's literature.

Activity:

1. Select high-quality children's literature that reflects a theme you are studying.
2. Children's literature that is read aloud should include setting, characters, theme, problem, resolution, and style in both text and illustrations.
3. Consider genre when making thematic literature selections. Expose children to a variety of genres, including fantasy, folklore, contemporary realistic fiction, historical fiction, biography, science fiction, poetry, and nonfiction.
4. Before reading, practice reading with intonation, pacing, and tone.
5. Join together in a comfortable setting. Be in clear view of all children.
6. When conducting the read-aloud, introduce the book to the class. Inform them why this selection was made. Share the book parts, such as title, print, pictures, copyright, and publisher.
7. Hold the book so children can see the pictures.
8. After reading a story, have children make personal connections with the text. Share personal reactions and comparisons between the current piece of literature and pieces read previously.

9. It is valuable to read aloud class favorites and texts that are rich in language multiple times.

10. Texts that become class favorites can be placed in a basket labeled "Old Favorites." Children will often return to these pieces of literature during independent reading.

Shared Reading

Purposes:

- Expose children to literature that fosters the development of concepts about print.

Materials:

- Access to a library (classroom, school, town, county) that shelves high-quality children's literature in enlarged form (big books).
- Chart paper.
- Markers.

Activity:

1. Select high-quality children's literature that reflects your theme. Shared reading materials should be enlarged texts (big books; poems and songs on chart paper; or pages of a small book copied onto transparencies and projected on an overhead projector).
2. Examine the literature for skills that can be taught within the context of the literature. Some skills that can be taught through the use of literature include letter identification, letter–sound correspondence, concepts about print, rhyming, predicting, understanding of story elements, and use of the three cueing systems.
3. Shared reading materials should contain repetitive phrases and rhymes. The pictures should be supportive of the text.
4. Read and have children chant predictable phrases and read familiar words.
5. As you read, track the print from left to right across the page with a pointer. Use a ruler, a chopstick, dowel with a pencil tip eraser, or the like.

Management Tip:

→ Use only one or two shared reading pieces a week. Literature selected will be used as a springboard for multiple skill and strategy lessons throughout the week.

Mini-Lesson: Comprehension

Purpose:

- Demonstrate how to put events in sequential order.
- Help students listen and respond to texts with comprehension.

Materials:

- Access to a library, as described above.
- Pocket chart.
- Sentence strips.

Activity:

1. The class gathers in the meeting area.
2. Remind the students that when they read, the events in a story occur in sequence or order.
3. Take a picture walk through the book with children and ask them to predict what will happen next throughout the story.
4. Read the story to the class.
5. Discuss the sequence of events in the story. Use words such as *first, then, after, next, last, finally* in your discussion.
6. Write the events on sentence strips.
7. Have the class help you put the sentences in sequential order in the pocket chart.
8. The activity can be placed in the Literacy Center for the children to use during center time.

Variations:

→ Have the children rewrite the story.
→ Have the students rewrite the story, cut it into strips and then put it back together again.
→ Have the children participate in a retelling of the story.

Thematic Tie:

→ The read-aloud can be theme-related.

INDEPENDENT WORK AT CENTERS

Independent work at centers should have a real purpose and allow students to authentically apply what they have learned. This work should be related to the current theme. It should be noted that not all the centers described in this section necessarily need to be set up in every classroom; adapt your selection of centers to your available classroom space, your resources, and your students' particular needs. The centers' names can also be changed, depending on your needs and preferences (e.g., Amy Holt calls her Writing Center the Author's Spot, as described in Chapter One). Moreover, not all of your centers will be used at the same time. As the teacher, you will decide which centers/activities would be most beneficial and useful for the students at any given time. Some activities will be "must do's" (those that the children must complete on a given day or within a given time frame), and others will be choices. Introduce each center gradually, and model the activities in the center as it is introduced to the class. Rules during center time must be clearly understood by the children and consistently enforced. Independent work at centers should last for 45–60 minutes (usually while you are having guided literacy instruction with different small groups).

Creating and Using a Center/Activity Chart

Purposes:

- Have students engage in practicing skills independently of you as the teacher.

Materials:

- Cardboard or poster board.
- Laminated icons for the various centers or activities.
- Index cards with children's names in heterogeneous groups.
- Velcro.

Activity:

1. The center/activity chart can be made of cardboard or poster board (see Figure 6 in Chapter 1 for an example).
2. The icons for the different centers or activities can be placed on the board with Velcro so they can be easily removed. (See Appendix A for sample icons.)
3. The group names are written on index cards and placed at the top of the board. Children are grouped heterogeneously for center activities.
4. Children locate their names on the board and go to the first center or activity listed for their group.
5. Each center contains some means for students to provide written accountability for their time.

Thematic Tie:

- → All activities should be tied to the current theme.

Management Tips:

- → The center/activity chart should be centrally located and placed at child level.
- → The group name card can be rotated to the right each day so the children can work at different centers.
- → The centers/activities should be changed weekly.
- → When you give a signal, groups rotate to the next center or activity.
- → Groups can change centers when guided reading groups change or after an appropriate amount of time.
- → You should model each center's activities.
- → If children don't finish an activity at a center, they place their work in folders to be completed later in the day when time permits.
- → Have a system to check center work.

Word Study Center

Purpose:

- Apply letter–sound relationships and word patterns of familiar words to read new words.
- Help children to use print concepts in developmentally appropriate ways.

Materials:

- Letter cubes.
- Index cards.
- Pencils.
- Cups.

Activity:

1. Organize an area for the Word Study Center (or whatever you choose to call it) within your Literacy Center.
2. Provide children with letter cubes.
3. Students work in pairs at this center. One student shakes the letter cubes, using a cup, and spills them out onto the table.
4. The children create as many words as possible using the letters.
5. The children write the words on index cards or a provided activity sheet as they make them.
6. They sort the words into categories (by onset, rime, vowel sounds, spelling patterns, meaning, etc.).
7. They write their word sorts on a piece of paper (or on the Word Study Center form that follows).

Variations:

→ Students manipulate individual letters on a magnetic board to create words. They begin by making two-letter words, then three-letter words, and so on. They write the words on index cards or paper and sort them when they finish.
→ You can provide the children with a long word or short phrase (e.g., *Halloween*, *amphibian*, *spring flowers*, etc.). The children are to make as many words as they can, using the letters in the given word or phrase. They write the words on index cards or paper and sort them when they are finished.
→ The children may use some of their words in sentences.
→ See Appendix B for more word study games.

Thematic Ties:

→ Children can be instructed to make as many words related to the current theme as they can with the letter cubes or magnetic letters.
→ You can provide the children with a theme-related word or phrase to make as many words as they can.

Management Tip:

→ To lessen the noise of the letter cubes, have the children roll them on a desk blotter or a piece of construction paper.

Name: _____ Date: _____

These are the words I made today.

1. _____   _____

2. _____   _____

3. _____   _____

4. _____   _____

5. _____   _____

6. _____   _____

7. _____   _____

8. _____   _____

9. _____   _____

10. _____   _____

Letter Study Center

Purposes:

- Build children's letter recognition.
- Foster children's discrimination of letter sounds.
- Promote proper formation of written letters.

Materials (many of these are described below in the "Activities" section):

- Sandpaper letters.
- Tracing paper.
- Laminated letter cards.
- Markers or wipe-off crayons.
- Supply of paper towels and/or baby wipes.
- ABC walk.
- Rice tray.
- Finger paint.
- Paper.
- Upper- and lower-case letter-matching puzzles.
- Sound puzzles.
- Alphabet Bingo game.
- Magnetic board and magnetic letters.

Activities:

1. Organize an area for the Letter Study Center within your Literacy Center. Then do any of the following:
2. **Sandpaper letters.** On sheets of fine-grained sandpaper, using a black permanent marker, write the letters of the alphabet. Use arrows to denote the proper formation of each letter. Children use their finger to trace over the letters or use thin paper to lay over the letters and trace. The traced letter has a bumpy feel to it.
3. **Laminated letter cards.** Cut up and laminate an ABC chart, laminate ABC flash cards, or record the letters of the alphabet on paper and laminate them. Add arrows to each letter to denote the proper formation. Use markers or wipe off crayons to trace over the letters. Create write-on, wipe-off activity cards that have children drawing lines to match upper- and lower-case letters and/ or to match initial consonant sounds to pictures.
4. **ABC walk.** On various colors of construction paper, draw and cut out 52 feet. On each foot, record an alphabet letter (upper- or lower-case). Laminate for durability. Place them in a plastic bag. Children pull a foot out of the bag, say the letter, and place it on the ground. They are to search for upper- and lower-case matches and sequence the alphabet.
5. **Rice tray.** Lay a piece of black construction paper on the bottom of an aluminum baking tray, and place enough rice on the tray to cover the black paper. Children may freely explore the tray, as they practice forming letters and/or writing words.

6. **Finger painting.** Children may freely explore the paint, as they practice forming letters and/or writing words.
7. **Upper- and lower-case letter puzzles.** From construction paper of one color, cut 26 rectangles measuring 8" × 4". On each rectangle, record an upper-case letter and the corresponding lower-case letter. Then, using scissors, create a unique cut through the middle of each rectangle, creating a one-of-a-kind puzzle piece. Laminate for durability. Children match the puzzle pieces. (See pattern on the following page.)
8. **Sound puzzles.** Prepare rectangles with pictures and their corresponding initial consonant sounds. Children match the letter to the picture that begins with its sound.
9. **Alphabet Bingo.** Use a commercially purchased Alphabet Bingo game or create one. Game boards should reflect both upper- and lower-case letters. Children can be the callers, further reinforcing letter identification.
10. **Magnetic board and letters.** Children may manipulate letters freely, or they may match letters to word cards to spell out their names and names of objects.

Thematic Tie:

→ This center can contain an activity that specifically has the children working with the first letter of a word the class is focusing on in the theme. For example, if a class's theme is "Popcorn/Maize," children can glue popcorn to a large prepared *P*.

Rhyming Center

Purposes:

- Help children to expand vocabulary as words are analyzed.
- Allow children to use print in developmentally appropriate ways.

Materials:

- Nursery rhymes on sentence strips (cut up so that one line is on each card).
- Enlarged nursery rhymes on poster board.
- Laminated copies of the nursery rhymes.
- Nursery rhyme books.
- Sets of rhyming words on cards.
- Cookie sheet.
- Magnetic alphabet tiles or letters.
- Markers.
- Paper.
- Writing implements.
- Rhyming Bingo game (commercially purchased or self-made).

Activities:

1. Organize an area for the Rhyming Center (or whatever you choose to call it) within your Literacy Center. Then do any of the following:

Upper- and Lower-Case Letter Puzzles

Fill in one upper-case and one lower-case letter on each blank puzzle piece. Enlarge and copy on colored paper. Cut and laminate.

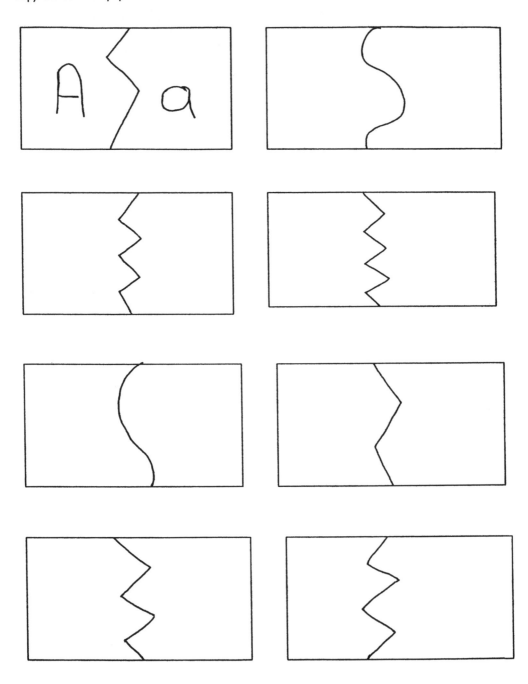

2. Children can read the nursery rhyme books.
3. They can take the enlarged version of a nursery rhyme and the cut-out nursery rhyme on sentence strips and match the words.
4. Using the sets of rhyming words on cards, children can play "Rhyming Memory."
5. Using the cookie sheet and the magnetic letters, children can create rhyming words for various word families.
6. Children should record rhyming words they have worked with, using the Rhyming Center form that follows.

Thematic Tie:

→ Sets of rhyming words can be created to match themes. For example, during a theme study on "Mail," children can do any of the above-described activities with the -*ail* word family.

Management Tip:

→ Index cards, sentence strips, and magnetic letters should all be kept in baskets or plastic bags that are labeled with their contents.

Name: _____ Date: _____

I rhymed today.
And if I may . . .
I'll share the words that I did say!

_____

_____

_____

_____

_____

_____

Rhyming Word Sort Activity

Purpose:

- Have students identify rhyming words.

Materials:

- Rhyming word cards.
- Pocket chart.
- Pencils.

Activity:

1. Have the students do this activity in the Rhyming Center.
2. Students are given two header cards (e.g., -at and -an) and rhyming word cards with the same endings (e.g., *hat, cat, man, fan*).
3. Students work independently or in pairs to sort the cards under the correct header on a pocket chart.
4. Students should record their word sorts on the Rhyming Word Sort Activity form that follows.

Variation:

➜ Additional headers (such as -ox, -ap, -ot) can be added to increase the difficulty of the activity.

Suggested Literature to Look for Rhyming Words: See Gerth (2000), Seuss (1976), and Carle (1999).

Rhyming Word Sort Activity

Name: _____   Date: _____

Today, I sorted the following rhyming groups:

        _____   _____

_____   _____

_____   _____

_____   _____

_____   _____

_____   _____

        _____   _____

_____   _____

_____   _____

_____   _____

_____   _____

Writing Center

Purposes:

- Help children develop and strengthen writing skills and strategies.
- Demonstrate how to compose texts for a variety of purposes.
- Enable children to write collaboratively and independently.

Materials:

- Hole puncher.
- Rings.
- Student journals.
- Paper.
- Pencils and erasers.
- Markers, crayons, colored pencils.
- Scissors.
- Stapler.
- Glue.
- Date stamp.
- Blank books.
- Writing folders.
- Computer, printer.
- Word-processing programs such as *StoryBook Weaver, Once upon a Time, Claris-Works for Kids*, or others.

Activities:

1. Organize a clearly defined space within your classroom's Literacy Center for the Writing Center (or Author's Spot, or whatever you choose to call it). It should provide a range of writing materials that are organized (in baskets, trays, shoeboxes, coffee cans, etc.) and labeled.
2. The Writing Center should contain reference materials (dictionaries, thesauruses, picture dictionaries, etc.).
3. Writing activities can be related to the teacher read-aloud, students' interests and experiences, or other topics.
4. Students place their work in writing folders that are kept in the center. Students' journals may also be kept in the Writing Center.
5. Invite five children to share journal entries they have just written, reading them from the Author's Chair.
6. Other possible writing forms for the Writing Center:

   - Story endings.
   - Scripts/plays.
   - Poetry.
   - Journal entries.
   - Letters.
   - Directions.
   - Newspaper articles.

- Signs.
- Stories from different genres (mysteries, personal narratives, fairy tales).
- Writing to instruct, persuade, inform, entertain.

Variations:

➔ A chart with a list of possible topics may be hung in the center for children who are having trouble thinking of something to write about.
➔ Topics can be kept in a "grab bag" for the students.

Thematic Tie:

➔ At least one writing activity should be related to the current theme.

Listening Center

Purpose:

- Increase students' listening comprehension.

Materials:

- Headphones.
- Tape recorders.
- Tape recordings of children's literature.
- Multiple copies of the literature itself.

Activity:

1. Organize an area for the Listening Center (or whatever you choose to call it) within your Literacy Center.
2. The center should contain a large variety of stories on tape.
3. Have each child listen to a story on tape and follow along with a print version of the story as he or she listens.
4. Have each child complete the Listening Center firm that follows about the story he or she has heard.

Variations:

➔ Have a library of tapes available that have been recorded by people who are familiar to the children:

- The principal.
- The custodian.
- The school nurse.
- The school secretary.
- Older children in the school.
- Other teachers.

➔ All readers should be models for fluency and expression.

➜ Children can make a written or picture response to an open-ended question after listening to a tape:

- "How did you feel when . . . ?"
- "What did you think was the . . . ?"
- "What would you have done in the story if . . . ?"
- "How would you . . . ?"
- "The part of the story I liked best was . . . ?"

➜ Children may tape themselves reading a familiar book and play the tape back
so they can hear themselves read.

Thematic Tie:

➜ The tape-recorded stories that are available should relate to the theme that is being studied.

Management Tips:

➜ Store tapes in large zip-lock-style plastic bags and label clearly.
➜ Copy the cover of each book, laminate it, and tape it to the plastic bag with the
tape in it, so young children can clearly identify the contents.

Name: _____ Date: _____

Title: _____

In this story, _____

_____

_____

_____

This is a picture of what happened in this story:

Buddy and Independent Reading Center

Purposes:

- Help students develop fluency through reading and rereading.
- Encourage independent reading.
- Encourage students to read a diversity of materials and texts.

Materials:

- Magazine holders.
- Cereal boxes for holding books.
- Plastic baskets.
- Multiple copies of books.
- Large selection of literature.
- Magazines.
- Newspapers.
- Rug or carpet squares.
- Beanbag chairs.
- Oversized pillows.

Activity:

1. Organize an area for the Buddy and Independent Reading Center (or Reading Center, Library Corner, or whatever you choose to call it) within your Literacy Center.
2. Do several book talks a week to acquaint your children with the books that are available in this center and to pique their interest in the books.
3. During center time, students read books either independently or with partners.
4. Have each child complete the Reading Center form that follows about the story he or she has read.

Thematic Tie:

→ Many books related to the current theme should be prominently displayed in this center.

Management Tips:

→ See the tips under "Buddy and Independent Reading" in the "Things to Do When the Students Arrive" section of this chapter.
→ Arrange this center so that there is a private area where children may read.
→ Be sure books are arranged in a student-friendly way—easy to access, placed at children's eye level.

Name: _____ Date: _____

Title: _____

In this story, _____

_____

_____

_____

This is a picture of what happened in this story:

Reading Activity: Reading the Room

Purposes:

- Expose children to a variety of print.
- Encourage children to read a variety of material.

Materials:

- Pointers.
- Glasses without lenses, or commercially made "Reading the Room" glasses.
- Classroom filled with print, including:

  - Word Walls.
  - Posters.
  - Charts.
  - Poems.
  - Big books.
  - Interactive writing.
  - Student stories.
  - Environmental print that you and the students have brought from home (household and grocery items, ads that are familiar to the children).

Activity:

1. Have children go to the morning meeting area (or some other convenient place) for this activity.
2. Use pointers to encourage children to read all the displays and environmental print around the room. Then have them do this independently.
3. Make sure that the room is full of environmental print located at students' eye level.

Variations:

→ Have children work with a partner.
→ Have children list the words read on a sheet of paper, or on the Reading the Room form that follows. They may then read their list to a partner or to you, or they may take it home to read to their parents.
→ Children may use some of the words they found in sentences.
→ Children can make vocabulary cards for some of their words. The children fold a piece of construction paper into four squares. In the first square, they write their word; in the second square, they write what it means; in the third square, they write a sentence using the word; in the fourth square, they draw a picture to go with their word.

Thematic Tie:

→ Children may look for as many words as they can find that are related to the theme.

Name: _____ Date: _____

Today I read these words in our room!

_____   _____

_____   _____

_____   _____

_____   _____

_____   _____

_____   _____

_____   _____

_____   _____

Technology Center

Purposes:

- Foster technological independence.
- Link classroom learning to the world of technology.

Materials (materials for this center are going to vary from classroom to classroom):

- Computers.
- Software.
- Digital cameras.
- Internet access.

Activity:

1. Organize an area for the Technology Center (or whatever you choose to call it)—either within your Literacy Center, or elsewhere in your classroom if the technology will be used to study other content areas (which is often the case).
2. If a class is studying an well-known author (e.g., Eric Carle, Margaret Wise Brown, Jan Brett, Ezra Jack Keats), access the author's Web site. If you enter a search for the author's name, the Web site is generally offered.

Thematic Ties:

→ Using a digital camera, work with the children to photograph items that relate directly to a theme or a particular letter that is being focused on. For example, during a theme study of "Leaves," a class can focus on the letter *L*. Photograph items around the room that begin with the *L* sound. These can be downloaded, and basic keyboarding can be used to create labels for the pictures. A class book can be made out of the pictures.

→ Using a clip art program, show students how to select and print out art related to a theme to use on a book cover for a story written by the author they are studying.

Story Props Center

Purpose:

- Help children develop an understanding of story structure through the means of oral retelling.

Materials:

- General stick puppets and felt board pieces.
- Story-specific stick puppets, felt board pieces, and corresponding pieces of literature.
- Felt board (see Chapter One).
- General and story-specific hand-held masks.
- Roll movie box and roll movies (see Chapter One).

- Story box dress-up clothes and corresponding literature.
- Tape recorder.
- Blank audiotapes.

Activities:

1. Organize an area for the Story Props Center (or whatever you choose to call it) within your Literacy Center.
2. When visiting this center, children may choose from a variety of activities:

   - **General stick puppets and felt board pieces.** Encourage children to develop their own stories, using stick puppets and felt board pieces that are not necessarily matched to a piece of literature.
   - **Story-specific stick puppets and felt board pieces.** Once a piece of literature has been shared with the class, stick puppets and felt board pieces corresponding to that literature can be made available so that children can retell the story. Always keep the piece of literature with the retelling pieces so children can refer to it.
   - **Roll movies.** Children can use the box, as well as the movies created by you and/or by the class to retell familiar stories.

3. Have children share their stories with a friend and then tape-record what they did in the center.

Thematic Tie:

→ **Story box dress-up.** In a box, keep a collection of dress-up clothes that children can use as they retell stories. For example, if a class's theme study is "Farm," old overalls, straw hats, flannels, animal costumes, and so on can be kept there to retell a variety of theme-related stories.

Management Tip:

→ Keep each piece of literature and the corresponding stick puppets and felt board pieces in a labeled plastic bag.

Science Center

Purposes:

- Integrate science and language arts through theme-related activities.
- Help children read and respond to a diversity of materials and texts with comprehension and critical analysis.
- In the particular activity described below, have children use all five senses to identify items.

Materials:

- Observation journals.
- Science materials related to each activity.

- Learning logs.
- Pencils.
- Subject-related books.
- Fish tank.
- Magnifying glasses.
- Plants.

Activity:

1. Organize an area of the classroom for the Science Center. (The Science Center is one of the content-area-related Learning Centers described in Chapter One. Space precludes a description of all of the centers.)
2. Model the task to be completed during center time.
3. Place an activity card in the center for students to work on, along with a form for students to record their work (see the sample card and form that follow).
4. Students finished and unfinished work can be placed on a tray or in the science folder in the center.

Sample Activity: Five Senses

Materials:

- Paper.
- Pencil.
- Paper bags and plastic containers.
- Objects that have a distinct feeling.
- Foods that have a distinct taste and smell.
- Tapes of sounds.
- Enlarged pictures of objects.

Activity:

One day of the week is set aside for each sense.

1. **Touch:** Students will touch several objects hidden in numbered paper bags (pine cones, hairbrushes, toothbrushes, acorns, screwdrivers, etc.). They will guess each object and write their guesses on paper.
2. **Smell:** While blindfolded, students will smell numbered containers and guess what's in them (chocolate, cinnamon, honey, vanilla, almond, lemon juice, peanut butter, garlic, etc.).
3. **Taste:** While blindfolded, students will taste things in numbered containers and guess what they've tasted (marshmallows, salt, chocolate, honey, peanuts, orange, powdered sugar, coconut, etc.).
4. **Hearing:** Students will listen to different sounds on tape (horn, squeaking brakes, thunder, lightning, rain, dog, baby crying, etc.). They will write down what they think the sounds are.
5. **Sight:** Students will look at enlarged pictures of objects. They will guess each object and write it down.

Thematic Tie:

➜ The activities in the science center should be related to the current theme.

Management Tips:

➜ Each child can work with a partner.
➜ Partners should be instructed to work in "whisper voices."
➜ The partners can assist each other with their written responses.
➜ The partners can compare their responses with each other.

Monday: Touch

On Monday, you will find some things hidden in paper bags at the Science Center. Feel each thing through the bag, and then guess what it is. Write down on the activity sheet what you think each thing is.

Tuesday: Smell

On Tuesday, you will find some things in little plastic boxes at the center. Put on a blindfold, and then open each box and smell what's inside. Guess what's in each box. Write down what you guess on the activity sheet.

Wednesday: Taste

On Wednesday, you will again find some things in little plastic boxes. Put on a blindfold, and then open each box and taste what's inside. Guess what's in each box. Write down what you guess on the activity sheet.

Thursday: Hearing

On Thursday, you will find a tape and a tape player at the center. Play the tape, and after you hear each sound on the tape, write on the activity sheet what you think the sound is.

Friday: Sight

On Friday, you will find some pictures of things that are much bigger than the things are in real life. Look at the pictures, guess what each thing is, and write down what you think it is on the activity sheet.

Name: _____ Date: _____

Touch

These are the things I think I felt:

1. _____   4. _____
2. _____   5. _____
3. _____

Smell

These are the things I think I smelled:

1. _____   4. _____
2. _____   5. _____
3. _____

Taste

These are the things I think I tasted:

1. _____   4. _____
2. _____   5. _____
3. _____

Hearing

These are the things I think I heard:

1. _____   4. _____
2. _____   5. _____
3. _____

Sight

These are the things I think I saw:

1. _____   4. _____
2. _____   5. _____
3. _____

Overhead Projection Center

Purposes:

- Encourage reading through a different medium.
- Have students read, view, and respond to a diversity of materials.

Materials:

- Overhead projector.
- Overhead pens.
- Large piece of white paper.
- Transparencies of stories and poems.

Activity:

1. Organize an area for the Overhead Projection Center (or whatever you choose to call it) within your Literacy Center.
2. Set an overhead projector to display on a piece of white paper located on the wall.
3. Students can read poems and stories on the overhead (these can be stored in plastic sheet covers to protect overheads and placed in folders).
4. Have each child complete the first Overhead Projection Center form that follows about the poem/story he or she has read.

Variations:

- → Plastic letters can be manipulated on the overhead to make words appear on the wall. (In this case, have each child complete the second Overhead Projection Center form that follows.)
- → Cut apart transparencies of familiar stories, and have the students match text and illustrations.

Thematic Ties:

- → The poems and stories should be related to the current theme.
- → Children can make theme-related words.

Management Tips:

- → Be sure the overhead projector is set up to project at a child's eye level.
- → Have each child work with a partner.
- → Partners should speak in "whisper voices."
- → Partners can read the poems, stories, or words to each other.
- → Partners can sign each other's accountability forms to show that they heard each other read.

Overhead Projection Center

Name: _____ Date: _____

This is the poem/story I read today:

_____

_____

_____

_____

_____

_____

_____

_____

Name: _____ Date: _____

These are the words I made today:

_____

_____

_____

_____

_____

_____

_____

_____

Word Wall Scavenger Hunt Activity

Purposes:

- Have children practice finding words on the Word Wall(s).
- Help children record words with correct spelling.

Materials:

- Word Wall or Walls.
- Paper.
- Pencil.

Activity:

1. Have children go to the morning meeting area (or wherever the class Word Wall or Walls are located) for this independent activity.
2. Children work together to locate old and new words on the Word Wall(s).
3. Each student records the words found each day on the Word Wall Scavenger Hunt form that follows.
4. Students review each other's work for accuracy before handing in their activity forms.

Variation:

→ Children take turns acting as the leader in a game of word "I Spy" with the other students. The leader locates a word and reads it to the others ("I spy the word . . . "); the other children find the word on a Word Wall and record it on the activity form.

Word Wall Scavenger Hunt

Name: _____ Date: _____

These are the words I found today:

Monday

_____   _____   _____

Tuesday

_____   _____   _____

Wednesday

_____   _____   _____

Thursday

_____   _____   _____

Friday

_____   _____   _____

GUIDED READING

Guided reading is the heart of the LAB. During guided reading, individual needs are met by working with children in small groups at their instructional levels. To organize guided reading, needs are assessed, groups are formed based on need, and appropriate materials are selected to address these needs. Each guided reading group lesson lasts about 15–20 minutes, for a total of 45–60 minutes if three groups are seen each day.

Grouping for Guided Reading

Purpose:

- Select groups for guided reading.

Materials:

- Running records. (See Chapter Six for a detailed description of these.)
- Observational notes.

Activity:

1. Guided reading is one of the only times children are homogeneously grouped. Texts are chosen for their appropriateness for each group.
2. The number of guided reading groups in a particular classroom will vary, depending on the range of student ability. A typical reading classroom has between four and six groups. A guided reading group with no more than five or six children seems to be the most manageable. The lowest-ability groups should contain no more than four students.
3. Children are placed in guided reading groups based on the results of several assessment measures and on your own observations. The groups are dynamic and are expected to change as the students' needs change.
4. You should meet with three or four groups each day. The lowest-ability groups should be seen daily. A different child should sit next to you each day; this is the child you will focus on that day for assessment purposes.

Assessing Students

Purposes:

- Determine each student's appropriate group, materials, and instructional needs.
- Measure children's progress throughout the year.

Materials:

Multiple assessment measures, which include but are not limited to the following:

- Motivation Interview.
- Letter Recognition form.
- Concepts about Print and Word Study form.
- Phonemic Segmentation form.

- Running records.
- Story retellings for comprehension (Morrow, 1985, 2001).
- Anecdotal records.
- Emergent Reading Behaviors form.

See Appendix C for assessment forms.

Activity:

1. At the beginning of the school year, evaluate students on several measures to determine skill needs and reading level. Use this information to select materials and form groups.
2. During the school year, the assessments listed above, as well as any additional assessments that are appropriate, are carried out within the small group setting or individually.
3. While working with each group, select a child to focus on for assessment purposes.
4. Rotate children so you focus on a different child each time the group meets.
5. Every child should be assessed quarterly on all appropriate measures.

Management Tip:

→ A chart that can be duplicated each quarter for record-keeping purposes is helpful. (See the reproducible chart that follows.) Place checks in boxes to indicate completed assessments. If a score is taken, record it in the box.

Guided Literacy Assessment Chart

Student: _____   Teacher: _____

Grade: _____   Date: _____

Motivation Interview				
Letter Recognition				
Concepts about Print and Word Study				
Phonemic Segmentation				
Running Records				
Story Retelling				
Anecdotal Records				
Emergent Reading Behaviors				

Selecting Materials

Purpose:

- Meet the instructional level of the children in each guided reading group.

Materials:

- Leveled books from early emergent to fluent reading levels.

Activity:

1. Multiple copies of leveled books are needed for guided reading instruction.
2. Select the appropriate leveled books for each guided reading group, based on your needs assessment.
3. The reading material must be carefully chosen to match the instructional level of the students. The children should be able to read the text with a 90–95% accuracy rate.
4. Books are assigned a level rating based on these criteria:

   - Number of words in the book.
   - Length of the book.
   - Number of different words.
   - Print size and layout of the text.
   - Length of the sentences.
   - Predictability of text and picture support.
   - Number of high-frequency words.
   - Language patterns and language structures used.

5. Purchase leveled books from the following publishers:

   - Benchmark Word I.D., 2107 N. Providence Rd., Media, PA 19063.
   - Rigby, 100 Hart Rd., 3rd Fl., Barrington, IL 60010-2527.
   - Sundance Publishers, 243 Taylor St., Littleton, MA 01460.
   - William H. Sadlier, 9 Pine St., New York, NY 10005-1005.
   - The Wright Group, 19201 120th Ave., Bothell, WA 90811-9512.

Guided Instruction for Emergent Readers: Suggested for Kindergarten

Purposes:

- Have children practice a directed reading and thinking strategy.
- Help children develop concepts about print.
- Teach children to recognize letters.

Materials:

- Multiple copies of a leveled text.
- Note-taking forms.
- Multiple assessment measures.
- Various tactile tools for skill development (magnetic boards, magnetic letters,

chalk, white boards, white board markers, tactile letters, pictures to be used in letter–sound sorts, framing devices, etc.).

Activity:

Sample Lesson 1—Practicing a Directed Reading and Thinking Strategy

Before the reading:

1. Before a new book is introduced, take time to revisit and chant a book that is known to the children.
2. Provide an introduction to the new text. Activate students' prior knowledge. Discuss book parts.
3. Give children their own copies of the new text. Lead the students on a "picture walk" through every page in the book, and discuss their predictions. Draw attention to frequently used letters or words. Encourage children to use the information in the pictures. Continually have children relate what they are observing in the book to their own lives.
4. It may be necessary to read the story to the children. As this is done, encourage children to follow along in their books, as well as join in.
5. An echo reading may also be necessary. For an echo reading, read a page of the book (modeling word-to-word matching). The children then echo both the reading and the word-to-word matching.

During the reading:

1. Following this scaffolded introduction, children are asked to read the new text together and out loud. The emergent readings may be considered reenactments or chanting of the text, rather than actual decoding of the text. With these readings, the children are practicing concepts about print, such as book-handling skills. They are using storybook language, pictures, text directionality, and memory to read.
2. During the reading, if students are ready to attend to the text, encourage pointing to the words as they are read.

After the reading:

1. Praise students for their successes and talk about the story with the group. Students may check their predictions or react personally to the story or information.
2. Instruct the students to return to the text for a teaching opportunity. For example, the book may contain numerous words that belong to the -*in* word family. Have students use magnetic letters to create various words in the -*in* family.
3. Following this, children read the text with a partner to practice fluency. Upon completion, the books are placed in students' browsing boxes/"Very Own Miniature Libraries."
4. Have students bring home their books and practice reading them with their families. Books should be returned to school the next day, or at most within 2 days.

Sample Lesson 2—Recognizing Lower-Case Letters (Auditory Sounds and Visual Representation)

1. Sing the ABC song with the children. As this is done, point to the letters on an alphabet strip.
2. Point to the lower-case *m*. Ask the children to identify it.
3. Give each child an index card with a lower-case *m* written on it. Have the children trace the letter with their fingers over and over again.
4. Lay out four alphabet cards, one being the lower-case *m*. Ask children to locate the *m*. Do this again; replacing the three other letters with other alphabet letters. Repeat a few times.
5. Share a short poem/song with the children. The poem/song should contain numerous lower-case *m*'s. A sample poem follows:

> Five little monkeys sitting in a tree,
> Teasing Mr. Alligator, "Can't catch me."
> Along came Mr. Alligator quiet as can be,
> And snapped a monkey right out of the tree.

6. Have the children locate the *m*'s in the poem and highlight them with highlighting tape.
7. Echo-read the poem with the children.
8. Send the poem home for the children to read with their families.

Guided Instruction for Conventional Reading: Suggested for First Grade

Purposes:

- Help children develop prediction strategies and comprehension skills.
- Help children increase fluency.
- Build children's sight word vocabularies.
- Have children practice rhyming words.

Materials:

- Individual copies of a leveled text.
- White boards.
- Markers.
- Magnetic letters.
- Magnetic boards.
- Forms for observational note taking.
- Assessment tools (running record).

Activity:

Before the reading:

1. Select an appropriate leveled book for the guided reading group.
2. Before you introduce a new book to the group, have the students read some-

thing familiar for fluency. Either they can read the familiar book together, or one child can read aloud to the group.

3. Preview the new piece of literature, in order to interest the students in the book and relate it to their experience. Discuss the title and author, and give a brief synopsis of the story.

4. Give each child a copy of the new book. Then ask the students to "picture-walk" through the book. The group discusses predictions of what the story may be about and asks questions.

5. During the reading, you can focus on one child for assessment purposes. Choose a different child during each lesson. You can take a running record on a child during the rereading of the story.

During the reading:

1. The children should read silently. At a signal from you (e.g., a tap on the shoulder), they should "whisper-read" so you can hear their processing. Take notes on the reading strategies the children are using. Use these strategies as teaching points after the reading.

2. The children in the group should be able to read the story at about the same rate and level of success.

After the reading:

1. The group discusses the story together. Encourage students them to ask questions, offer comments, and give opinions. When the group discusses the story, you can determine how well the students comprehended the story.

2. A lesson is then taught, focusing on a phonics skill or something that the students struggled with. The students may use magnetic boards and magnetic letters during this lesson. You may ask students to create words using the letters.

3. After a lesson is taught, you may have students practice their writing skills. This can be done using white boards and markers. You may ask them to write a personal response to the story or rewrite the story. The retelling can be cut up into sentence strips for the students to reassemble. This strengthens their sense of sequential order and sentence structure.

4. When students have finished, they can read the story with a partner to practice fluency. When the instruction is over, the books are placed in students' browsing boxes.

Sample Guided Reading Lesson

Purposes:

- Help students use and develop reading strategies when reading unfamiliar text.
- Help students become successful independent readers.

Materials:

- A "big book" copy of *The Great Big Bug Book* (Williams, 1988).
- Multiple copies of *The Great Big Bug Book*.

- White boards.
- Running records.

Activity:

Before the reading:

1. Begin the lesson by reading, along with the students, a "big book" version of a familiar story called *I Know an Old Lady Who Swallowed a Fly* (Westcott, 1980). It can be done as a choral reading.
2. Now Introduce sight words from the new story and place them on a Word Wall titled "Insects" (the theme being studied is "Insects"). The Word Wall will include *mosquito, bee, ladybug, butterfly, grasshopper, spider,* and *caterpillar.*
3. Introduce the students to the "big book" copy of *The Great Big Bug Book.* Provide the students with information about the story. Discuss the plot, title, important ideas, and vocabulary pertaining to the story.
4. Give the students smaller copies of the book.
4. Take the students on a "picture walk" of the story. Students make predictions about what the story will be about. They also discuss the illustrations.

During the reading:

1. Children may need assistance, so it is important to pay close attention to their reading.
2. Take notes on strategies the children are using. Use these strategies as teaching points after the reading.

After the reading:

1. The group discusses the story. Students talk about predictions they had made, ask questions, and so on.
2. Use the story to teach a skill. For example, focus on rhyming words. Both you and the students find words that rhyme in the story. Next, provide each child with a white board. Say a word and ask the students to write down a word that rhymes with the word. The students may be asked to place that word in a sentence.
3. Students will store their copies of the book in bags with their names on them. The students are aware that the materials for guided reading will be in the bag.
4. You can take a running record on a child during the rereading, or hold one child back to take a running record after the group is dismissed.

Management Tips:

→ Place your chair in the guided reading group so that you can see the entire class.
→ The guided reading area needs to be well organized. All teaching materials should be within easy reach of your chair.
→ Children who are not participating in a guided reading group should be engaged in meaningful, theme-related independent activities at centers.
→ Children rotate to a new center/activity after each guided reading group.

Book in a Bag

Purpose:

- Organize guided reading materials.

Materials:

- Chosen reading materials.
- Large plastic bags for each child.
- Materials to teach skills (such as sentence strips, index cards, etc.).

Activity:

1. Before the guided reading lesson begins, each child receives a large plastic bag with his or her name on it.
2. The children are encouraged to browse through their bags to find out what materials are inside.
3. The children are told that the bags contain materials needed for each guided reading lesson and independent work.
4. When the lesson is over, the materials are returned to the bags.
5. Change the material in the plastic bags when necessary.
6. Bags are stored in individual holders.

Variation:

→ Large envelopes or folders can be used instead of plastic bags.

WRITING WORKSHOP

The Writing Workshop is a block of time set aside for independent writing activities. Each session includes time for whole-class, small-group, and individualized instruction. This enables you to meet each child's individual needs and to assess individual mastery of procedures, skills, and strategies.

Mini-Lessons

Mini-Lesson 1: Suggested for Kindergarten

Purposes:

- Introduce students to specific procedures, skills, and strategies necessary for writing.
- Model and present each writing task.

Materials:

- Chart paper.
- Writing basket.

- Markers.
- "My Very Own Writing Folder" (one for each child—these house pieces the children are working on).

Activity:

1. Mini-lessons are conducted with the whole class. They cover a variety of procedures, skills, and strategies: good use of time in the Writing Workshop, material usage (stapler, tape machine, etc.), paper selection, pencil grip, paper position, topic selection, picture creation, cooperatively working with a buddy, using invented spelling/"kid spelling," concepts about print (leaving spaces between words, proper usage of upper- and lower-case letters), rhyming, syllabication, sounding words in a sentence, describing words with multiple meanings, journal entry idea selection, publishing, use of environmental print/the Word Wall, letter formation, composing a friendly letter, and so on.
2. Introduce the task being focused on in each mini-lesson.
3. Discuss the rationale and function of the task.
4. Demonstrate how to incorporate the task into personal writing.

Sample Mini-Lesson: Spacing between Words

Purpose:

- To introduce children to the idea of spacing between words.

Materials:

- As above, plus "Space Makers" (see the description below).

Activity:

1. Introduce "Space Makers." Inform children that the Space Makers will help to remind them to put spaces between words. Space Makers are decorated Popsicle sticks.
2. Describe how spaces help readers to see where words begin and end.
3. Model using a Space Maker as you write a sentence or two on chart paper. See example:

Once upon a time

4. Tell children that they can help themselves to Space Makers as they write.

Mini-Lesson 2: Suggested for First Grade

Purposes:

- Teach specific procedures, skills, and strategies needed for writing.
- Model and present each writing task.

Materials:

- Overhead transparencies.
- Easel pads.
- Chart paper.
- Markers.
- Paper.
- Pencils.
- A writing folder for each child.

Activity:

1. The mini-lesson is taught in a whole-group setting.
2. The mini-lesson emerges from what you notice the students need to learn. This information is gathered from observing students writing, conferring with them, and reviewing their writing folders.
3. Introduce each task by using a written example (such as a poem, short story, etc.).
4. Mini-lessons focus on a procedure, skill, or strategy.
   a. Procedural lessons focus on the rules and routines of the Writing Workshop. Examples:
      - Rules for conferring with peers.
      - Where to find writing resources.
      - Procedures for writing a final copy.
      - Organizing and using the writing folder.
   b. Skill lessons focus on the mechanics of writing. Examples:
      - Using capital letters for names and the beginnings of sentences.
      - Leaving spaces between words.
      - Saying words slowly and recording their sounds.
   c. Strategy lessons focus on what authors and illustrators do to communicate their messages to readers. Examples:
      - Providing details.
      - Choosing a title.
      - Writing a good lead or ending.
5. Show the students how that day's procedure, skill, or strategy can be incorporated into their writing.
6. Assign a writing task and model it.
7. Children are given materials to complete the writing task. When the students have finished the assignment, they work on pieces kept in their writing folders. The writing kept in the folders includes those begun after completing the assigned writing task. The folders allow children to use the skills they have learned or to experiment with other types of writing.

Management Tip:

→ Often, introduce a procedure, skill, or strategy that can go onto a class chart or into student notebooks for future reference.

Sample Mini-Lesson: Using Capital Letters for Names and at Sentence Beginnings

Purposes:

- Have students practice using capital letters.
- Show students how to review and correct their own writing.

Materials:

- Sample teacher writing in first-draft form.
- Student writing in first-draft form.
- Pencil.

Activity:

1. Using a sample piece of your own, demonstrate how to search for names of people by rereading sentence by sentence.
2. Change names beginning with lower-case letters to capital letters by using the standard triple-underline editing mark.
3. Return to the beginning of the passage and model rereading for capital letters at the beginning of each sentence. Show students how to search for end punctuation, and encourage them to listen to their voices as they read aloud to themselves.
4. Again change lower-case letters by using the appropriate editing mark.
5. Give students an opportunity to work on this skill during the Writing Workshop that day. Monitor students working on this skill.

Buddy Writing

Purpose:

- Have children work cooperatively to develop writing strategies.

Materials:

- Writing paper.
- Pencils.
- Pens.
- "Work in progress" folders.

Activity:

1. After you assign the writing task, encourage children to share their ideas with the children around them.
2. The children then return to their seats, and children pair off as buddies to discuss ideas further.
3. Each child takes a turn discussing his or her ideas.
4. The children exchange ideas until they feel confident enough to begin writing.
5. The children continue to share with their buddies during the writing process.

6. After each child has met with the teacher independently, the buddies continue helping each other.
7. When the children have finished the assignment, they have the opportunity to finish writing pieces in their folders or to start a new piece based on a previous Writing Workshop mini-lesson.
8. Unfinished work can be placed in the "work in progress" folder.

Teacher-Guided Writing

Purpose:

- Meet the individual writing needs of each child.

Materials:

- Pencils.
- Paper.

Activity:

1. Meet with groups of children who have similar needs, while the other children are working with their buddies on the assigned writing task.
2. First, discuss the assigned writing task presented during the mini-lesson.
3. Review a procedure, skill, or strategy that the students seem to be struggling with.
4. Ask the students to review what they have written thus far and to make any necessary corrections.
5. Answer any questions from the group.
6. Finally, the group works on the assigned writing task at your table. This gives the children a chance to work with you individually if the need arises.

Conferences with Individual Students

Purpose:

- Help individual students write in clear, concise, organized language.

Materials:

- Paper.
- Pencils.
- Children's first writing drafts.

Activity:

1. Meet with individual children during the guided writing groups.
2. Begin by complimenting the child on a specific aspect of his or her writing.
3. Choose one or two points to discuss with the child on how to improve his or her paper. The points are designed to make the child's writing better in the future.

The goal of the conference is to help the child become a better writer, *not* to make this particular paper perfect.

4. After the conference, the student may seek advice from his or her buddy.
5. After you have had a conference with each child in the group, call a new group.
6. Each group should be seen before the assignment is completed.

Sharing

Purposes:

- Allow children to speak for a variety of real purposes and audiences in a variety of contexts.
- Encourage children to listen actively in a variety of situations, in order to receive and respond to information obtained from a variety of sources.

Materials:

- Author's Chair (a specially labeled chair in which a person sits while reading his or her writing).

Activity:

1. The children gather on the carpet in the meeting area.
2. Ask for volunteers to share their writing pieces. Sometimes a student shares a "published" piece. More often, students read from a first draft that they have just written.
3. One child reads from the Author's Chair at a time.
4. You should also share your own writing with the class.
5. After a child has read a piece, he or she calls on peers to tell something that they liked about the piece.
6. End the sharing session with your own comments about the work that the class is doing.

Variations:

→ Display compositions routinely on the wall or bulletin board.
→ Have an Author's Night, in which parents are invited to read and comment on the compositions students have created and selected for display.
→ Assigns all children one day of the week on which they get to share in the Author's Chair.

Management Tip:

→ Model useful comments for the students to offer their peers. Examples:
  - "I love the way you described . . . "
  - "I wonder why the character . . . "
  - "The way you began the story was . . . "
  - "I think your story would be easier to understand if . . . "
  - "Could you add some more description to . . . "

Publishing

Purposes:

- Build confidence and motivation in young writers.
- Enable children to produce work for an audience.

Materials:

- Pencils.
- Paper.
- Blank books.
- Crayons, markers, colored pencils.
- Computer, printer.
- Computer programs such as *ClarisWorks for Kids, Writing Center, Once upon a Time,* or *StoryBook Weaver.*

Activity:

1. Once children have produced three to five first-draft pieces, they choose one they want to publish.
2. They get advice from others and revise their writing to make it as clear and interesting as possible.
3. Students choose a friend to help them with the editing.
4. Students have conferences with you for help with the final editing.

Variations:

- → Children's work can be sent to children's magazines (such as *Highlights for Children*) for publication.
- → Papers can be assembled as a class book.
- → Class books can be shared at home with the family.
- → Children's work can be published on the Web.
- → Children's work can be displayed on class bulletin boards.
- → Children's books can be placed in a special area in the classroom or school library.
- → Children can share chosen work during a "Meet the Author Day." Family members can be invited to attend.

Poetry Writing: Concrete Poems

Purposes:

- Model writing tasks to be completed by the students.
- Encourage students to write in poetic form.

Materials:

- Writing folders.
- Pencils.

- Crayons, markers.
- Paper.
- Author's Chair.
- Collection of poetry, including concrete poems.
- Pictures or cutouts of various shapes.

Activity:

1. Introduce the students to the idea of a "concrete poem," which is a poem that takes the shape of its subject matter.
2. Show the class an example of a concrete poem, and explain how to create such a concrete poem.
3. Create a concrete poem with the class.
4. The students are sent back to their seats to think about a subject for their poem.
5. Children choose a subject and practice writing a concrete poem.
6. When the students have finished their poems and feel comfortable about sharing them, they take turns reading them from the Author's Chair.

Keeping an Idea Notebook

Purposes:

- Provide a place for children to record their thoughts, questions, and ideas.
- Encourage children to compose texts that are diverse in content and form for different audiences.

Materials:

- Small spiral notebooks.
- Pencils.

Activity:

1. Students maintain notebooks (these can be titled "Treasure Chest" or the like) for recording their thoughts, ideas, questions, conversations, and so on.
2. Students write in their notebooks on a regular basis.
3. Children are reminded to refer to their notebooks often.
4. Students can choose an idea from their notebooks when they need something to write about.
5. Students can share their ideas with buddies.
6. Students are encouraged to write in many different genres.

Independent Writing

Purposes:

- Encourage children to write on self-selected topics.
- Allow children to engage in the writing process for an uninterrupted period of time.

Materials:

- Various kinds of paper.
- Pencils.
- Crayons, markers, colored pencils.
- Journals.
- Blank books.

Activity:

1. Following the completion of the Writing Workshop tasks, children engage in independent writing. Independent writing time is the time for a child to personally select writing topics and writing forms. It is the time for him or her to integrate all the procedures, skills, and strategies learned in class into writing pieces that are personally meaningful.
2. Children may select a piece from their writing folders to continue working on, choose to begin a new piece, or choose to write in their journals.
3. Children may publish a piece at this time. Before publishing, it is necessary for a child to have a conference with you about the piece that the child wishes to publish. A published piece should be error-free.

FIVE

Second-Grade Case Study

INTRODUCTION TO THE TEACHER, JILL SAWYER

Jill Sawyer (a composite of several teachers) studied early childhood education and English as an undergraduate. She is currently working on her master's degree in reading, leading toward certification as a reading specialist. Jill has taught second grade for five years in the same school district.

The community where Jill teaches is economically and ethnically diverse. The socioeconomic levels range from lower-middle to upper-middle. Jill's classroom is also representative of the ethnic diversity of the community. The ethnic backgrounds of her 24 students are as follows: 12 European, 4 Native, 4 Asian, and 4 African. Six of these children speak more than one language at home.

In the classroom, 15 children are reading between a second- and fourth-grade level. Three children spend time during the day receiving services in the school's Resource Center, while the child study team is observing three others as potential candidates for these same services. In addition, three other children are in the school's Basic Skills Program for reading and writing, and meet with this teacher for the LAB twice a week.

Teachers in Jill's district are strongly encouraged to participate in continuing education opportunities. Teachers are reimbursed for courses successfully completed at the graduate level; and they have the opportunity to take several in-district courses offered in the fall, spring, and summer for salary guide credit. The school district also schedules five delayed-opening days during the academic school year for staff development, which usually focuses on grade-level curriculum. In addition, teachers are encouraged to cooperate and collaborate with one another on a regular basis.

TEACHING PHILOSOPHY

When asked about her philosophy of literacy instruction, Jill says:

> "Literacy instruction occurs throughout the day in our classroom. Extended periods of time are set aside daily for the language arts curriculum, and the use of children's literature, writing activities, 'book talks,' etc., are integrated into all content areas. I use both fiction and nonfiction trade books, as well as poetry, to enhance the children's understanding and enjoyment of content material.
>
> "I have created Literacy Centers in the classroom to encourage the children to

Teachers confer with each other and collaborate on a regular basis.

work collaboratively and to direct much of their own literacy learning. I plan center activities that allow for a range of abilities; it is important for all children to learn to work independently.

"Along with the child-directed learning activities, I integrate explicit teaching of skills and hold the children accountable for demonstrating these skills. Although in second grade we use a developmental report card to indicate to parents whether certain reading and writing behaviors have been acquired, I also introduce the children to rubrics. These rubrics show the children on a number scale the assessment expectations for a specific assignment. I have found that children in second grade want to know 'how well' they have done, and it helps them to see specifically what they need to work on."

THE PHYSICAL ENVIRONMENT IN THE CLASSROOM

Several large footprints taped to the floor of the hallway lead to the door of Jill's classroom. Across the doorway is a banner that reads, "Oh, the Places You'll Go—Journey

Jill uses both fiction and nonfiction trade books, as well as poetry and other genres of children's literature, to enhance children's understanding of content material.

through Second Grade." On the wall outside the room is a large drawing of the characters from Dr. Seuss's book (1990) *Oh, the Places You'll Go!*

Inside the classroom, the theme continues on a bulletin board in the class library. This bulletin board is entitled "Featured Author." Shel Silverstein's poem "Where the Sidewalk Ends" (from his book of the same name; Silverstein, 1974) is written on a large piece of chart paper in the center of the board. Around the poem are copies of other poems by Shel Silverstein, as well as pieces of biographical information about him. Below the bulletin board is a book display with a sign above it that reads, "Where the Sidewalk Ends and *Your* Journey Begins." Throughout the year, different authors and their works are featured here. Students are encouraged to make use of the featured works to discuss similarities and differences between individual pieces, as well as to investigate how an author's life may have influenced his or her writing.

In the Library Corner, there are beanbag cushions, a rocking chair, several pillows, puppets, and stuffed characters of popular children's books. This is an inviting place where children can easily select books for independent and buddy reading. Built-in bookcases and stackable crates hold books arranged according to genre. Jill's classroom collection includes fiction, nonfiction, poetry, fairy tales, folklore, and reference works. Commercial library stickers help the children to locate and replace books that belong within these categories; different-colored stickers in the inside back cover help children to find books at their appropriate reading level.

Some of the most popular books in the library are not purchased books, but books written by individual children in the classroom. Within the bookcases where the trade books are stored, each child has a small shoebox to house his or her published stories. "I like the children to feel as though they are as much authors of books as any other authors featured in the class library," Jill reports.

The Library Area in Jill's classroom is used more than any other area in the room. Not only does it serve as a place to find and read books, but also it is a gathering place for instruction and a place to work on word study and create stories. Magnetic letter trays, word games, poetry boxes, and writing/drawing materials are all stored in shelves in the Library Area.

The Library Area is defined on one side by an easel with chart paper, a white board, a felt board and a magnetic board. These boards are used for teacher-led instruction, as well as for some independ-

In the Library Corner, there are beanbag cushions, a rocking chair, pillows, and puppets to invite children to select from the many books present.

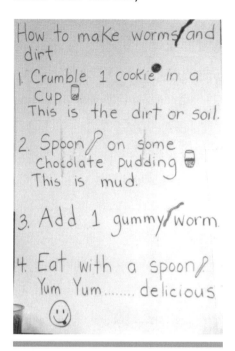

How to make worms and dirt

1. Crumble 1 cookie in a cup.
This is the dirt or soil.

2. Spoon on some chocolate pudding.
This is mud.

3. Add 1 gummy worm.

4. Eat with a spoon.
Yum Yum........ delicious

(☺)

A chart integrating literacy, science, and the study of worms.

ent work during center time. A stand with pocket charts sits on the other side of the library. These pocket charts are often used for sorting words, creating poems, and displaying book titles that are categorized for similarities. For example, one pocket chart is reserved for book titles that fall under the category "text-to-text connections," a comprehension strategy. Children write titles and explanations and put them in the pocket chart. Two sentence strips read, "Paul Bunyan and Swamp Angel are alike because they are both big and do things that normal people can't do," and, "Junie B. Jones and Ramona the Pest are alike because both characters get into trouble with their teachers."

Jill encourages the children to work together during many activities and lessons throughout the day. To facilitate this goal, the desks are arranged in groups of four where "teams" of children with mixed abilities sit. A Word Wall stretches across the blackboard near the groups of desks. "Tricky" words such as *because, really, where,* and *were,* as well as other commonly misspelled words, are stapled to sentence strips that hang from each letter on the alphabet placard. Jill also includes words on the Word Wall as they are introduced and talked about in math, science, social studies, and health, such as *dinosaur* and *culture,* so that the children are able to look for them and spell them when needed.

Next to the Word Wall are word charts that reinforce skills. One of these charts shows words in which -s and -es are added to form plural words. Another chart that is continually evolving is entitled "Homophones." It begins with Jill's writing of words such as *see* and *sea* and continues with words written in by the children such as *where* and *wear.* A third wall displays word endings. As "chunks" or vowel rimes/word endings are taught, lists of words are created for each rime. The lists are hung around the room for the children's use.

A small bulletin board is designed like a board game with a winding path and stopping points. The stopping points are labeled with science and social studies topics that the children will "visit" throughout the year. Each unit has related children's books and poems that are stored near the board, and the children's work from the current unit is displayed. This is an area where children can revisit previous topics and look forward to new ones.

Children's work is also displayed in the Computer Center. During center time, one computer is designated as a publishing area; the other two are used for creating *PowerPoint* slide shows, for illustrating stories, and even for playing word games such as *Carmen Sandiego* and *Word Detective.*

Jill has created a center/ activity chart to help students select independent work.

CLASSROOM GUIDANCE AND DIRECTION

In Jill's classroom, the children are working on a range of activities during the LAB. The children are busy working on stories and plays, working with manipulative word materials, creating comic strips, and reading in different areas of the room, to name a few! Good guidance and direction are necessary in order to allow all these activities to run smoothly. "The key to managing the LAB," Jill says, "is to plan well, establish literacy routines, and generate enthusiasm. When children are engaged, I have very few problems to deal with." Jill's own enthusiasm motivates the children to stay engaged and on task.

Jill finds that beginning the LAB with all the children in the Library Area helps build a sense of community. On one particular day, she began by asking the children whether they had ever had a really horrible day in which everything went wrong. After a few children shared stories, Jill read the story *Alexander and the Terrible, Horrible, No Good, Very Bad Day* (Viorst, 1972), making it come alive with felt board characters. The children laughed at the problems that the boy in the story had, and recited the repeating lines "It was a terrible, horrible, no good, very bad day," and "I think I'll move to Australia." Jill followed up by leading a discussion about when things go wrong in school and what students should do when this happens. This then led the class to create classroom rules—an appropriate activity for the beginning of the year.

After the whole-class meeting, it was time for the children to move independently to the centers around the room. Jill has developed a routine to help manage the independent work at the centers. On a half-piece of laminated poster board, Jill has placed Velcro squares with pictures of the different centers and activities on them. These icons tell the children what centers are open for use that day. Jill selects activities she knows that the children need to practice. The children are to look at them early and think about what they would like to work on. When a child selects a center, Jill records it and hands the child a clothespin with his or her name on it to attach to the icon. Jill keeps track of the time each child spends at each center. This ensures that the children are encouraged to explore all the centers, and don't always go to the same ones.

When problems arise that can't be resolved by the children, Jill will ask what happened and how the situation can be improved. Children receive a warning for inappropriate behavior. If it continues, Jill hands the child a form that begins, "Dear [Mom, Dad, or other guardian], Today I had a problem. This is what happened." The child writes a letter explaining the problem and describing what he or she will do differently if the problem happens again. Jill comments, *Completed during that time not recess*

> "I've found that when children write about a problem in the classroom, they have to sit and really think about it. It's not like missing recess. When the children have a consequence like missing an activity, they're just mad about missing the activity—they don't always make the connection between the poor behavior and the punishment."

Jill's classroom is a productive place where children are constantly interacting with one another. To maintain an appropriate noise level in the classroom while still encouraging the children to work together, Jill uses a silent signal that means voices are too loud. Near the small-group table is a meter taped to the wall. It is divided into three parts: green, yellow, and red. When the children get too loud, Jill moves the arrow to the yellow area. The children seem to notice it immediately and quickly "shush" the others around them. If the arrow does not move into the red area, then the children earn a marble for the marble jar. Jill states,

> "The marble jar is the greatest way I've found to get the children to work together. The children have the goal, or challenge, of earning 30 marbles in the jar. When they work well as a team and monitor the noise in the room, they earn a marble. When they have reached their goal, we celebrate their hard work and accomplishments."

The children in the classroom are accountable not only as team members, but also as individuals during center time. At the end of the LAB, the children record on a sheet for the week the activities they have participated in and the centers they have visited. They rate their effort for each day on a scale of 1 to 3.

A predictable environment is important in classroom management at the second-grade level. This requires both a carefully constructed physical environment and well-practiced routines. Paper, pencils, crayons, erasers, scissors, and other materials are set out on a table for easy access, and the children take responsibility for gathering appropriate materials for lessons. A schedule is posted in the Library Area to help the children follow the events for the day. Attention to this level of detail in the room helps the bustle of classroom activity run smoothly.

TYPES OF READING EXPERIENCES AND SKILL DEVELOPMENT

The children in Jill's classroom are exposed to many different reading experiences throughout the day. The children participate in whole-group mini-lessons, engage in small-group guided reading lessons, and read both independently and with buddies.

Jill presents mini-lessons based on objectives that satisfy the needs of her children. For example, Jill found early in the school year that many children in the class, even the very fluent readers, needed explicit teaching and practice with phrasing. For the next mini-lesson, she chose the book *Cloudy with a Chance of Meatballs* (Barrett, 1982) to read aloud. Before she began the book, she asked the children to listen closely to *how* she read the words—the pauses she took and the expression she used. When she finished reading the story, she picked up two sentence strips taped together. Prior to the lesson, she had written on the long strip a sentence from the book, but without its original interior punctuation: "That night touched off by the pancake incident at breakfast Grandpa told us the best tall-tale bedtime story he'd ever told." She read the sentence without taking any pauses, then asked the children about what the sentence was telling the reader. The children had a hard time understanding the sentence. Jill then put in the two commas that were originally printed in the sentence. She told the children that the words before each comma had to go together; she then had a child cut the first two words from the sentence strip and put it in the pocket chart. Another child then cut the next part of the sentence that went together and placed it next to the first. The class then read the sentence together, pausing at the correct places. Jill had also prepared sentence strips with other sentences from the book for extra practice.

During center time, the children can participate in independent and buddy reading, while different groups of children engage in guided reading with Jill. During independent and buddy reading, the children select books from the classroom library, as well as books read during previous guided reading lessons. They find a comfortable place in the classroom, such as a quiet corner or a spot under a table, to enjoy the book. Another activity set up for independent reading time is the "I Bet You Didn't Know" board. If the children choose a nonfiction book, and learn something new that they believe no one else knows, they write it up on the board and share it with the class during sharing time. Children are also asked to write their findings on a sheet provided to account for the reading they have done. Statements written on the board range from "All food chains begin with grass" (taken from a "Let's-Read-and-Find-Out" book) to "Tyrannosaurus Rex was a scavenger, not a killer" (taken from an article in a children's magazine). At the beginning of the school year, children are only able to read silently for about 10–15 minutes. By the end of the school year, when many are reading longer chapter books, they will read for 20–25 minutes.

Guided reading allows for small-group instruction. The groups are flexible and arranged according to common needs. Children are called to a table in the room to learn or practice a reading skill or concept based on these needs. Jill carefully chooses books that will complement the children's—or, in some cases, a particular child's—needs. For example, one guided reading lesson was planned for only one child, who was reading at a beginning first-grade level. In a previous book, the child had had difficulty with the -*ai* vowel combination, and some explicit instruction was needed.

In another guided reading lesson, Jill met with five children and introduced a new book to them. The objective for this lesson was to explicitly teach the skill of making connections between the reader and the story, and to record those connections in a Venn diagram. Jill began the lesson:

JILL: Today we are going to read a story about going on a journey or a trip. What kind of trips have you gone on with your family?

STUDENT 1: We went to the beach over the summer.

JILL: Why did you think your parents wanted to go to the beach?

During center time, children can participate in independent and buddy reading.

STUDENT 1: We all like it there. We can swim, build sand castles, and ride bikes on the boardwalks.

JILL: I asked you about trips you've taken because, as I mentioned, the book I'm going to read is called *Grandma's Jenny's Trip*. In this story, the main character tells of a trip that her family takes, but it's a little different from the trips you take. (*Pause to pass out books*) What things are you thinking about as you look at the cover?

STUDENT 2: That the story is going to be about American Indians.

STUDENT 3: That it might take place at another time, because there is a wagon, not a car.

JILL: Okay, let's open the book and take a short walk through the pages. You will see that the grandmother is telling the story. While you read the story, I want you to think about how your trips are the same as the grandmother's; also think about how they are different. When you make a connection, I want you to use a Post-it Note in the book—you can even write a note on it—to remind you of the connection you made.

When the children returned to the table after reading *Grandma's Jenny's Trip* (Spang, 1997) independently at their seats, Jill handed out sheets with Venn diagrams drawn on them. She reminded the children that a Venn diagram compares two things. In this case, the children were going to compare their family trips with the family trip the grandmother told about in the story. Jill directed each child to write his or her name at the top of one circle and "Grandma" at the top of the other. She further instructed them to go back through the pages of the story to find the parts in which they made "self-to-text" connections. After the group discussed how these connections helped the children to remember part of the story, each child wrote his or her own connections in the center of the diagram. They also discussed with one another how their trips were different from the character's, and then completed their diagrams.

TYPES OF WRITING EXPERIENCES AND SKILL DEVELOPMENT

Although Jill's students engage in a wide variety of writing experiences throughout the day, writing time is most concentrated just before and during the Writing Workshop.

The activities during this time include whole-class mini-lessons, small-group shared writing, and independent writing in which the children are encouraged to follow their own interests.

Jill often precedes the Writing Workshop with a word study or spelling lesson, which helps link the reading and writing activities. She chooses to call this lesson "word study," because she explains that the focus is not on memorizing a list of words, but on learning and understanding how words are blended together and segmented apart.

Each week, Jill introduces new vowel rimes (word endings), such as -at and -ack, written as headers on pieces of chart paper. She asks the children to look at the letters in each "chunk" and listen carefully as they say them with her. The children then sit in pairs with magnetic boards of letters. She then asks them to add a consonant such as c to the -at chunk to build the word cat. The lesson always begins with simple instructions, since the children still need specific directions when adding and deleting letters from chunks. The discussion then turns to a chart of "blends" and "digraphs." The teacher encourages the children to look at the chart and explore with the blends and digraphs to see what new words they can create. As the children work together, words begin to fill the chart—ranging from simple words such as chat and flat, to more sophisticated words such as atlas and acrobat. The charts are posted, and words are added during the week as children discover them.

Next, the children move into the Writing Workshop. Jill often begins the workshop with a brief mini-lesson, which is usually followed by a shared writing activity. One particular lesson focused on identifying the "problem" and "solution" in a story, and then on teaching the children how to create a writing plan for problems and solutions in their own stories.

JILL: Who would like to tell us about one of your favorite stories?

STUDENT 1: The story "Pudding like a Night on the Sea" from *The Stories Julian Tells* [Cameron, 1989].

JILL: What was it that made you enjoy that story so much?

STUDENT 1: Julian and his brother ate the pudding when they weren't supposed to and knew they were going to get in trouble. It was funny.

JILL: You knew something was going to happen to them, right? Were you asking yourself questions about what was going to happen?

STUDENT 1: Yeah. They were hiding under the bed and they heard their dad coming to find them, and I wondered if he would, and if he did, what would he say?

JILL: There was a "problem" in the story that made it exciting. Great stories always have a problem in them. Something happens and the characters have to try to figure out what to do. What is the problem in *Lilly's Purple Plastic Purse* [Henkes, 1996], the story we read yesterday?

STUDENT 2: She gets her purse and shimmering glasses taken away.

STUDENT 3: And her shiny coin. She gets really mad at the teacher for taking them away.

JILL: Doesn't that make you want to know more? Now, let's think about writing a story about a little boy on his first day of school. What could be a problem the little boy faces in school?

STUDENT 4: He can't find his classroom.

STUDENT 5: He comes to school and finds out that all the teachers are vampires!

The conversation continued, and Jill listed the possible problems on chart paper. The children later returned to their seats with a predrawn writing plan to define the characters and the problems for their own stories.

Lessons during the Writing Workshop time vary and include instruction on creative writing, persuasive writing, poetry, and even simple expository writing.

CROSS-CURRICULAR CONNECTIONS

In all areas of the curriculum, it is evident that Jill brings literacy instruction and practice into most of her lessons. The year-long theme "Oh, the Places You'll Go—Journey through Second Grade" is intended to give the literacy curriculum a thematic focus, but it also extends beyond that to include and tie together content material that is part of the science and social studies curriculum.

Jill says about her cross-curricular connections,

"The beginning of the year is full of stories about characters going on a journey or a trip, and the children can easily write stories about their own journeys, especially since most of them go on summer vacations. The theme is explored in science and social studies units. I find all kinds of fiction and nonfiction stories to go along with the content material. I even managed to tie the science unit on water into the theme of 'Journeys' through the book *The Magic School Bus at the Waterworks* [Cole, 1986]. This book goes through the process of the water cycle, in addition to the process of the water purification process. The children all became students on the Magic School Bus, and we explored additional content in the unit. The children had the responsibility of writing their own Magic School Bus stories to cover the content that was not included in the book."

Word study also comes up often in units of study. For example, when teaching the science lesson on the water cycle, Jill pointed out the letter combination *-tion* as it looks and sounds in the words *evaporation, condensation,* and *precipitation.* As the unit on water progressed, many other words were added to the list of *-tion,* words such as *water purification* and *reaction.* One child even made the observation that many words in science have *-tion* in them.

One science lesson involved Jill's giving the children a question from an activity that required the children to give reasons for the answer they chose. The activity was from their science unit on matter, and called for the children to mix cornstarch with water. When the children scooped it up and rolled it between their hands, it took on the properties of a solid—it became hard. When they stopped rolling it, it took on the properties of a liquid—it dripped through their fingers. The question on the board asked the children: "Is the mixture a solid, a liquid, or both? Explain." Jill told the children that

"Explain" meant they had to think of reasons for their answer. She then passed out a writing plan that structured how to answer this type of question. At the top were lines to write the first sentence, which included the children's answer to the question in a complete sentence, and below were three blocks in which the children could write their reasons. The children later wrote the expository piece in their writing journals.

The LAB itself often begins with a poem or song related to a theme being studied in a content area. In keeping with the theme "Journeys," and tying in the social studies units "Maps" and "Cultures," Jill shared "Poetry around the World." For each continent studied and traveled to, the children learned and wrote different types of poems, such as acrostic poems, haiku, rhyming couplet poems, and free verse.

Math at the school is taught from a scripted lesson that is part of a math program in the school district; however, Jill often begins new concepts with children's literature written for that particular concept. *Eating Fractions* (McMillan, 1991) and *Gator Pie* (Mathews, 1979) are titles she uses to illustrate how fractions can be recognized all around us.

TEACHABLE MOMENTS

Lessons in Jill's classroom involve a great deal of dialogue. Children feel comfortable asking questions and sharing ideas and stories; these often inspire teachable moments. Jill takes advantage of such moments by allowing for vocabulary and concept development. For example, the class was studying dinosaurs, and an activity included sorting the dinosaurs being studied into those that walked on two legs and those that walked on four. One student raised his hand when he came upon this information and said:

STUDENT 1: Look, this book shows the same thing we're talking about, but the words are different—*bipedal* and *quadrupedal*.

JILL: You're right. Look, everyone, Tim found different words for dinosaurs that walk on two legs and four legs. What do you notice about the word *bipedal*?

Jill wrote the word in large letters on the white board, with a small space between the *bi* and *pedal*.

STUDENT 2: It looks like *bicycle*.

JILL: (*Writing the word* bicycle *on the board with a space between the* bi *and* cycle) It certainly does. Why do you think I'm putting a small space in the word? (*Pause*) How many wheels does a bicycle have?

STUDENTS: Two!

STUDENT 3: Those are dinosaurs with two legs.

JILL: Right. *Bi* means "two," and *pedal* means "feet."

STUDENT 4: Then *quadrupedal* means "four feet," because *quad* means "four."

JILL: Are there other words you can think of that have *quad* in them—words that mean "four"?

STUDENT 5: *Quadruple.* Like in math.

STUDENT 6: *Quadruplets.*

STUDENT 7: What about a *quadrilateral*? We just finished talking about that in math.

As the children gave words, Jill wrote them on the white board. These brief diversions from the immediate topic are common in this classroom, and often increase or expand students' understanding of the materials.

DAILY SCHEDULE

The daily schedule in Jill Sawyer's classroom is as follows:

8:25–8:35:   Children put away belongings and settle in for the day. Attendance and lunch count are taken.

8:35–8:50:   Morning message. 15 min.

8:50–9:00:   Daily jobs and jokes/riddles.

9:00–9:15:   Review of schedule and sharing.

9:15–9:55:   "Specials"—P.E., music, art, computers, school library.

9:55–10:15: Beginning of LAB—minilesson before independent work at centers and guided reading.

10:15–11:00: Independent work at centers and guided reading.

11:00–11:20: Word study (spelling).

11:20–11:35: Writing Workshop—mini-lesson.

11:35–12:05: Writing Workshop—small-group shared writing and independent writing time.

12:05–12:45: Lunch.

12:45–1:00: Silent reading.

1:00–2:00:   Math

2:00–2:35:   Science, social studies, or health.

A TYPICAL DAY IN SECOND GRADE

When school began, the children lined up outside the classroom and were greeted by Jill. As the children came into the classroom, they followed the routine of hanging up coats, taking homework folders (and any other necessary items) out of their book bags, and placing their book bags in the laundry baskets assigned to their table groups. The baskets were then placed in the coat closet for the remainder of the day.

The children's day immediately began with an independent literacy activity—the morning message. The few sentences that made up the morning message were written on the board, as well as printed on a strip of paper for each child. The morning message included grammatical, spelling, and punctuation errors that the children corrected, using editing marks taught in several lessons early in the year. Jill reminded them, "Use three lines under a letter that should be capitalized; put a line through a misspelled word and write it the correct way over it; use a 'carrot' to put words in that were left out." She then told them to put their papers in their homework folders to share with parents at home. (Because each morning message is about what is going on during a school day, it is a great way for parents to begin a conversation with their child about what they did during the day.)

As most of the children made their way to the library area, others began daily "housekeeping" jobs. Until everyone came together, Jill prepared a riddle with clever word play. She read from the book *When Riddles Come Rumbling* (Dotlich, 2001): "I soar and fly, but have no wing—I dip and dive from a trail of string." The children made many guesses, and Jill quickly wrote on the white board, "fly but no wing" and "trail of string." One child yelled out, "Kite!" Jill then commented on how the words "soar" and "dive" might make the reader immediately think of a bird, but that the author used those words in the riddle to make the comparison between the movement of birds and the movement of the kite. She explained that the reader had to think of what else might move in such a way.

In the 10–15 minutes remaining before the children went to their "specials" (P.E., music, art, computers, the school library), Jill reviewed the schedule for the day. She listed and briefly talked about all of the activities (independent work at centers/guided reading, word study, writing workshop, etc.), along with the times each activity began. ("The children feel comfortable when they know what to expect," Jill says. "They know how to plan for the next activity and to be prepared for it.")

After the children returned from their "specials," the rest of the morning was reserved for the LAB. Jill began with a read-aloud to reinforce the comprehension strategy of "questioning," which had been introduced in a previous lesson. She began by introducing a book, *The Frog Prince, Continued* (Scieszka, 1991a). She looked at the cover, then put the book down in her lap. "I wonder," she said as she looked up, "what the author meant by *Continued*? What do you think?" The children made predictions about why the author chose that title, most thinking that the author had written a second part to the story. Jill then began reading the story, inviting the children to raise their hands when a question about the characters or the events popped into their heads. Each time the Frog Prince came up to a witch to ask her to change him back into a frog, the children were raising their hands to ask "I wonder" questions about the anticipated events. Jill ended the lesson with a reminder that good readers ask many questions about the story as they read, and that the students would be practicing that strategy in their guided reading groups.

Next, Jill presented the choices available for center time and asked each child to plan his or her time. Then she walked around the room helping the children get started. Children had to complete two of the four activities. Two children chose to take the book just read, *The Frog Prince, Continued* (Scieszka, 1991a), to buddy-read together. Other children chose to listen to books on tape in the Listening Center and answer questions posed, to work with word study manipulatives, or to work on writing and publishing stories.

Juan chose to write a new version of *The Frog Prince, Continued* during center time.

While the children worked, Jill began guided reading by calling a group of four children to the small-group table. This group of children had just made the transition from reading picture books to chapter books, and they needed some work on blending words with multiple syllables. The children used magnetic letters to practice segmenting words with multiple syllables and blending them together. Jill then introduced them to the book *Horrible Harry in Room 2B* (Kline, 1990), a short chapter book. They read the first chapter and discussed the events. Jill highlighted a few multisyllabic words and asked the children how they figured them out. She then sent them back to their seats to read the second chapter and write one question they had in their minds at the end of their reading assignment.

After meeting with two more groups, Jill gave a 5-minute warning to "wrap up." She walked around the room to watch as the children put back materials "the way they found them," and then joined the children in the Library Area. Some children chose to share finished stories and interesting things they read about; other children shared ideas of things they were continuing to work on.

Jill then turned her attention back to the morning message for a brief word study lesson. She explained that she had included the word *found* in the message, and spelled it incorrectly as *fownd*, because she noticed many children were spelling it that way. She acknowledged that the *-ow* makes the same sound in many other words and that it was a good first try at spelling the word, but she asked the children, "If I were to *read* this word, would it *look* like this? Close your eyes and try to picture the word in your head." The children did so, and Jill asked a student to take another try at writing the word. When the child wrote *found*, Jill underlined the *-ou* in the word and explained that it was another way to make the same sound as *-ow*." *She wrote the word on a piece of sentence strip and stapled it to the Word Wall. "Take a good look at this word," she reminded the children. "I want to see this word written like this all the time."*

In the remaining 45 minutes of the LAB, the children engaged in the Writing Workshop. The mini-lesson prior to the children's independent writing focused on writing dialogue. Jill had noticed that the children were writing dialogue in their stories, but were having trouble with the mechanics. She prepared on chart paper a brief piece of dialogue without any punctuation marks. She asked the children what type of punctuation they noticed when characters were speaking. Immediately a few children yelled out, "Talking marks." Jill explained that in second grade they were going to call them "quotation marks," and she wrote the phrase on the board for the children to see. She further explained that quotation marks go around any words that "come out of a character's mouth." She then introduced where commas needed to be placed. When the children went back to their seats to work on new stories or stories in progress, Jill had conferences with individual students, helping them to write dialogue with appropriate punctuation.

Reviewing the day that Jill planned for her students, it is clear that they are engaged in literacy activities all day long. Jill uses varied strategies and structures to engage her students. Her classroom is a literacy-rich environment that provides literacy-rich experiences.

SUMMARY

Jill's classroom supports literacy learning. The purposeful construction of the physical environment, as well as the carefully thought-out lessons, units, and thematic connections, work together to encourage such learning. Instruction is balanced to include direct and explicit whole-class skill instruction, as well as group collaboration and independent discovery. In addition, the range and quality of the materials used to support the instruction further enrich the children's literacy learning experiences.

Predictable, practiced child guidance techniques and routines carefully control the many different activities that occur throughout the day in Jill's classroom. As a result, there is minimal disruption of the literacy learning process.

It is apparent from observations of Jill's classroom that effective literacy instruction and learning aren't about simply selecting the right materials, or developing a model lesson type, or having a well-thought-out physical environment, or maintaining careful control of the classroom. Not just *one* of these, but all of them carefully working together, support the common goal of maximizing literacy learning for children.

The teacher holds individual writing conferences during the Writing Workshop.

SIX

Second-Grade Activities and Plans

GETTING STARTED

Language Arts Block Time Schedule

As in Chapter Four, note that this schedule covers the LAB *only*, not the entire instructional day.

9:00–9:30:   **Things to do when the students arrive**
Lunch count/attendance board
Classroom journals
Classroom Web page

9:30–10:00:   **Morning meeting**
Class news
Integrating math and language arts into the morning meeting
Geography journals
Shared reading
Poem of the week
Home journals

10:00–11:10:   **Guided reading instruction/independent work at centers**
Guided reading
Literature Circles
Listening Center
Story Props Center
Working with Words Center
Author's Corner
Social Studies Center
Science Center
Computer Station

11:10–11:30:   **Independent classroom reading**
Checking out books
Response journals

11:30–12:10:   **Writing Workshop**
Working through the writing process
Prewriting
Drafting
Revising
Editing
Publishing
Self-assessments in writing
Writing across genres
Poetry writing

Tools for Teaching Language Arts

Classrooms contain many materials—some supplied by the demands of the curriculum and the school district and some supplied by your own preference and personal ingenuity. You may have a fully stocked classroom, or you may have one with only a minimum of materials. Be creative with what you have. And be creative when your needs go beyond what is readily available to you. Don't be afraid to ask students to bring in anything from crayons to fabric to glitter and beyond! The following list is intended to help you get started. Then it's up to you!

- Classroom computer, printer, and programs.
- For the Listening Center: tape recorder, headsets, audiotapes, and books.
- Pocket chart and stand.
- Leveled books.
- Big books.
- Book bins/book boxes.
- Felt board and felt board storytelling pieces.
- Roll movie box and roll movies.
- Materials for making felt board pieces and roll movies.
- Overhead projector.
- Chart paper.
- Easel.
- Small chalkboards or wipe-off boards.
- Writing journals.
- Blank books.
- A variety of writing materials.
- Crayons, markers, colored pencils, glue sticks, construction paper.
- Comfortable furnishings in an attractive Library Area, Reader's Corner, or whatever you choose to call it.

Ideas for Classroom Organization and Management

Purposes:

- Use time efficiently and effectively.
- Provide structure to a classroom setting.
- Make smooth transitions from one activity to the next.
- Gain the children's attention.

Methods for Gathering Attention:

Some of the methods for gathering attention described in Chapter Four may be used.

- Clap two times and say, "Clap two times if you can hear me." The students who heard the signal stop what they are doing and clap two times. Repeat your clapping. After two or three times, the entire class should be focused on the teacher.
- Ring a bell, or just say "Ding, ding" if you do not own a bell.
- The sound of chimes is a soothing, calming way to get children's attention. The students enjoy listening to it. Sometimes you can even start to play a song, and

they will be very quiet so they can hear it. The chimes are very soft and cannot be heard unless they are quiet.

- Teach students that when they hear classical music, all must be silent.

Keeping Track of Other Students When You Are Working in Small Groups:

- If you are rotating the students at centers between guided reading groups, or if it is time to clean up centers in preparation for whole-class instruction, use a signal such as the ringing of a bell to get the students' attention.
- Create bathroom passes for the students to use when they need to use the lavatory. (This cuts down the number of times that you are disturbed while you are working with groups.)

  - Color, cut out, and laminate the gingerbread boy and girl passes (see the diagrams that follow). Attach a piece of Velcro to the back of each pass.
  - Use a matching piece of Velcro to hang the passes somewhere in the room. If a student needs to use the bathroom while you are working with a group, the student should take the appropriate pass and leave it on his or her desk.
  - When the student returns from the bathroom, he or she should return the pass to its place in the classroom. By looking for bathroom passes placed on the children's desks, you can easily tell which students are using the lavatory at any given time. It is a good idea to limit the number of times the students are permitted to use the pass during small-group work (except, of course, for emergencies!).

Boys

Girls

THINGS TO DO WHEN THE STUDENTS ARRIVE

This section includes meaningful literacy activities for children to do when they enter school. These activities should be planned to cover a period of about 30 minutes.

Lunch Count/Attendance Board

Purposes:

- Create an organized system for taking lunch count and keeping track of attendance.
- Demonstrate the ability to gain information from a variety of media.

Materials:

- Laminated poster board, divided into columns labeled with the lunch choices being offered, plus "Absent."
- Monthly school lunch calendar.
- Laminated name tags.
- Velcro.

Activity:

1. Write each student's name onto a laminated name tag.
2. Place a piece of Velcro on the back of each name tag.
3. Place matching pieces of Velcro under each heading on the poster board.
4. Hang the poster board in an accessible area of the classroom. Hang the monthly school lunch calendar nearby.
5. Begin taking lunch count/attendance by placing all of the students' name tags under the "Absent" column.
6. Explain to the students that each morning, they will read the posted school lunch calendar to find out what is for lunch. Then each child will place his or her name tag under the appropriate lunch column. (See the illustration that follows.)
7. Refer to the lunch count/attendance board each day to find out what the students will be eating for lunch. You can easily tell who is absent for the day by looking to see whose names are left in the "Absent" column.
8. Appoint a student to tally up the lunch count and to verify that those students whose names are listed in the "Absent" column are indeed out.

Management Tips:

- → Be sure to use a permanent marker and write each student's name on the name tag *after* it has been laminated. This way, the name tags may be used from year to year. Simply use nail polish remover to erase an old name and write in a new one.
- → Appoint one student to move the name tags back under the "Absent" column at the end of each day.

Hot Lunch	Cold Lunch	Brought Lunch from Home	Absent
▦	▦	▦	▦
Marge	Stuart	Michael	Moira
Alex	Alyson	Timmy	John
Eric	Jen	Ed	▦
Julie	Jeff	Eileen	▦
Viola	Doug	▦	▦
Sandy	Kevin	▦	▦
Tommy	▦	▦	▦
Carole	▦	▦	▦
▦	▦	▦	▦
▦	▦	▦	▦

Classroom Journals

Purposes:

- Have students write in clear, concise, organized language that varies in context and form, for different audiences and purposes.
- Enable students to speak for a variety of real purposes and audiences.

Materials:

- Classroom journals, such as these:

    a. Ouch Book.
    b. Birthday Book.
    c. Official Report Book.
    d. Tooth Journal.
    e. Share Your World Book.

Activities:

1. Starting at the beginning of the year, integrate each journal into classroom use, one at a time. Explain its purpose and use in the classroom, and leave journals in an accessible place.

a. **Ouch Book**—Whenever children have an "ouch" (hurt themselves or do something they aren't happy about), they can write and draw about it in the Ouch Book.

b. **Birthday Book**—On a child's birthday, the child can use the Birthday Book to tell how he or she will celebrate.

c. **Official Report Book**—When children have a conflict with each other, they can use the Official Report Book. Students can write and draw about the problem, and use their entry to help foster a discussion among each other. Put on the directions page that once they have completed their page, their report is now "official!"

d. **Tooth Journal**—When a child loses a tooth, he or she tells how it fell out in the book.

e. **Share Your World Book**—This book is used in a version of "Show and Tell" called "Share Your World." Students share objects with the class that are important to them. Students take home the Share Your World Book in a canvas bag on their assigned day. In the book is a form for each child to fill out after selecting an object.

- The child completes the form and places the object in the bag to bring to school the next day.

- On the form, the child writes three hints about his or her object, indicates why he or she chose it, and draws a picture of the object.

- All of the pages from preceding children remain in the book all year, so that the children and parents can look back and read previous entries.

- Send home directions for the project before sending home the bag, so parents know what to expect.

Thematic Tie:

→ The "Share Your World" idea can be extended to incorporate classroom themes. For example, if the current theme is "Gorillas," you can send home a book about gorillas, a toy gorilla, and a Gorilla Journal. Students can read the book, enjoy the toy, and write on the topic. Writing topics can include the following:

a. Write three facts about gorillas that you have learned.

b. Write the main idea and three supporting details from the story.

Management Tips:

→ The following instructions should be posted on the inside cover of all the books:

a. Write the date.

b. Write your name.

c. Write/draw your entry.

→ You can make these books by binding paper together or by using hard-cover composition books.

Classroom Web Page

Purpose:

- Use technology to encourage development of speaking, listening, writing, and reading to assist with viewing.

Materials:

- Computer.
- Internet access.

Activity:

1. If your school has a Web site, you can set up a Web page for your classroom and teach your students to access it daily.
2. Students can learn to independently turn on the computer and the printer each day; to navigate, using the mouse onto the Internet; and then to access the school's Web site.
3. Once on the school's Web site, students can easily access the classroom's Web page. Students can view any information that is on the page, as well as check any incoming e-mail messages.
4. If there is new e-mail, students can print out new messages to share with the class and the teacher.

Management Tips:

➜ This activity will need to be modeled several times before students can do it independently.
➜ A volunteer can come to the classroom to help the students gather the day's news from the Internet.

MORNING MEETING

The morning meeting is a 30-minute block of time that is packed with many valuable literacy and math opportunities for your students. It is a time for your students to take leadership roles, bond with each other, and show what they know. It is also a time for sharing, discussing, planning, recording, reading, writing, and problem solving.

Class News

Purposes:

- Enable students to speak and listen for a variety of real purposes and audiences.
- Help students to compose print.

Materials:

- Chart paper or white board.
- Easel.
- Markers.

Activity:

1. The children are seated on the rug in front of the easel.
2. Children are selected in advance to share any personal news with the class.
3. The students orally share a few sentences of news.
4. Act as scribe for each child as he or she begins by saying aloud the first word of a sentence. The words are said slowly, one at a time, "stretching" them in order to hear the separate sounds in the words.
5. Have the child tell you how to write the words he or she is sounding out.
6. Use this time of writing sentences to go over various topics (grammatical structure, punctuation, basic sight words, spelling, consonant blends, short and long vowels, silent letters, spacing of words, etc.).

Variations:

→ When students are called on to share news, those particular students can come up and write it themselves. They may serve as teachers by asking the class how to write, or they may write independently and the class can edit it.

→ After gathering class news from a few students, you can simply ask the class, "Observations?" Students may begin to notice similarities, differences, and patterns in the class news.

→ The students can type class news on computers, with each student typing his or her own news, or students can type up news from selected children. If there are not enough computers, you can gather news in the same manner as described above, and type it up for the class. Programs such as "ClarisWorks for Kids" are great for word processing. The news can be printed out and added to a notebook titled "Class News." Each week's class news can be added to the book. This book can be kept in the reading area throughout the year. Students will be intrinsically motivated to read it, because it is about them and their lives.

Thematic Tie:

→ Ask students to share what they have learned about the current class topic/theme, and record their data in the same manner as detailed above.

Geography Journals

Purposes:

- Have students use speaking, listening, reading, and viewing to assist with writing.
- Help students become familiar with the names of, locations of, and facts about the 50 states.

Materials:

- Large United States map.
- Geography journal page (see below).
- Star stickers.
- Children's geography books such as *United States Atlas for Young People* (Smith, 1991) and *First Facts about the States* (Stienecker, 1996).

Could do during Unit 6 in Place of Word Know

Activity:

1. During morning meeting time, a helper chooses a state and places a star on the large map of the United States.
2. Read from a children's geography book about the chosen state. Include the location, direction from your state, and miscellaneous facts in the read-aloud.
3. The students then go to their seats and locate and color the state on the map in their geography journal (see the sample map that follows).
4. They then write sentences about the state, including the capital and other facts that were discussed.
5. For a culminating activity, each child randomly chooses a state to research at home. This involves making a flag and map of the state, as well as completing a state information form (see the sample form that follows the map). *—Use for investigation*

Variation:

→ Students can write to the Department of Tourism to request information about their state (and to practice their letter-writing skills!). This information, as well as research of the computer, will be used to create their flag, map, and data. When this is complete, the students will compile the data to form brochures about their state.

Management Tip:

→ Be sure to have your children write to the Department of Tourism several weeks before their project is due. This would be a good way to start the unit.

United States Geography Journal

Today's State _____

160

State Research

Your name: _____

Name of state: _____

Capital: _____

Population: _____

State bird: _____

State flower: _____

State tree: _____

State song: _____

State nickname: _____

In what part of the country is it located?:

_____

Resources/products: _____

_____

Places of interest: _____

_____

_____

_____

_____

Any famous people that are from this state:

_____

_____

Sports teams that play in this state:

_____

_____

_____

_____

At least four other interesting facts about this state: (You may use the back.)

_____

_____

_____

_____

_____

_____

_____

Shared Reading

Purposes:

- Involve all students in a rewarding, enjoyable reading experience.
- Help students read material and text with comprehension and critical analysis.

Materials:

- Big books.
- Easel for holding a big book.
- A pointer.

Activity:

1. Use big books because the text and illustrations are larger, and because they make it easier to engage students in the stories.
2. Select a big book depending on which reading skill or theme you wish to focus on.
3. Begin with an introduction to the book. Review challenging words and their meanings prior to reading the story. Include a "picture walk" for a few pages, and ask for predictions.
4. While reading the story, track the words so children can follow along more easily.
5. Read with a dramatic, enthusiastic voice. Engage children in the characters, humor, conflicts and plot. Encourage choral reading during repetitive parts of the text.
6. Read through to the end of the story, keeping a rhythm. Fewer interruptions during the first read-aloud aid in student comprehension.
7. After the story, go back and savor some of the children's favorite parts of the book. Ask critical thinking questions that are open-ended, to engage the group in a meaningful discussion. Children can retell the story from memory when finished or can share observations.

Thematic Ties:

→ The shared reading experience should tie into the current classroom theme. Have children do any of the following:

- Paint a mural of the story, using information from the story and theme.
- Act out the story (with or without props or puppets), or put on a play at the end of a theme.
- Compare and contrast related characters or stories in a Venn diagram.
- Do a related art project, such as clay figures or watercolor paintings.
- Keep and post a list of all the titles of books that you have read for that theme.
- Create a "museum" or area in your classroom to display theme-related activities and books.

Poem of the Week

Purposes:

- Encourage students to gain an appreciation for poetry.
- Help students read various materials and texts with comprehension and critical analysis.

Materials:

- Chart paper.
- Pointer.

Activity:

1. Students can read a poem, song, or chant that has been written on chart paper and posted. The poem should be related to a theme or a current area of study in the classroom.
2. On the first day with a new poem, read it aloud while tracking print. Go over any unfamiliar vocabulary, meaning, or the like. Then have the class read the poem along with you.
3. Since the same poem is used for 1 week, it is a shared reading experience, and the children participate in the reading of the poem more each day. A different student can lead the reading of the poem each day
4. After the class reads together, one or two students can volunteer to read it aloud.

Variations:

→ Think of actions to go along with the poem. Have students act out the poem while it is being read.
→ Have students write new versions of the poem.
→ Teach a particular phonic or literacy skill or strategy (rhyming words, word families, use of repetition, etc.).

Home Journals

Purposes:

- Enable children to respond to poetry in writing.

Materials:

- Poems on chart paper.
- Poems typed and reproduced for each child.
- Marbled composition books.
- An explanation letter inside each child's journal (see the sample letter that follows).
- Glue sticks.
- Crayons, pencils.

Activity:

1. The home journal is a collection of poems, songs, and chants taught during the school year that goes home after each use. It connects the family and school by enabling parents and children to share the reading and enjoyment of the same poems and songs. Children learn to take leadership roles by reading and teaching the poems to their families.
2. In the beginning of the year, provide each child with a notebook to use as a home journal.
3. Provide a letter explaining the purpose and use of the home journal inside the front cover.
4. As part of the morning meeting, read a weekly poem (see "Poem of the Week," above).
5. Students read the poem and discuss what the poem means to them.
6. Children receive a copy of the poem to paste into their home journals.
7. Students write and/or draw their response to the poem on the opposite page.
8. Students take their journals home for one or two nights to read the poem to their families and share their response.

Variation:

→ Throughout the year, invite parents to write their own thoughts about the poem in the journal or add to their child's work.

Dear Parents,

This is your child's home journal. The purpose of the home journal is to share with you many of the songs and poems that we learn in second grade.

After singing a song or reading a poem for approximately one week, children paste a copy of it inside their journals and illustrate and/or write about what the song or poem means to them.

Once your child has illustrated/written about the poem or song, the journal is sent home for one or two nights. Encourage your child to teach the songs and poems to the family! Increase your child's language skills by singing and reading the songs and poems together.

This journal creates a wonderful literary connection between home and school, and encourages children to take leadership roles in their learning. I welcome any of your comments, if you wish to include them inside the journal.

Please be sure to send the journal back to school within one or two days. Thank you and enjoy!

Sincerely,

Integrating Math and Language Arts into the Morning Meeting

Purposes:

- Enable students to speak for a variety of real purposes and audiences.
- Encourage students to listen actively in a variety of situations to information from a variety of sources.
- Help students view, understand, and use nontextual visual information.

Materials:

- Snap or Unifix cubes.
- Three cups to represent ones, tens, and hundreds.
- Stirrer straws.
- Rubber bands.
- Markers.
- Real or fake coins.
- A Velcro or shelved unit to hold coins.
- Drawing paper.
- Flip chart numbers.
- Chart paper or journal.

Activities:

The children are gathered on the rug in front of a bulletin board labeled "Morning Meeting" or "Morning Matters."

1. **Odd and Even.** If the date is September 10, have one student count out 10 cubes and attach them to make a stack. The student then breaks the stack in half and lines up the halves. Showing this to the class, the student asks the class "Is 10 odd or even?" If the halves are even, then the number is even. If the stack is uneven, the number is odd. On each day of school, a new cube is added to the stack until the end of the month. At the beginning of each new month, begin again with one cube. Every stack of 10 cubes should be a different color for easy counting.

2. **Place Value Chart.** Have students count and write the number of days that they have been in school. One way to keep track of the days of school is with a place value chart. It consists of three containers to represent ones, tens, and hundreds. Small flip charts with the numbers 0–9 are displayed in each container. Each day, a student adds a straw to the place value chart and adjusts the flip chart to show the appropriate number.

3. **Number Train.** Write the number of school days either on cash register tape or on small seasonal cutouts, such as apples and pumpkins. Watch the train get longer and longer until 180 school days are reached! The train can also be used as a time line for recording significant events, if students write or draw significant events of that day on the "cars" of the train.

4. **Tally Sheet.** Students keep track of the days of the month with a tally sheet. For example, on May 20, have a child add a tally to the tally sheet to show 20 tallies.

5. **Recording of Events.** The morning meeting should be a time when students

take leadership [role]... [p]rovide students with an oppor[tunity]... [d]uring the meeting. This can b[e] done individually by each child in a math log/journal; one or two students [can]... share it with the class; or the en[tire]... scribe.

Handwritten note:
Write number on chart
Write a way to name
that number
(target #)   words
             number sent.
             expanded
             tally marks
             money
model at first, then
release to them to do
during workshop time

Thematic Ties:

→ To include yo[ur current classroom theme in the]..., you or the students can incl[ude a fact of the]..., newspaper article, or the lik[e]...

→ The lesson pla[n]... [e above] can also relate to the t[heme]...

INDEPENDENT WORK AT CENTERS

As emphasized throughout this book, classroom centers should be designed so that the students can work independently on activities while you are meeting with guided reading groups. The time spent at centers will depend upon how many groups you meet with during the LAB. It should average 60 minutes per day. Centers and activities should be introduced gradually and modeled by you. The directions for each center/activity should be clearly displayed.

Here are some other suggestions for using classroom centers:

• Students change centers or activities when the guided reading groups change.
• Post a colorful sign with each center's name and an appropriate icon near each center area. This allows the students and classroom visitors to locate the learning stations easily.
• If classroom space is limited, make portable centers. Use cloth bags, colorful gift bags, and plastic containers to store center materials. The bags may be hung from self-adhesive hooks around the classroom.
• Carefully monitor the materials placed at the classroom centers. Too many materials may overwhelm the students, while not enough may leave them looking for something to do.
• Train classroom volunteers to assist the students during center time. This will help to decrease the number of times that you are disturbed during guided reading groups.
• Have accountability at each center. The children must complete a written product or report that you will check.
• Each child should have a center/activity folder to organize his or her work. Incomplete work should be kept in this folder. Completed work should be turned in to you.

Finally, keep in mind (1) that the number and type of centers/activities you offer for independent work should be tailored to your available resources and your students' needs, and (2) that you can call centers and activities by any names you prefer (as noted in Chapter Four).

Creating and Using a Center/Activity Pocket Chart

Purposes:

- Create a system for student rotation to the various classroom centers/activities.
- Establish an environment where small groups of children can work together on multilevel activities without teacher guidance.

Materials:

- Brightly colored, laminated library card pockets.
- A bulletin board or piece of sturdy poster board.
- Popsicle sticks or tongue depressors for the students' names.
- Permanent markers.

Activity:

1. To create the pockets, label the bottom of each laminated library card pocket with the name of a center (or activity within a center), using a permanent marker. The use of brightly colored library card pockets allows for clear visibility once the Popsicle sticks are placed in them. (These library pockets are often sold in teacher or office supply stores.)
2. Attach the pockets to the bulletin board or poster board. (See Chapter One for a photograph illustrating this.)
3. Write each child's name on a Popsicle stick or tongue depressor. Make sure that it is written high enough for the name to be visible once the stick is placed in a pocket.
4. Place the sticks in the pockets to group the children heterogeneously for center activities. The sticks may be moved either vertically or horizontally to rotate the students to different centers.
5. Children look to the pockets to find which centers/activities they will be working in while you are meeting with guided reading groups.

Thematic Tie:

→ You may wish to develop centers to reflect classroom themes. For example, if the class is studying dinosaurs, you may wish to turn the Science Center into a Dinosaur Center. Because the pockets are laminated, center names can be changed when necessary. Use nail polish remover to erase the old names and write in the new names.

Management Tips:

→ If centers/activities are rotated when the guided reading groups change, the students can be taught how to move the popsicle sticks from one pocket to the next. You may choose to appoint a new student each week to do this job.
→ Be flexible when it comes to rotations. There may be times when some of the students will need to remain at a center/activity for more than the allotted time. For example, if a student is creating a felt story at the Story Props Center, he or she will probably need to spend more than one day at that center.
→ Hang the pocket chart in a central classroom location at the children's eye level.

Sample Center/Activity Pocket Chart:

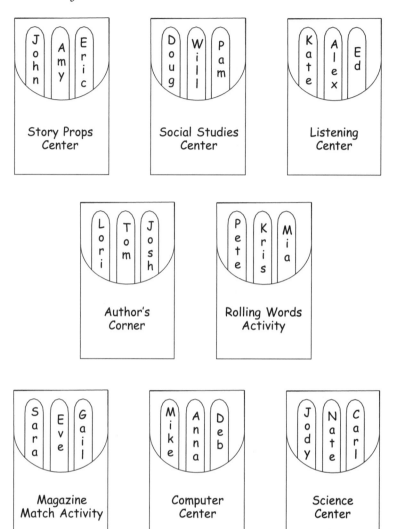

Keeping Track of Independent Work at Centers

Purposes:

- Create an organized system for keeping track of independent work at centers and for storing related activity sheets.

Materials:

- Two-pocket folders that can also hold loose-leaf paper (one per student).
- Copies of "My Center Work" form (see the form that follows; one per student).
- Three-hole puncher.

Activity:

1. Label each pocket in the two-pocket folders as "Still Working" and "Finished."
2. Punch holes in the "My Center Work" form and attach it to each folder.
3. Distribute the folders to the class. Tell the students that the folders will be used for keeping track of their independent work at centers.
4. At the end of center time each day, the students will complete the "My Center Work" form. They will write the date, the name of each center where they worked, and one or two sentences stating what they did at each center.
5. The folder pockets will be used to store activity sheets. Sheets that the students have not finished will be stored in the "Still Working" pocket. Sheets that the students have completed will be placed in the "Finished" pocket.

Thematic Tie:

➜ Develop classroom centers that reflect thematic units of study. Have the students keep track of their work at these thematic centers, as well as the permanent classroom centers. For instance, if the class is studying the rain forest, create a Rain Forest Center. Include goods that come from the rain forest, posters, a map of the world's rain forests, rain forest books, and related activity cards.

Management Tip:

➜ Periodically check the students' folders to assess their work at the classroom centers.

Name: _____

Week of _____

Day	Center	What I Worked On
Monday		
Tuesday		
Wednesday		
Thursday		
Friday		

Listening Center

Purposes:

- Encourage children to listen for enjoyment and for obtaining information.
- Expose children to a wide range of literature.

Materials:

- Tape recorders and headsets.
- Multiple copies of books, which represent a variety of difficulty levels.
- Cassette recordings of the books.

Activity:

1. Designate an area for the Listening Center (or whatever you choose to call it) within your Literacy Center, near an electrical outlet. Include a table, or a few desks, and enough chairs to seat the number of children who will be using this center.
2. To promote student choice, place about five different book/cassette sets at the center. Be sure to include multiple copies of each book. The five sets should be rotated periodically.
3. Model how the tape recorders should be turned on, how to rewind and change tapes, and so on, before allowing the students to use the center independently.
4. Have children complete an accountability sheet that requires a short critical review of the story on tape.

Variations:

→ Commercially prepared book and cassette sets are frequently available through book clubs. Using "bonus points" to obtain these materials helps to offset the cost of establishing a Listening Center.
→ Invite parent and student volunteers to record the text for books that you would like to include at the Listening Center. Encourage them to read with expression when creating these tapes.
→ Allow students to create listening tapes to go along with the stories they write during Writing Workshop. Include these stories at the classroom Listening Center.

Thematic Tie:

→ You may choose to use Listening Center materials that reflect current classroom themes. For example, if the class is learning about animals, you may wish to place a variety of books and cassettes about animals at the Listening Center.

Management Tip:

→ Individual portable cassette players (such as Sony Walkmans) can be used to increase the number of listening spots.

Story Props Center

Purposes:

- Help students practice comprehension skills and strategies.
- Foster enjoyable experiences with literature.

Materials:

- A variety of reading materials, in a range of genres and difficulty levels.
- Small dry-erase board, markers, and erasers.
- Puppets, stuffed animals, and the like.
- Felt board and felt board characters.
- Materials for students to make their own felt board pieces.
- Roll movie box and roll movies.
- Blank roll movie paper.
- Writing supplies.
- Blank notebook titled "Recommended Books."

Activities:

1. Organize an area for the Story Props Center (or whatever you choose to call it) within your Literacy Center.
2. Have students use the dry-erase boards to write down interesting words that they have found in the books at the center. Encourage them to look for rhyming words, compound words, words with the same vowel sound, and so on.
3. Create displays including books and corresponding props that may be used to retell stories. The props can be made or purchased.
4. Include a felt board and felt board story pieces at the Story Props Center. A copy of each featured book should be placed near the related felt board pieces. Place materials that may be used to make new felt board stories at the center. These materials can include felt, construction paper, sandpaper (to help the paper pieces stick to the felt board), glue, crayons, and markers.
5. Place a roll movie box and stories at the Story Props Center. Copies of the books that the roll movies are based on should also be available. Allow the students to create their own roll movies by leaving blank roll movie paper at the center.
6. Use the blank notebook to create a class list of "Recommended Books." Instruct the students to pretend that they are book critics and write about their favorite books in the notebook. Ask them to include the book title, the author, and why they are recommending the book to other students.
7. Allow students to share their Story Props Center creations (roll movies, felt board stories, etc.)

Thematic Ties:

→ Highlight thematic books at the Story Props Center by grouping them in a separate container.
→ Create felt board stories and roll movies that coincide with classroom themes.

Working with Words Center

Purposes:

- Have students manipulate letters to create words and sentences.
- Build students' word analysis skills.

Materials:

- Magnetic letters.
- Magnetic words and punctuation marks.
- Small magnetic boards or cookie sheets.
- Newspapers.
- Notebooks.
- Index cards.
- Letter stickers.
- Telephone.
- Dictionary.

Activity:

1. Use a desk or small table and a few chairs to create the Working with Words Center (or whatever you choose to call it) within your Literacy Center.
2. After new reading or spelling words are introduced, students use plain index cards to draw a picture representing one of the new words. On the other side, students write the word and its meaning. Place finished index cards at the Working with Words Center. Students will use each other's illustrations to guess the words that they represent. Also, leave blank index cards at the center to use when illustrating new words.
3. Have students cut out specified words from the newspaper and then look for various types of words (rhyming words, words with given vowel sounds, consonant blends, etc.). At the top of each page in a blank notebook, tell the students the types of words that they should be looking for—for instance, "How many long-*i* words can you find in the newspaper?" Students paste the words into the notebook.
4. This center may be used to reinforce spelling words. (Place a dictionary at the center to assist in the spelling of words.) The following are activities that may be used to practice spelling skills:

    a. Invite the students to use the magnetic letters and a magnetic board or cookie sheet to build spelling words.
    b. An old telephone may be used to practice spelling words and math skills. The students should use the telephone keypad to assign numbers to each letter in a spelling word. (You will have to insert the letters Q and Z, since telephone keypads do not include these.) The students then add up the numbers to determine the word's total. Encourage them to find which of their spelling words has the highest total value and which has the lowest.

1	2 ABC	3 DEF
4 GHI	5 JKL	6 MNO
7 PQRS	8 TUV	9 WXY(Z)
★	0	#

Most:
6 + 6 + 7 + 8 = 27

5. The students can put words together to build sentences as follows:

   a. Magnetic words and punctuation marks may be used to practice sentence construction. (These letters and punctuation marks can be purchased from teacher supply stores or can be handmade, using laminated construction paper and magnetic tape.) The students can create their sentences on a magnetic board or cookie sheet, or on the side of a nearby filing cabinet.

   b. The students can cut out individual words and punctuation marks from newspapers to create new sentences. Have them glue their new sentences into a blank notebook or onto a piece of construction paper.

Thematic Tie:

→ Encourage the students to work with words that are related to current thematic units at the Working with Words Center. Ask them to create vocabulary index cards using these words (activity 2). Include the thematic words on magnetic tape for the students to use in sentences (activity 5a).

Mystery Words Activity

Purposes:

- Have students decode unfamiliar words.
- Help students recognize small chunks in larger.

Materials:

- Chalkboard.
- Chalk.
- Paper.
- Pencils.

Activity:

1. This activity is meant to assist children in decoding unknown words by recognizing familiar chunks.
2. Write an unfamiliar word, such as *paleontologist,* on the chalkboard.

3. Tell the class that they are going to attempt to read this "mystery word" by looking for smaller chunks that they recognize. (Ask those children who can already read the mystery word not to share it with the rest of the class.)

4. Have the children come to the board to circle and say the smaller parts that they can read in the mystery word. These parts may be little words or even groups of letters and blends in the larger word. For example, in *paleontologist,* the students may recognize the word *pale* or the *-ist* ending.

5. Once the students have located several smaller words or chunks, ask them to attempt to read the mystery word.

6. Use this activity to reinforce vowel sounds, blends, and so forth, and also to point out any irregularities that occur in the longer mystery words.

7. After doing several examples as a class, have the students use the blank paper and pencils to try to decode more mystery words as an independent activity at the Working with Words Center. Later, discuss the different ways that the children broke the words apart.

8. Reinforce this method of decoding unknown words during guided reading groups.

Thematic Tie:

➜ This activity may be used to introduce thematic vocabulary. For example, when the class is working on a science unit about dinosaurs, you can use it to introduce tricky dinosaur names.

Rolling Words Activity

Purposes:

- Have students use letter dice to build words.
- Encourage students to work cooperatively in a small group.

Materials:

- Blank wooden or foam cubes (these can often purchased at craft stores).
- Permanent markers.
- Empty plastic cups.
- Score sheet.
- Pencils.

Activity:

1. Students will be placed into groups of four at the Working with Words Center for this activity.

2. Using the blank wooden or foam cubes, you will need to prepare four letter dice for each group. Using a permanent marker, program the cubes with letters. At least one die should consist of the vowels *a, e, i, o, u,* and *y.* One die should be programmed with letter combinations that reflect spelling patterns or sounds that are being studied. For example, if the class is working with *r*-controlled vowels, the six sides of one die may be labeled *ar, or, ir, er, ur,* and "Roll Again."

("Roll Again" may always be used if you do not have enough letter combinations for all six sides of a die.) The remaining two dice may be programmed with the consonant and/or vowel combinations of your choice. You may also want to label one side of a die "Lose a Turn" to make the game more interesting.

3. In their groups, the students will take turns rolling the dice. (The students may use the plastic cups to shake up their dice.) If a player lands on "Roll Again," then he or she rolls that particular die again. If a player lands on "Lose a Turn," then that player loses his or her turn altogether.

4. The object of the game is to try to create words, using the faces of the four dice that have ended up on top. Once a word is formed, the student should record the word under his or her player number on the group's score sheet. (Players are allowed to "challenge" each other if they think that a word is not legitimate.)

5. If a player cannot create a word using the four faces that are on top, then that player loses his or her turn.

6. Points are earned based on the number of letters in each word created. For example, if a student creates a two-letter word, he or she earns 2 points for that word; a four-letter word will give the student 4 points; and so on. The sheet that follows can be used for keeping score.

7. The game is over and points are tallied after a set amount of time or a certain number of turns.

8. The winner of the game is the player with the most points.

Variations:

→ This game can be made more challenging by *requiring* students to include the die that contains the spelling patterns or sounds being studied in words that are made. If the student cannot create a word that includes this particular die, then the student loses his or her turn.

→ The number of players can also be varied. This game can easily be played with the entire class. Place students into teams. List the team names on the chalkboard. When it is their turn, have each team work together to come up with words, using the letter dice. Record words and points earned on the chalkboard.

Rolling Words Activity Scoresheet

Player 1	Player 2	Player 3	Player 4

Score _____ | Score _____ | Score _____ | Score _____

Magazine Match Activity

Purposes:

- Have students find specific spelling and/or sound patterns in print.
- Encourage students to work cooperatively with partners.

Materials:

- Magazines.
- Newspapers.
- Scissors.
- Glue.
- Construction paper.
- Crayons.

Activity:

1. After introducing a certain spelling pattern or sound to the class (e.g., the /ü/, *ough, ew, ue* sound and patterns), explain to the students that they will be hunting for words with similar patterns in magazines and newspapers.
2. Place students with partners at the Working with Words Center.
3. Distribute construction paper, crayons, scissors, glue, magazines, and newspapers to the pairs of students. They should label their construction paper, using crayons, to reflect whichever pattern or sound is currently being studied. One column should also be labeled "Irregulars." For the /ü/, *ough, ew, ue* example, their construction paper might look like this:

/ü/ Words			
ough	ew	ue	Irregulars

4. Partners will then look through their newspapers and magazines to find words that fit the pattern of study. The words will be cut out and glued onto the construction paper under the appropriate heading. Any word that follows the spelling pattern, but does not have the specified sound should be placed in the "Irregulars" column.
5. Allow the students to share the words that they have found with the class.

Author's Corner

Purposes:

- Have students write on self-selected topics in a variety of literary forms.
- Encourage students to write collaboratively and independently.

Materials:

- The students' Writing Workshop folders.
- Various types of paper.
- Blank notebooks.
- Typewriter.
- Pencils.
- Rulers.
- Stapler.
- Glue.
- Scissors.
- Dictionary.
- Wordless picture books, such as *Tuesday* by David Weisner.
- Art materials (construction paper, crayons, markers, colored pencils, stencils, etc.).

Activities:

1. Locate the Author's Corner (or Writing Center, or whatever you choose to call it) in a quiet area of your Literacy Center.
2. Place a wide range of writing instruments and paper at the center.
3. Art materials should be available for the students to design book covers and story illustrations.
4. Place a wordless picture book, such as *Tuesday* (Weisner, 1991) at the center. Invite the students to write a story accompanying the pictures.
5. Create a class story at the Author's Corner. Leave a blank notebook with an interesting sentence or two to begin the story.
6. Invite visitors to the Author's Corner to help create the story by adding their own sentences to what is already written.
7. Other projects that the students may wish to work on while they are at this center:

   a. Letters to friends and relatives.
   b. Greeting cards.
   c. Narratives.
   d. Nonfiction.
   e. Sequels to stories read in class or read independently.
   f. Plays.
   g. Comic strips.
   h. Poems.

Variation:

➜ A computer may be placed at the Author's Corner for the students to use when composing writing pieces.

Thematic Tie:

➜ To connect the Author's Corner with a current thematic unit, display related posters, word lists, and story starters at the center. For example, if the class is learning about magnets, include a word list that contains words such as *pole*, *force*, *attract*, and *repel*. Display a writing prompt, such as "There once was a magnetic boy . . ."

Management Tips:

→ Use trays, shelves, pencil holders, and the like to help keep the center neat and organized.
→ Store the students' writing folders in this area for easy access.
→ Allow the students to work independently or collaboratively at the center.

Social Studies Center

Purposes:

- Have students use literature to research social studies information.
- Help students read a variety of materials and texts with comprehension and critical analysis.

Materials:

- Globe.
- Maps.
- Postcards.
- Compass.
- "North," "South," "East," and "West" signs.
- Trade books that represent the current unit of study.
- Activity cards that correspond with the trade books placed at the center.

Activities:

1. Designate an area of the classroom as the Social Studies Center. (This is one of the content-area-related Learning Centers described in Chapter One.)
2. Display a globe and a variety of maps at the center. Place postcards in a small bin, along with a sign that reads, "Can you find these places on a map or globe?" The students use the maps and globe at the center to locate places shown on the postcards.
3. Place books and materials that reflect the current unit of study at the Social Studies Center. Create research activities and task cards to coincide with the literature placed at the center. For example, if the class is studying the 50 states, books, puzzles, and flashcards about the 50 states should be placed at the center. Activities should also correspond with the theme of the 50 states (see the sample activity cards and research activity form that follow).

Thematic Tie:

→ Change the Social Studies Center to reinforce current classroom themes. For example, during Women's History Month, place books by and about influential women at the center. Display related posters, and provide activities that high-light notable women.

Management Tips:

→ Copy "North," "South," "East," and "West" signs onto colored paper. Cut them out, laminate them, and hang them in the appropriate areas of the classroom (use a compass to help with this). These will serve as a constant reminder of the four directions and will come in handy when students are doing social studies activities that involve the directions.

→ Tape a laminated map (world, U.S., etc.) to the table. This will serve as a nice workspace for the students.

Activity Card: The 50 States

Use the books and materials at the Social Studies Center to answer the following questions:

- Which of our 50 states is the largest?
- How many states begin with the letter N? Write their names.
- What was the last state admitted to the United States of America?
- What is New Jersey's state bird?
- What city is the capital of Florida?
- Name two products that come from California.
- Which four states touch Texas?
- If you could live in any state, which state would you choose? Give four reasons for your choice.

Activity Card: The 50 States

1. Choose a state that you would like to know more about.
2. Complete a "K-W-L" chart (see below) for the state.
3. Use the books in the Social Studies Center to find information on your state to complete the chart.

What I know	What I want to know	What I learned

Use the books and materials at the Social Studies Center to learn more about your favorite state.

State name: _____

Capital city: _____

State bird: _____

State flower: _____

State motto: _____

Draw a picture of the state flag:

This state is my favorite because: _____

_____

_____

Which books/materials did you use to help with your research?

_____

_____

_____

_____

_____

Science Center

Purposes:

- Have students use literature to assist in researching science information.
- Reinforce science concepts through independent and small-group work.

Materials:

- Magnifying glass.
- Trade books that represent the current unit of study.
- Activity cards that correspond with the trade books placed at the center.
- Theme-related flashcards, posters, file folder games, and the like.
- A sign that reads, "What on Earth?"
- A decorated ballot box.
- Scraps of paper.

Activity:

1. Designate an area of the classroom as the Science Center. (This is another of the content-area-related Learning Centers described in Chapter One.)
2. Place materials at the Science Center that are consistent with the current unit of study. For example, if the class is studying insects, the science center should contain activities and books about insects, and it can be called the Insect Center during this unit. The following can be included at the Insect Center:

    a. Insect posters.
    b. Insect trade books.
    c. Plastic insects.
    d. A pet insect, such as a butterfly.
    e. Products that come from insects, such as honey.

3. Place an unusual or hard-to-recognize object at the Science Center. Again, the object should relate to the current theme. For example, if your Science Center has ocean materials, place some dried fish scales in a magnifying box. Post the "What on Earth?" sign near the unusual object. Ask your students to speculate what the peculiar object is. (Encourage them to use the books at the Science Center to assist with this task!) Each student should record his or her guess on the blank paper and then place the paper into the ballot box. Toward the end of the unit, share the answer to the "What on Earth?" challenge with the class.

Variation:

➜ Teach the students how to look up science information on the Internet. For example, if the class is studying animals, investigate Web sites that contain information about animals. Encourage the class to use the Internet to help them complete the activity cards and research the "What on Earth?" challenge.

Thematic Tie:

→ Create activity cards that coincide with the current theme. (See the sample activity card for insect study that follows.) Provide books and materials related to the theme that will help the students successfully complete each card.

Management Tip:

→ Use large plastic bins to organize and store your Science Center materials. Designate one bin for each unit of study. As you acquire theme-related books and materials throughout the year, place them into the appropriate containers. Keeping all theme-related materials in one central location simplifies the process of setting up the Science Center.

Activity Card: A New Insect Has Been Found!

Pretend that you are an entomologist who has just discovered a new insect. Draw a picture of the insect and label its parts:

- Head
- Thorax
- Abdomen
- Six legs
- Antennae

Write a paragraph that tells about the new insect.

The following are some questions to consider when you write your paragraph:

- What did you name the insect, and why did you give it that name?
- Where was the insect found?
- What does the insect like to eat?
- Does the insect have any special traits or characteristics?

Computer Station

Purposes:

- Encourage students to use the Internet as a means of gaining information.

Materials:

- Computer, keyboard, printer, and so on.
- Educational software.
- Poster that labels and explains the parts of a computer (mouse, keyboard, etc.)

Activity:

1. Set up the Computer Station (or Computer Center, Technology Center, or whatever you choose to call it) in an area of the room—either within your Literacy Center, or elsewhere in your classroom if the computer will be used to study other content areas (which is often the case).
2. Display a poster that labels and explains the parts of a computer.
3. Install an age-appropriate language arts program onto each available computer. Some titles geared specifically toward second-grade students are *JumpStart 2nd Grade* (Knowledge Adventure Products), *Reader Rabbit 2nd Grade* (The Learning Company), *Smart Steps: 2nd Grade* (DK Multimedia), and *Madeline 1st and 2nd Grade Reading* (Creative Wonders).
4. Have the students work at the Computer Station during center time. (You may wish to invite a parent volunteer to work with the students at this station.)
5. Have students print out the work done.

Variation:

- → Install word-processing software onto the classroom computers for the children to use during the Writing Workshop. Allow the students to print their published stories.

Thematic Ties:

- → Include theme-related software at the Computer Station. For example, the *Magic School Bus* series, by Microsoft, has good science-related titles on such topics as dinosaurs, the ocean, the solar system, and animals.
- → Create *PowerPoint* presentations that reinforce concepts being learned in class. Allow the students to view the presentations at the Computer Station.

Management Tips:

- → Have only one or two students at a time work at each classroom computer during center time.
- → Work with the students in small groups to review the parts of a computer (use the poster to assist with this).
- → Demonstrate how to use the installed software programs.

GUIDED READING

As noted in Chapter Four, guided reading is the heart of the LAB. During guided reading, individual needs are met by working with children in small groups at their instructional levels. To organize guided reading, needs are assessed, groups are formed based on need, and appropriate materials are selected to address these needs. Each guided reading group lesson lasts about 20 minutes, for a total of 60 minutes if three groups are seen each day.

Grouping for Guided Reading

Purposes:

- Provide flexible grouping for children who are reading at a similar text level and who have similar instructional needs.
- Have students read and respond to a diversity of materials and texts in discussion and writing.

Materials:

- Running records (see below).
- Observational notes.
- Recommendations from faculty members (reading specialists, students' earlier teachers).

Activity:

1. Guided reading is one of the only times children are homogeneously grouped. These need-based groups, however, are different from traditional reading groups. Children grouped for guided reading do not read a fixed sequence of books. Texts are chosen for their appropriateness for the group.
2. The number of guided reading groups in a particular classroom will vary, depending on the range of student ability. A typical reading classroom has between four and six groups. A guided reading group with no more than five or six children seems to be the most manageable. The lowest-ability groups should contain no more than four students.
3. Children are placed in guided reading groups based on the results of running records taken on leveled books and on your observational notations. If leveled books are not accessible at your students' ability level, evaluate the book based on length of story and chapters, size of print, number of words on a page, and difficulty of concepts and vocabulary presented. The groups are dynamic and are expected to change as the students' needs change.
4. You should aim to meet with three groups each day, depending on scheduling. The lowest-ability groups should be seen daily. A different child should sit next to you for each lesson; this will be the focus child on that day.

Guided Reading Instruction

Purposes:

- Enable students to identify elements of a story, such as characters, setting, and sequence of events.
- Expand students' vocabulary by using appropriate strategies and techniques, such as word analysis and context clues.
- Help students read a variety of materials and texts with comprehension and critical analysis.

Materials:

- Magnetic letters.
- Magnetic white board or chalkboard.
- Reading response journals.
- Individual copies of a leveled text. The sample lesson below uses *Frog and Toad Are Friends* (Lobel, 1970).
- Story elements organizer.

Activity:

Sample Lesson: Comprehension and Word Analysis

1. *Frog and Toad Are Friends* is an early chapter book at level K, which is a mid-second-grade reading level. This lesson is designed for Chapter Three, "A Lost Button," in *Frog and Toad.*
2. Begin the lesson with a familiar read. Have the children return to Chapter Two to read a part of the story that they feel is funny.
3. Introduce Chapter Three by telling the children that in this chapter Frog and Toad go for a walk in the meadow and Toad loses something.
4. Continue the book walk by introducing unfamiliar or challenging vocabulary. You may wish to introduce *meadow, sparrow, square, trouble, sewing/sewed.*
5. Set a purpose for reading by having the children read the chapter silently to find out what Toad lost and what Frog did that showed he was a good friend to Toad, and what Toad did that showed he was a good friend to Frog.
6. It is important to hear the children read aloud during the first reading. Use a predetermined signal to indicate to individuals that you want them to read aloud. While each child reads aloud, take notes on the strategies that the children are using to solve problems.
7. After the first reading, return to make two teaching points based on the observations you made.
8. Briefly discuss the purpose questions set in step 5.
9. Show children how words they know can help them read new words. Build the following words with the children, using the magnetic letters.

but	*all*	*in*	*am*
button	*small*	*thin*	*slam*
		thick	*slammed*

10. Have the children return to their seats to reread the chapter and write in their reading response journals about a time they did something special for a friend.

Variations:

→ The next time the group meets, have the children share their journals.
→ Have the children complete a story map that includes the name of the characters, the setting, the problem, and the main events leading up to the solution.

Management Tips:

→ Children can use highlighting tape when new vocabulary is introduced.
→ You can take a running record on a child at the end of the reading group.
→ To signal children to read aloud, you may tap their shoulders, stand behind them, sit next to them, or touch their hands.

Running Records

Purposes:

- Record and analyze a child's reading to learn what strategies he or she uses to problem solve
- Determine what strategies need to be developed.
- Document a child's reading growth and reading level over time.

Materials:

- Leveled readers.
- The first 100 words of the book typed double-spaced (referred to as a "recording sheet") or any blank piece of paper.

Activity:

1. Based on what you know about the child's reading level, select a book that you feel is at his or her instructional level (i.e., a book the child will be able to read with 90–95% accuracy).
2. Record the child's reading, using the following conventions:

   a. Record a check mark for each word that is read correctly (see the illustration of running record symbols that follows).
   b. If a substitution error is made, write the word that the child said above the actual word.
   c. If a word is omitted, place a dash above the actual word.
   d. If a word was inserted, place it over a dash.
   e. If words were repeated, underline them.

    f. Record a "T" for words given by you (the teacher).

    g. Record an "SC" for words the child self-corrected.

3. Score the running record as follows (see the form that follows the illustration of symbols):

    a. A substitution is counted as one error.

    b. If there are multiple attempts of the same word, only one error is counted.

    c. Each omission, insertion, and word that was given by you counts as one error.

    d. Repetitions are not errors.

    e. Self-corrections are not errors.

4. To determine the accuracy rate, subtract the number of errors from the number of words. Divide by the number of words and multiply by 100 (Morrow, 2001).

    Below 90% accuracy = difficult (frustrational).

    From 90% to 95% = instructional.

    95% to 100% = independent.

Variations:

➜ During a guided reading group, take one running record for a focus child sitting next to you throughout that lesson.

➜ Do running records instead of meeting with guided reading groups, or do three running records and meet with three groups each day.

Running Record Symbols:

Type of error or miscue	Symbol	Description
Accurate reading	✓✓✓✓	For each word read correctly, a check or dash is placed above the word. Some teachers prefer no marking to mean accurate reading.
Self-correction (not counted as an error)	his | SC her |	The child reads the word incorrectly, pauses, and then corrects the error.
Substitution (counted as an error)	boat barge	The student substitutes a real word that is incorrect.
Refusal to pronounce word (counted as an error)	— | table | T	The student neither pronounces the word nor attempts to do so. The teacher pronounces the word so that testing can continue.

Type of error or miscue	Symbol	Description
Insertion (counted as an error)	at ———	The student inserts a word or a series of words that do not appear in the text.
Omission (counted as an error)	——— rat	The student omits a word or a continuous sequence of words in the text, but continues to read.
Repetition (not counted as an error)	The horse ran away.	The student repeats one or more words that have been read. Groups of adjacent words that are repeated count as one repetition.
Reversal	he said w as	The student reverses the order of words or letters.
Appeal for help (counted as an error)	— App house T	The child asks for help with a word he or she cannot read.

Running Record Form

Name: _____ Date: _____

Book: _____ Book level: _____

Words: _____ Error rate: _____ Accuracy rate: _____

Errors: _____ Self-correction rate: _____

			Cues used					
			E			SC		
E	SC	Text	M	S	V	M	S	V

M, meaning; S, structure; V, visual; E, error; SC, self-correction.

Reading level

Independent: 95% to 100% accuracy

Instructional: 90% to 95% accuracy

Difficult (or frustrational):   Less than 90% accuracy

Reading proficiency: Fluent _____ Word by word _____ Choppy _____

Retelling

Setting: Characters _____   Time _____   Place _____

Theme: Problem or goal _____

Events: Number included _____

Resolution: Solved problem _____   Achieved goal _____   Ending _____

Creating Book Bins for Books from Guided Reading

Purposes:

- Create and use boxes for storing books that are at a child's reading level.

Materials:

- Cereal boxes with the tops cut off at an angle.
- Optional decorating materials: paint, wallpaper, contact paper, wrapping paper.

Activity:

1. Students will bring in cereal boxes. Each student will decorate his or her box with any of the above-listed art materials and label the side of the box with his or her name.
2. Leveled readers that are used during guided reading can then be placed in the children's book bins for later rereading. This will ensure that students have access to and are reading books at their specific reading level.
3. Place books in plastic bags before putting them in book bins.

Variation:

➜ Corrugated cardboard magazine holders can be used as book bins.

Reading Interviews

Purposes:

- Assess how children view themselves as readers and writers.
- Enable children to speak for a variety of real purposes and audiences.

Materials:

- Interview questions.

Activity:

1. The following questions are for three separate interviews, which are given to children during different times in the school year. The interviews can be used to help you understand and assess the reading and writing development of your students. The interviews are shared with parents at conference time. At the end of the year, copies of the interviews are sent to the parents, and a copy is saved to share with the child's next teacher.

Reading Interview Questions

During the first week of school:

1. Can you read?
2. How did you learn?
3. What does someone do to learn to read?

4. Can you write?
5. Who do you know is a good reader?
6. What makes this person a good reader?

During December:

1. Can you read and write?
2. How do you choose your topics for writing?
3. What can you do now in writing that you couldn't do when school started?
4. If you had to tell somebody what was most important about writing, what would you tell them?
5. Tell me about reading.
6. How did you learn to read?
7. What's your favorite book that you've learned to read?
8. What do you want to learn to do next in reading?
9. How about in writing?

During the first week of June:

1. Tell me about yourself as a reader.
2. How do you choose books?
3. What's your all-time best book?
4. What will you do to become an even better reader?
5. Tell me about yourself as a writer.
6. What is your best piece of writing?
7. What would you tell someone who asked you about becoming a reader and a writer?
8. Do you have a favorite author?

Variations:

→ Interview responses can be typed up and saved under a child's name in a word-processing program such as Microsoft *Word*. Open the file each time you need to interview the child, and add the results.
→ The Motivation Interview in Appendix C can also be used.

Literature Circles

Purposes:

- Have students read various materials and texts for critical analysis.
- Encourage students to listen actively to others and demonstrate comprehension of others' thoughts.

Materials:

- Paper or index cards.
- Index cards with the names of different jobs.

- Multiple copies of a book.
- Post-it Notes or bookmarks.

Activity:

1. Explain the different jobs that children can do in the Literature Circle.
2. Introduce the story.
3. Introduce vocabulary.
4. Have students make story predictions.
5. Students read the selection silently and then complete their jobs.
6. When the group is finished, each child discusses the Literature Circle activity that he or she has completed. The children are encouraged to discuss their findings and differing opinions.
7. Describe the jobs to the children as follows (this list is based on Daniels, 1994):

   a. **Passage Picker**—Pick parts of the story to read aloud to your group. Mark the parts you want to share with a Post-it Note or bookmark.
   b. **Summarizer**—Prepare a brief summary of today's reading. You are expected to give a quick statement that conveys the gist, the key points, and the main idea of the piece.
   c. **Discussion Director**—Write down good questions that you think your group will want to talk about.
   d. **Word Finder**—Look for special words in the story. When you find a word you want to talk about, mark it with a Post-it Note. Ask your group questions such as "Does anyone know what this word means?" and "How does this word fit into the story?"
   e. **Artful Artist**—Draw anything about the story that you liked. During group sharing, don't tell what your drawing is. Let them guess and talk about it first.

Thematic Tie:

→ Books that are selected for Literature Circles can be thematically based, to tie in with a theme being taught at that time.

Management Tip:

→ Have students practice their jobs with a small group before they work alone.

INDEPENDENT CLASSROOM READING

During independent classroom reading, which should be a daily activity lasting about 20 minutes, students are permitted to read books or magazines of their choice. You yourself should also be engaged in free reading during the independent classroom reading period.

Designing a Classroom Library

Purposes:

- Provide a variety of materials for children to read.
- Create an organized system for housing and categorizing classroom literary materials.
- Foster a love of reading through a supportive and inviting environment.

Materials:

- Containers for book storage (bookcases, shelves, crates, baskets, wire book racks).
- Comfortable seating (carpet, pillows, rocking chair, beanbag chairs).
- Children's literature of multiple genres, both narrative and expository.
- Reading-related posters.
- "Dot" stickers, like those used to mark prices, in various colors.
- "Author/Illustrator of the Month" sign.

Activity:

1. Make the classroom library a warm and inviting space. Provide comfortable seating. Include home-like touches, such as bookends, plants, and stuffed animals.
2. Provide a wide range of reading materials at a variety of difficulty levels. Include books of different genres, children's magazines, big books, student-made books, brochures, newspapers, and narrative and expository text.
3. Use shelf space or a book basket to highlight a particular author or illustrator each month.
4. Place books by the chosen author or illustrator in this area.
5. Hang up the "Author/Illustrator of the Month" sign near the book display of the author's or illustrator's featured work.
6. Display Caldecott, Newbery, and Coretta Scott King award-winning books. Explain the reason for each award.

Thematic Tie:

→ Change the library environment to reflect current classroom themes. If the class is learning about oceans, turn your classroom library into a "beach." Include beach chairs, beach blankets, and ocean-related posters and books at the Library Corner (or whatever you choose to call it).

Management Tips:

→ To simplify the process of locating books, it is important to establish a system for categorizing your collection. There is no "right" way to do this.

→ You may choose to organize the books according to difficulty level. Place red dot stickers on the spines of the most challenging books, blue dots on those books that are less challenging, and green dots on the least challenging books.

→ Or, you may wish to organize your books according to genres or subject matter.

Use red dot stickers on biographies, blue dots on realistic fiction, yellow dots on poetry, and so on.

→ Hang a sign at the library that explains what each colored dot represents.

Checking Out Books

Purposes:

- Establish an organized system that allows students to check out classroom library materials quickly.
- Provide a variety of reading materials for children.

Materials:

- Library card pockets (one per student).
- Bookmarks.

Activity:

1. Label each library card pocket with a student's name.
2. Hang the pockets in the classroom library. (They can be mounted on poster board, tacked to a bulletin board, or simply hung separately.)
3. Give each child a bookmark. Instruct the children to put their names on their bookmarks.
4. Explain to the students that whenever they borrow a book from the classroom library, their bookmark should be kept in the book. If a student does not have a book in his or her desk, the bookmark belongs in that person's library card pocket. You can easily tell who has borrowed a book simply by looking for empty library card pockets at the library.

Management Tips:

→ Emphasize making good choices when picking out library books.

→ Explain and model the five-finger rule to the students. ("Try reading a page from the book that you are considering checking out. Put a down a finger each time you cannot read a word. If by the time you are finished reading the page, you have more than five fingers down, you may want to think about selecting a different book. The one you are looking at may be too difficult.")

→ If the students are permitted to check out more than one library book at a time, give them more than one bookmark to keep in their library pockets.

→ If you wish to keep track of the book titles that the students check out of the library, simply put up a sign-out sheet at a central location (see the sheet that follows).

→ Appoint a classroom librarian to keep track of books being checked out for in-school and out-of-school reading. The librarian can be responsible for making sure that all books are checked out and returned on time and in good condition.

Library Sign-Out Sheet

Name	Book Title	Date Out	Date In

1. _____
   _____

2. _____
   _____

3. _____
   _____

4. _____
   _____

5. _____
   _____

6. _____
   _____

7. _____
   _____

8. _____
   _____

9. _____
   _____

10. _____
    _____

Independent Reading

Purposes:

- Have students read independently a variety of literature written by authors of different cultures, ethnicities, genders, and ages.
- Encourage students to express thoughts and ideas about the books they read independently.

Materials:

- A well-stocked classroom library, which includes a variety of reading materials in a range of genres and difficulty levels.
- A system for checking out books.
- Student response journals.

Activity:

1. During the independent reading time, the students should be permitted to read a book or magazine of their choice. You should also be reading during this block of time.
2. You should do periodic book talks to highlight materials from the classroom library.
3. The students should write about the books they are reading during independent reading time in their response journals. (See "Response Journals," below, for more information about organizing these notebooks.)

Thematic Tie:

→ Highlight theme-related books and reading materials during independent reading time. Include a supply of these thematic materials in your classroom library and highlight them during book talks. Encourage the students to read these materials during independent reading.

Response Journals

Purposes:

- Keep track of books students read during independent reading time.
- Have students use prior knowledge to extend reading ability and comprehension, and to link aspects of the text with experiences and people in their own lives.

Materials:

- Notebooks (one per student).
- List of possible response questions (photocopy one per student).
- Pencils, markers.
- Chart paper.

Activity:

1. Explain to the students that their response journals are for responding to the books they read independently.
2. Read the list of response questions (see the activity card that follows) with the class. Emphasize that these questions can help students decide how to respond to a book. The list of questions should serve only as a guide. Students should not be required to answer every question. Encourage them to comment on anything that they notice or are thinking about the book.
3. Use the chart paper and marker to model a response journal entry of a book shared with the entire class. Begin with the date, title of the book, and author of the book. Elicit student responses and write them down on the chart paper.
4. Allocate time at the end of each independent reading period for the students to write in and share their response journals.
5. Meet periodically with individual students to discuss their written responses and the books that they are reading.

Thematic Tie:

→ Students can keep response journals to reflect upon books related to specific thematic units. (These thematic journals may be as simple as a few blank pages stapled together with a decorative cover.) For instance, if the class is studying animals, you may require the students to keep "Animal Journals." The students may respond to animal books read—both books that you read and ones that they read independently.

Management Tips:

→ Paste the list of possible response questions into the front of each child's notebook. This will serve as a point of reference for those times that students cannot think of anything to write about.
→ Early in the year, it may be helpful to give the students sentence starters for their response journals:

- "The part of the book I like the most was . . . I liked it because . . . "
- "This book reminds me of the time . . . "
- "The funniest part of the book was . . . "
- "I decided to read this book because . . . "

Response Journals Activity Card

Name: _____ Date: _____

The following are some questions to think about when you are writing in your reading response journal. (Do not limit yourself to answering only these questions!)

1. Why did you decide to read this book?
2. How does this book make you feel? Why?
3. Does this book remind you of anything that has ever happened to you?
4. What is your favorite part of the book? Why?
5. Was there anything that you didn't like about the book?
6. What would you ask the author about the story?
7. Who is your favorite character in the story? Why do you like this character? Does this character remind you of anyone that you know?
8. If I were the author of this book, I would . . .

WRITING WORKSHOP

Each day, about 50 minutes should be set aside for writing. The students engage in both independent and collaborative writing activities. You will have conferences with individual students to assess specific needs. Areas that need to be reinforced are addressed through individual conferencing and language mini-lessons.

Rules for Good Writers

Purposes:

- Identify the characteristics of proficient writing.
- Create a classroom display of authorship rules that students may refer to when they are working on writing activities.
- Encourage students to write in clear, concise, organized language that varies in content and form for different audiences and purposes.

Materials:
- Chart paper.
- Marker.

Activity:

1. Discuss the characteristics of good writing. (Encourage students to think about books they have read. What did they notice about the authors' writing?)
2. Record the students' ideas on chart paper, using the heading "Good Writers . . .". Some possible rules might include the following: "Good Writers . . . "

   - include a lot of details in their stories."
   - have a beginning, middle, and end."
   - use capital letters correctly."
   - use punctuation marks correctly."
   - spell words the best that they can."

Variation:

→ Authorship rules can be created for different genres of writing. For example, if the students are studying fairy tales, chart their ideas for writing fairy tales. If the class is focusing on a poetry theme, you may wish to create a chart entitled "Rules for Writing Poetry."

Management Tips:

→ Post the chart in a highly visible area of the classroom.
→ Continue to add rules to the chart throughout the year (especially after relevant mini-lessons).
→ Review the chart periodically so that students will refer to it when they are writing.

Working through the Writing Process

Purposes:

- Introduce and model the five steps in the writing process.
- Provide the students with the opportunity to practice the steps in the writing process.
- Have students write from experiences, thoughts, and feelings.

Prewriting

Purposes:

- Model the process of selecting a topic or subject to write about.
- Have students use a variety of strategies and activities, such as brainstorming, listing, discussion, and journal writing, for finding and developing ideas about which to write.

Materials:

- Overhead projector.
- Blank transparency paper.
- Transparency markers.
- Chart paper.
- Markers.
- Student journals and writing folders.

Activity:

1. Explain to the students that the class will be working together to create a story. The first step in creating the story is to select a topic to write about. Brainstorm possible writing topics with the children. Encourage them to look through their daily journals to get ideas. Since this is going to be a class story, encourage them to select topics that the rest of the class will be familiar with. The topics can be related to everyday school occurrences, such as programs, classroom visitors, or holiday parties.
2. Using the overhead projector, blank transparency paper, and transparency markers, record some of the students' topic ideas.
3. Before selecting the topic to write about, analyze the topics brainstormed with the students. Encourage them to think about the following questions when looking at each topic:

   a. "Do we have enough information to write about this topic?"
   b. "If not, where will we get the necessary facts?"
   c. "Is the topic too big to write about? How can we narrow it?"
   d. "Is the topic too small to write about? How can we expand it?"

4. After each topic has been analyzed, select one to write about with the class. Discuss and identify the purpose (e.g., descriptive, informational, etc.) and audience of the writing piece.

5. Use the chart paper to create a web to organize the ideas to be drafted. For example, if the class decides to write about the first day of second grade, the web might look something like this:

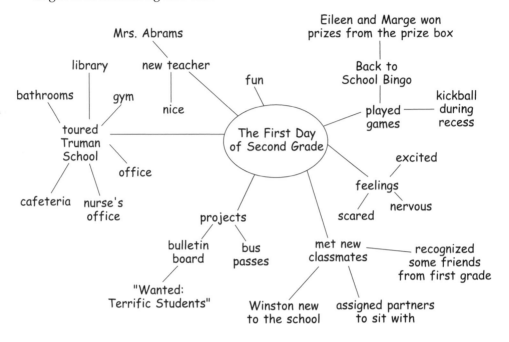

6. After the prewriting stage has been modeled with the class, allow the students to go through the steps in the process for themselves. Encourage them to revisit their daily journals when thinking about possible writing topics. Have them store their ideas in their writing folders.

Thematic Ties:

➜ Topics can be tied to the current theme.
➜ You can begin the prewriting lesson by reading a theme-related book to stimulate the writing.

Management Tips:

➜ Children can work in small cooperative groups to brainstorm for topics.
➜ Brainstorming should be limited to about 5 minutes.
➜ If the brainstorming and follow-up discussion take too long (close to 30 minutes), the web should be saved for the next day.

Drafting

Purposes:

• Model the use of a prewriting web to create a first draft.
• Have students work independently to create a first draft.

Materials:

- The prewriting web created in the previous lesson.
- Chart paper.
- Markers.
- Writing folders.

Activity:

1. Display the class's prewriting web, and then use the web to write a story. Tell the students, "We may or may not want to include all of the ideas that are on our web. We may wish to include new ideas." Discuss how the piece should begin, what should come in the middle, and how it should end. Also, remind the class of the purpose and audience.
2. Use the blank chart paper to create a draft of the class story with the students. Engage in "free writing"—record all of the students' sentences about the topic. (Include grammatical and spelling errors in this first draft.) Point out the importance of writing on every other line. (This makes it easier to make changes during the revision and editing stages.)
3. Throughout the drafting process, encourage the class to use words that create a clear picture in the readers' mind of the sights, sounds, and other sensory images in the composition. The draft for the story "The First Day of Second Grade" might look like this:

The first day of second grade was a lot of fun. We had a really fun day. We lked meeting our clasmates and recognized some students frum first grade but winston was new to truman school. Mrs abrams put us with partners to sit with in our new classroom We workd on a lot of fun progects like the "Wanted: Terrific Students" bulletin board and our bus passes. We felt nrvous and scared and excited. We played some games like Back to School Bingo and kickball during recess. Eileen and Marge one prizes frum the prize box! the class tuk a tore of truman school. we saw the bathrooms and the library and the gym and the office and the cafeteria and the nurses office it turned out to be a grate day!

---

4. After modeling the drafting stage, invite the students to create their own drafts, using their prewriting webs as organizational tools for the writing. The students' drafts will be stored in their writing folders.

Revising

Purposes:

- Have students revise content, organization, and other aspects of writing, using collaborative feedback from themselves, their peers, and you (the teacher).
- Model the revision process.

Materials:

- First draft of the class story.
- Markers.
- Individual student drafts (stored in their writing folders).
- Colored pencils.

Activity:

1. Post the chart paper draft of the class story. Discuss with the students what they like about it and what they would change. Encourage them to look for ideas that are repeated and those that are best left out of the piece. Where would they add details and include new points to improve the composition? The revised "The First Day of Second Grade" story might look like this:

2. Using a different-colored marker from the one used in the original draft, revise the class story with the students.
3. Distribute the colored pencils. Invite the students to use them to revise their own writing pieces. After the students have finished revising their own work, place them with partners to discuss and revise each other's pieces. Encourage them to point out the positive aspects of each other's work, as well as the things that they would change.

4. While the students are working independently and with partners, have conferences with individual students about their compositions.

Management Tips:

→ Model for the children how to give constructive criticism about another person's work.
→ When modeling, be sure to use "think-alouds" so the children can hear how an author thinks while he or she is writing.
→ Post-it Notes may be used to mark passages that need to be revised.

Editing

Purposes:

- Have students edit writing for developmentally appropriate syntax, spelling, grammar, usage, and punctuation.
- Have each student work independently, with a partner, and with you (the teacher) to edit a piece of writing.
- Teach students to identify and use proofreaders' marks.

Materials:

- Revised class story.
- Markers.
- Poster of proofreaders' marks.
- Individual student stories (in their writing folders).
- Colored pencils.
- Dictionaries (one per student).
- Post-it Notes.

Activity:

1. Post the revised class story. Explain to the class that the next step in the writing process is editing. "Editing" means looking for errors with syntax, spelling, grammar, usage, capitalization, and punctuation.
2. Create and display a poster of proofreaders' marks. Discuss each mark and how it is used.

Proofreaders' Marks	
℮	Take out
∧	Add
≡	Make a capital letter
/	Make a lower-case letter
¶	New paragraph

3. Edit the class story together. Editing may be done with Post-it Notes to mark where errors are found and to make corrections; thus the paper is not marked up. Model the use of a dictionary to assist in spelling misspelled words. The edited "The First Day of Second Grade" piece might look like this:

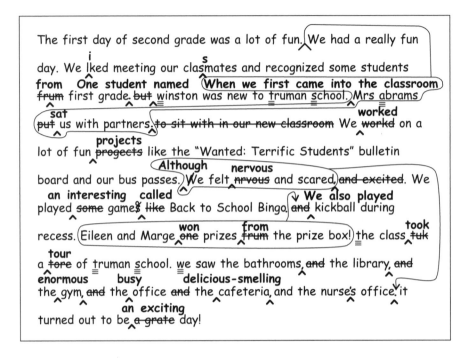

5. Invite the students to use colored pencils or Post-it Notes and dictionaries to edit their own pieces. Once they have finished looking at their pieces independently, place them with partners to edit each other's work.
6. During this time, continue having conferences with individual students.

Variations:

→ Use the students' own work to practice the revision and editing processes. Make transparencies of the children's first drafts. Use an overhead projector to revise and edit their writing pieces with the class. (Be sure to get the student/author's permission before sharing his or her composition with the rest of the class.)
→ You may wish to train parent volunteers to assist with the individual conferences during the Writing Workshop.

Publishing

Purposes:

- Model the process of publishing.
- Enable children to publish their writing in a variety of formats.
- Provide the opportunity for student/authors to share their work.

Materials:

- Edited class story.
- Chart paper.
- Assorted types of paper.
- Computer, equipped with a word-processing program.
- Author's Chair.

Activity:

1. Read the edited class story with the students. Make sure they are satisfied with the final piece before it is published.
2. Rewrite the story onto a new piece of chart paper.
3. Invite the students to add illustrations that coincide with the story. Display the finished product somewhere in the classroom. The published "The First Day of Second Grade" story might look like this:

The first day of second grade was a lot of fun. When we first came into the classroom, Mrs Abrams sat us with partners. We had a really fun day. We liked meeting our classmates and recognized some students from first grade. One student named Winston was new to Truman School. We worked on a lot of fun projects like the "Wanted: Terrific Students" bulletin board and our bus passes. We played an interesting game called Back to School Bingo. Eileen and Marge won prizes from the prize box! We also played kickball during recess. The class took a tour of Truman School. We saw the bathrooms, the library, the enormous gym, the busy office, the delicious-smelling cafeteria, and the nurse's office. Although we felt nervous and scared, it turned out to be an exciting day!

---

4. Allot time for the children to publish the pieces they have been working on during the Writing Workshop. Make available various types of writing paper and art supplies to be used for publishing. Permit the students to use the computer to type out the text of their stories.
5. At the end of the writing period, allow the students to share their published pieces with the rest of the class. Those who are sharing should sit in the Author's Chair.

Variation:

→ The classroom computer may be utilized in other ways for the Writing Workshop. The following are some ideas:

- Have the students send letters to pen pals via e-mail.
- Use word-processing software to work through the writing process.
- Encourage the students to use the Internet to research information that they would like to include in their writing pieces.

Thematic Ties:

→ Consider classroom themes when modeling different types of writing. For instance, if the class is learning about animals, model informative writing. Provide a range of nonfiction animal books that may be used by the students to write their own informative pieces.

→ If the class is studying a topic such as rain forests, you may wish to introduce persuasive writing. Encourage the students to write persuasive letters to political figures, asking them to assist in stopping the destruction of the rain forests.

Self-Assessments in Writing

Purposes:

- Help students write in clear, concise, organized language that varies in context and form for different audiences and purposes.
- Have students look critically at their own work to determine its quality.

Materials:

- Class checklist (one copy per child).
- Journal goals sheet (one per child).
- Portfolio forms.

Activity:

1. During the Writing Workshop, students write independently on a topic of their choice or on a given topic.
2. Because each student has different abilities, each student has his or her own "journal goals" sheet, which states the minimum number of sentences needed for each day, and a class "checklist," which pinpoints different components that should be included in each day's writing. These documents are referred to as "tools" for writing and are stored in each child's writing folder.
3. When the end of the Writing Workshop is near, the children are asked to take out their "tools" to assess their own work.
4. Students can also work with partners to check each other's work, using the journal goals and the checklist as guides.

Management Tips:

→ The goals sheet can be laminated, and the number of sentences can be written in wipe-off markers, so the numbers can be changed throughout the year.

→ When a child experiences writer's block, he or she should speak to the teacher, so the teacher will know why there may not be writing on a particular day.

→ A form may be provided for children to complete when they wish to place pieces of writing in their portfolios.

→ The form should include why a child wants to place this particular piece of writing in his or her portfolio.

→ After completing the form, the child clips it to his or her work and places them in a basket labeled "Ready for Writing Portfolios."

→ After you have conferenced with the child, the child places the writing in his or her portfolio.

Writing across Genres

Purposes:

- Help students write in clear, concise, organized language that varies in content and form for different audiences and purposes.
- Have students engage in writing expository text.

Materials:

- Children's books that include different genres.
- Writing journals/writing papers.

Activity:

Sample Lesson: Reading and Writing in a "Scientist" Voice

1. Your second-grade class is learning about mealworms.
2. Read nonfiction books to the students, and discuss the nonfiction genre and how it differs from fiction.
3. Have students brainstorm what they notice about the nonfiction books they have read about mealworms.
4. After doing an observation of their mealworms, ask the children to write "As scientists" to document what they have seen.
5. If a child begins to write, for example, "Sammy was eating a leaf. Sammy was happy," respond: "When we are writing like scientists, we need to use the word *mealworms* when writing about them, and we also need to write only what we observed. We do not know for sure that the mealworm is happy, so let's think of what we actually did see and write about that."

Variations:

→ When you are exposing students to different genres (nonfiction, plays, poetry, memoirs, biographies, etc.), students can begin to notice the different purposes in writing, and try out some of these voices or genres in their own writing.

→ Students can write on the computer, through the use of word-processing programs for children. Most of these programs also enable students to add graphics and/or create their own pictures to go along with their writing.

How to Motivate Writing

Purposes:

- Motivate children to write.

Materials:

- Author's chair.
- "Meet the Authors" bulletin board.
- Writing portfolios.
- A basket labeled "Writing to Share with the Class."
- Young Author Awards.
- "Work of the Week" board.

Activities:

1. A decorated, special Author's Chair can be labeled and used as the "chair of honor." As noted in Chapter Four and earlier in this chapter, when a child has writing to share with the class, he or she should sit in the Author's Chair.
2. Create a year-round bulletin board for your classroom titled "Meet the Authors." Design an oval picture frame for each child. Post a photograph of each student inside the frames. When children have writing to display, they hang it near their photos. The writings should rotate regularly.
3. Writing portfolios hold what the children feel is their best work. One way to make a writing portfolio is for each child to bring in a small pizza box. The pizza boxes are painted by the children and labeled with their names.
4. Always have a basket in the classroom labeled "Writing to Share with the Class." You can share your writing, too!
5. Young Author Awards can be given to children for great writing (see the example that follows). A little decorative paper award goes a long way to increase a child's self-confidence!
6. Exemplary writing can be hung on a special board labeled "Work of the Week." Try putting this board out in the hall outside your classroom door so all can admire the work! Be sure that everyone gets to display work during the course of the school year.

Young Author Award

to

_____

for

_____

_____

_____

_____
(signed)

_____
(date)

Poetry Writing: Ecphrastic Poetry

Purposes:

- Articulate the connection between visual and verbal messages.
- Demonstrate the ability to gain information from a variety of media.

Materials:

- Photos, paintings, illustrations.
- Writing paper.
- Pencils.
- Author's Chair.

Activity:

1. "Ecphrastic" is a little known technical term used by classicists and art historians, referring to the long tradition of poetic responses to great works of art.
2. Ways to write ecphrastic poetry:

    a. Describe what you see, step by step.
    b. Address a subject in the work.
    c. Take on the identity of a subject in the work.
    d. Reflect upon what you see.

3. Students are given a work of art to look at and analyze.
4. When analyzing art, students can work as a class, in small groups, as partners, or individually.
5. Students brainstorm, collaborate, and discuss the image and the message that is being conveyed, using the instructions above as a guide.
6. Students then use the work of art as inspiration for writing a poem.
7. When the poems are complete, students share the work of art and their writing with the class, reading from the Author's Chair.

Thematic Tie:

→ Ecphrastic poetry is a wonderful way to integrate writing into social studies or history. When studying themes within these subjects, gather works of art that relate to your theme, and do an ecphrastic poetry activity with your class. You'll be surprised at the insight and motivation your students possess when a work of art is provided for them as "fuel for the fire"!

SEVEN

Third- and Fourth-Grade Case Study

INTRODUCTION TO THE TEACHER, NANCY KIMBERLY

The school that Nancy Kimberly (a composite of several teachers) teaches in is considered low-middle-class in an urban/suburban setting, and her students are ethnically diverse. Nancy has been teaching in the same district for 7 years and has been a teacher for 13 years. Previously, she had taught in the primary grades; only in the last 5 years has she taught in fourth grade. Her class for this academic year is an inclusion class; out of 21 students, 7 are classified as developmentally disabled. The students' ethnic backgrounds are representative of the community: There are 12 children of European, 5 of Asian, 5 of Native, 1 of African, and 1 of Hispanic origin. There are 10 girls and 11 boys in the class. For approximately half the day, there is a special education teacher in the room with Nancy. This teacher provides some direct instruction, but acts more as a support teacher.

TEACHING PHILOSOPHY

When asked to talk about her philosophy of literacy instruction, Nancy says:

"Our classroom encourages students to function as a community of learners. The atmosphere is one of acceptance and encourages children to be academic risk takers;

Nancy's classroom encourages students to function as a community of learners.

Nancy's students take academic risks and responsibility for their learning.

their ideas are shared and valued. Students are given and accept responsibility for their learning, and contribute as members of a family. In our classroom, all students are viewed as capable learners who progress at their own developmental level. As much as possible, I use extended, uninterrupted periods to devote to the language arts daily. Literacy instruction in my classroom involves the integration of the language arts into content area themes. Skills need to be taught within a meaningful context, and in an explicit manner when necessary. Therefore, I meet in small groups based on the specific needs of children. I know that all of this will work for my students only if there is a positive and supportive attitude in my classroom to motivate children to learn."

THE PHYSICAL ENVIRONMENT IN THE CLASSROOM

As one enters Nancy's classroom, it becomes immediately apparent how much value she places on literacy. There is an area set aside in the classroom labeled "Book Nook," with an easy chair set on a rectangle of carpet, surrounded by numerous floor cushions and large beanbag chairs where students can settle in to read. Right next to the easy chair is a book cart with a variety of books from which Nancy or the students can choose. The cart has many types of books, from light reading such as *Squids Will Be Squids* (Scieszka, 1998) to the more serious *When I Was Young in the Mountains* (Rylant, 1982). A Word Wall, made of felt containing different parts of speech, takes up a good portion of the wall in the Book Nook. Posters of popular books, such as *Harry Potter and the Sorcerer's Stone* (Rowling, 1998), cover the remainder of the wall. Next to them are book reviews written by students for the class to read. Posters that promote good reading hang on the walls, file cabinets, and bookcases. Charts with writing guidelines (prewriting, drafting, revising, conferencing, editing, and publishing) and definitions of literary terms, such as *onomatopoeia* and *alliteration*, hang from a rope strung diagonally across the room. The blackboard takes up most of the front wall, but around its periphery are varied smaller posters of other literary terms, the class rules, and the bell schedule. On the back wall of the room is another Word Wall, which displays the most commonly misspelled words.

When one enters this classroom, it becomes apparent how much value is placed on literacy. The Literacy Center includes a lounge chair, beanbag chairs, and a large supply of books for independent reading.

There are many bookcases, filled with hundreds of books of all levels and genres. Books are labeled according to type, such as "Reference," "Fiction," "Nonfiction," and "Science." In the nonfiction section, there are books on fossils, dinosaurs, planets, and stars, to name a few topics. The reference section contains a set of encyclopedias, several dictionaries, and other resources. Prominently displayed on an open shelf is a book rack with "Personal Choice" books. Popular books by well-known authors of children's literature are part of the collection, such as *Nighty Nightmare* (Howe, 1987), *Tales of a Fourth-Grade Nothing* (Blume, 1972), and *Ralph S. Mouse* (Cleary, 1982). They share space with trendy series books, such as Pascal's *Sweet Valley Kids* books and Stine's *Horror Series*. The remaining open shelves under the windows contain books grouped by specific type; science topics being studied are next to biographies of U.S. presidents used for social studies. The science topic currently being studied is "Natural Disasters." There are 20 books on the shelf about volcanoes, tidal waves, hurricanes, and earthquakes. Most titles are single copies, but there are multiple copies of several, such as *The Magic School Bus inside a Hurricane* (Cole, 1995) and *Earthquakes* (Simon, 1991). On the wall near the shelf of science books is a corkboard with posters of the earth, weather patterns, earthquakes, hurricanes, and similar topics.

Easels and bulletin boards are placed throughout the room with various topics. On one easel is a list with the headings "Said Is Dead" on the top half and "Fun Is Done" on the bottom half of the paper. Beneath the respective headings are synonyms students have put on the chart that can be used in their written work instead of the overused *said* and *fun*. Some of the synonyms suggested by students for the word *said* are *replied*, *uttered*, and *bellowed*. Synonyms for *fun* are *outstanding*, *excellent*, and *extraordinary*.

The students' desks are grouped in clusters of four. In addition, there are several tables where individuals or groups can work. Nancy's desk is toward the back of the room. Near her desk are a computer and printer. Though there is only one computer in the classroom, there is access to the Internet. Students use the Internet frequently for research, and the computer is used a great deal for word processing.

Nancy encourages students to use this literacy-rich environment she has created, which accommodates the differences in reading ability in her classroom (from first-grade to ninth-grade reading level). The first time I walked into the classroom, it was apparent that every student was totally engaged in reading and using the environment during a "sustained silent reading" (SSR) period. Some students were reading at their desks, others were at tables, and a few were found under the tables.

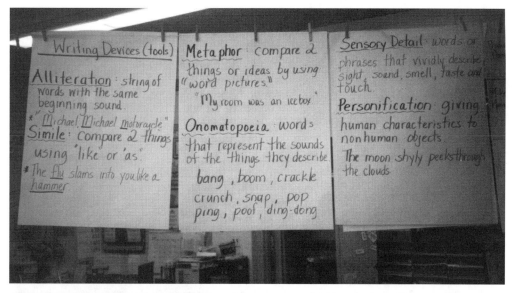

Charts and Word Walls fill the room with writing guidelines, as well as vocabulary words from novels the students have read.

CLASSROOM GUIDANCE AND DIRECTION

Good management is evident in exemplary classrooms, and Nancy sets an exceptional example. "I hammer home my expectations for the classroom routines in the first 2 weeks of school," says Nancy. "After that, the class is able to function on its own." Occasionally she needs to remind the students to stay on task or to quiet down, but it is just that—a reminder that has immediate effect. On several occasions Nancy redirects students simply by asking, "What are you supposed to be doing?" That question is indicative of her teaching style; She doesn't give the students the answers; they have to figure them out themselves with her support and encouragement. Nancy states that a 1-2-3 count to get the attention of the class is a lifesaver. During my observation period, however, she never had to count past 2 before getting the attention of her students.

In the beginning of the school year, Nancy lays out four basic rules that she requires of the class:

1. Do things the *first* time you are asked.
2. Respect the rights and properties of others. Keep hands, feet and other objects to yourself.
3. Have all appropriate materials at your desk and be ready to work when class begins;
4. Raise your hand and wait to be called on before you speak.

Without a lengthy list of "musts," the students seem to be able to focus on the few key items that make the class run smoothly. Nancy has set up the classroom environment to facilitate good behavior during the daily activities. Classroom materials are accessible throughout the room. Paper is kept by the chalkboard, as are boxes and cans of frequently used items, such as rulers and erasers. As noted above, desks are arranged in groups of four; the students at each cluster constitute a "team." This allows Nancy to work with small groups without constantly having to create them, greatly reducing time spent on getting organized. She also dismisses students by teams, which speeds up the process. To encourage good behavior, Nancy awards points to these teams. For example, after she has told the class to get ready for dismissal, Nancy never repeats herself. All she has to say is this: "Ten points for this first team. Good job for getting ready so quickly." That gets the attention of the other students, who scramble to be the next team ready. For the second team, Nancy will award 5 points, then 3. Points earned for good behavior result in rewards. Approximately once a month, Nancy changes the teams to allow the students to work with different classmates, and to try new roles within the new groups.

Planning is part of classroom guidance and direction, and again this is an area in which Nancy is always prepared with the materials, resources, and background information for daily lessons. She posts the schedule on the chalkboard, so students know what is coming up and can be prepared for it. Consequently, students are usually ready for and productively engaged in interesting activities, which leaves little time to misbehave. If the class is working well, Nancy will stretch out the time for a given activity. Conversely, if something is not working, she will shift gears and move on to the next. A key to keeping students engaged is to make sure they know what to do when they finish with an assignment. Nancy has several projects that students can work on independently when they have free time; for example, they can write in their journals, and they are always encouraged to read.

TYPES OF READING EXPERIENCES

Nancy provides for SSR daily. During this time, students can read whatever material they choose. They know that they are allowed to read during SSR in various spots around the room—some alone, some with a partner, and some in a group. Students can also be found curled up on the rug reading in the Book Nook. It is quiet during this period since students are quite absorbed. Occasionally a student will read something he or she wants to share, in which case a whispered conversation may take place. *Scary Stories 3* (Schwartz, 1991), *My Teacher Is an Alien* (Coville, 1989), *Where the Sidewalk Ends* (Silverstein, 1974), and Rowling's *Harry Potter* books, are examples of books that students choose to read during SSR.

Students read for a half hour, and when the time is up they reluctantly return to their desks to begin the next activity. The motivation to read clearly comes from Nancy herself. After SSR, Nancy has some students give a brief plug for the books they are reading. One day, when a student said she was reading *Minton Goes Driving* (Fienberg, 2001), Nancy bellowed, "Love that book!!" while pounding her hand on a table to punctuate each word. She followed up with "That is a *must-read*!" There wasn't a person in the class, myself included, who didn't want to read that book next. The atmosphere in her class is very much in keeping with her overall teaching philosophy: "My students have to read a lot, and they learn to love to it. It's my job to give them the strategies to get inside the book. It's about the joy of having a book in your hands and pulling meaning from it." Every summer before school starts, Nancy writes a letter to her

There is time for quiet book reading, and the teacher participates as well.

new students in which she says, "If you don't love to read now, you will by the time you leave fourth grade."

A second type of reading takes place in guided reading groups, which Nancy calls "Book Clubs." The Book Clubs meet in different sections of the room. The students are grouped according to similar reading needs and abilities. Nancy sets up the Book Clubs based on what skills need to be taught. Within the small guided reading group or Book Club, students are taught new skills, and old ones are reinforced.

A third type of reading occurs in "Literature Circles." Whereas in earlier grades teachers used Literature Circles as part of guided reading, at this age students can select their own books for reading and use circles independently. These groups meet to engage in discussions about books. Nancy has great expectations for how Literature Circles are utilized. Her students have been well trained about the different roles to play as a members of a Literature Circle. In fact, for at least the first 2 months of school, Nancy models Literature Circle behaviors and aspects of good book discussions with the whole group. After reading a book, students make up questions and think of thoughtful comments, which they write on Post-it Notes and place on the pages that the questions and comments refer to. When they meet for discussion, the Post-its facilitate the discussion. As the school year goes on, students are able to create their own discussion questions, and to carry out their Literature Circle discussions independently.

The fourth type of reading that is common in this classroom is partner reading. Students are asked to pair up to read for pleasure or to enhance content area reading. Pairs review books they have read and list the most important facts. To do this task, students must skim, analyze, and summarize the text together.

A fifth type of reading that occurs is reading a book aloud. In Book Clubs, students often take turns reading books aloud that Nancy has already read to the class. Nancy's rationale for her read-alouds is to "expose students to as many incredible authors as possible."

Children run their own Literature Circles independently.

Any reading activity that Nancy is engaged in is highly interactive with her students. She is constantly questioning and encouraging students to dig deeper into the text. The following dialogue was from a whole-class discussion of *The Big Wave* (Buck, 1948/1973):

NANCY: All right, let's find out what transpired in the reading.

STUDENT 1: (*Recaps the last chapter of the book.*)

NANCY: Why does he want to be Jiya's father?

STUDENT 2: Because Jiya doesn't have a family any more.

NANCY: Why is Kino's father willing to give up Jiya? That's an incredible sacrifice, don't you think?

STUDENT 3: It's like he's giving away his son.

NANCY: Yeah! Why do you think he would do that? What can Old Gentleman give Jiya that Kino's father can't?

Nancy's questions don't allow students to just retell the text. She asks, "Why?" and "What do you think about that?"—questions that force the students to reflect on what they are reading. The following dialogue occurred while Nancy was reading *Knights of the Kitchen Table* (Scieszka, 1991b) aloud to the whole class.

NANCY: (*After reading a few pages in the first chapter*) Crazy so far, huh? Now, does anyone have any questions about it?

STUDENT 1: How did they get back in time?

NANCY: Excellent question. They never said what happened, did they? What else?

STUDENT 2: How are they going to get out?

STUDENT 3: Is the knight good or bad? (*Students laugh.*)

NANCY: That's actually a good question. Usually the black knight is the bad guy, but it hasn't really been said, so we don't know yet. He could turn out to be good. Those are all good questions.

Even when she is reading aloud to the students, Nancy will stop and ask questions to get the students thinking. She often has the students assume the role of the teacher; they make predictions about the plot and ask questions that they would like answered from the text. The dialogue she encourages flows quickly and fluidly, always centered around the topic. If the focus starts to wander, Nancy will redirect the conversation to keep it productive and on track.

TYPES OF WRITING EXPERIENCES

In Nancy's class, the children's writing experiences are as diverse as their reading experiences. Often the day will start with the students writing a response in their literature response logs to questions posted on the chalkboard, such as this one: "What surprising things happened in the last chapter we read in *The Big Wave*? What do you think about it?"

After finishing the book *The Big Wave* (Buck, 1948/1973), each student in a team had to choose a section of the story and write a synopsis that included the most pertinent events in the plot. Nancy had the students use a writing process approach that included brainstorming in their teams (prewriting), drafting, revising, conferencing, and editing.

Journals are used for students to write responses to assignments from Book Clubs or other readings. Nancy reads the journals to check for comprehension of the text, as well as to assess the general thought patterns of the students. The following dialogue is an example of an assignment that was given during a Book Club meeting:

NANCY: What is aloneness? Why is the main character feeling this?

STUDENT 1: (*Begins to answer.*)

NANCY: No, listen, I want you to write in your journals. Wrap your head around this aloneness thing. Is the character really alone?

STUDENT 2: No, he's got his grandma there.

NANCY: So what does it mean he's alone? Why then, at that point in the story? He's not really alone. I know I've felt that before, though. Have you?

STUDENTS: (*Several affirmatives.*)

NANCY: It's interesting that you answered the way you did. Consider why you answered like that. Now get your thoughts on paper. This is pretty personal stuff, but later I'd like to ask if anyone is comfortable sharing.

Nancy also encourages the students to keep private journals to record thoughts, emotions and events. To show the students what a journal looks like, Nancy keeps a copy of *Amelia Hits the Road* (Moss, 1997). This is a mock journal that provides a good basis for students to start their own. One of Nancy's students showed me hers and explained its use to me: "It's a notebook, and you can put anything you want, like private thoughts and pictures and stuff in there. No one can look at it unless you let them." Her journal was decorated with photographs and drawings, both on the cover and inside. She showed me several photographs of her family, as well as a postcard that a friend had sent to her from the Netherlands. She pointed out numerous entries she had written as she flipped through the pages.

Nancy also has a Writing Workshop, in which students have a mini-lesson in a writing procedure or strategy and then are given time to write. The mini-lessons are based on the needs of the students and the whole class. Lessons range from learning about writing structural elements of a story to using new forms of punctuation. The following dialogue took place during a mini-lesson in preparation for writing an expository composition entitled "My Three Favorite Things."

NANCY: When you are getting ready to write your expository composition about your three favorite things, what will you write first?

STUDENT 1: An opening.

NANCY: Right. We also call it the introduction. And what comes at the end?

STUDENT 2: The closing.

NANCY: Yes. And what about the middle?

STUDENT 3: The paragraph on your favorite things.

NANCY: Good. Now are you going to have just one paragraph, or what?

STUDENT 3: You will have three paragraphs.

NANCY: Totally, because you have three things, right? You would probably do a whole paragraph on each thing. It's like a sandwich. There is the bread on the top and bottom; that's the introduction and closing. The meat is in the middle, which are the middle paragraphs for the piece. We would probably have to have meat, cheese, and lettuce because we have three paragraphs. Do you see how it looks like a sandwich?

Nancy drew a sandwich on the white board and labeled the top piece of bread the "introduction," the bottom the "closing," and the three layers of food in between the "middle." The class went on to discuss the content for each section. The whole mini-lesson took less than 10 minutes.

Students are encouraged to "publish" writings for the bulletin board or the classroom library. The class also publishes a student newsletter regularly.

The teacher carries out a mini-lesson during the Writing Workshop with a small group of children.

Nancy engages her students in writing poetry often. Over the course of several months, the students wrote different types of poems, such as haikus, cinquains, and sonnets. The students kept the poems, and when they had a collection, they typed them on the computer, published them, and bound them in an anthology. Taking the project a step further, Nancy turned the classroom into a coffeehouse for a day and had the students experience the beatnik scene (complete with hot chocolate instead of cappuccino, jazz music in the background, and poetry readings by students). Other types of writing in the classroom include summarizing texts, writing advertisements, and writing scripts.

CROSS-CURRICULAR CONNECTIONS

Nancy ties the other content area she teaches, social studies, to the language arts through thematic instruction. She says:

> "Using themes allows me to incorporate meaning into the curriculum. In my fourth-grade social studies curriculum, we study Japan. I can make that really interesting and meaningful for my students by selecting a piece of literature to read such as *The Big Wave*, which discusses a small Japanese fishing society that ties in so well with our work in social studies."

Social studies also incorporates a strong writing component. Whenever the class reads and discusses a text, or Nancy is teaching a lesson, the students take notes in a special social studies notebook. In one social studies activity, the students had to compare and contrast the lives of two different women they had read about, who lived in approximately the same time period but in different countries. They created graphic organizers and word webs with Nancy's guidance, and filled the various categories with similarities and differences that they were able to draw from the two texts.

TEACHABLE MOMENTS

Nancy rarely ignores a teachable moment. During a discussion of famous people, for example, one student brought up Tiger Woods and his placement on the "money list." Realizing that the student did not have a clear understanding of what a "money list" was, Nancy pursued the topic.

STUDENT 1: I was reading about Tiger Woods and that he just won. The check he received for $297,000 put him at 40th on the "money list."

NANCY: That's interesting. He's a really great player. Do you know what a "money list" is?

STUDENT 1: (*Hesitates.*)

NANCY: Can anyone help Mike with that?

STUDENT 2: Isn't it the money that he won?

NANCY: That's part of it, but it's more than just what a person wins once. For a tournament, the first-place winner might get $297,000, but doesn't the second-place winner also get something?

STUDENTS: Yes.

NANCY: Does second place get as much money?

STUDENT 3: No, they get less.

NANCY: How about third place?

STUDENT 4: They also get something, but it's less.

NANCY: Right. So someone might win first place twice and second place three times, and get money each time. Over the course of a year, the total amount of money that a person wins determines where he goes on the "money list." The number one on the money list has won the most money so far. Where can you find out who's on the "money list" and the rankings?

STUDENTS: In the newspaper.

NANCY: Where in the newspaper?

STUDENT 1: The sports section.

NANCY: Okay, Mike, your job tonight is to look through the newspaper and find the "money list." Bring it in and give us a report.

This example is typical of the way that Nancy handles such moments. The general framework of such episodes is similar: Nancy notices a weakness and asks questions to see the extent of the students' understanding. She explains when necessary, but nearly always makes the students do the work. The Tiger Woods example above took just a few minutes out of the planned discussion, but allowed her to add new vocabulary and understanding to the lesson. This sort of exchange is common in Nancy's classroom.

THE DAILY SCHEDULE AND A TYPICAL DAY IN THE FOURTH GRADE

The following is an outline of a fourth-grade day for Nancy's class. A description of a typical day, highlighting the language arts activities, is then provided.

Children enter school
>   Classroom jobs.
>   Journal writing (free writing, skill practice).
>   Buddy reading.

Social studies (students stay with their teacher)

Read-aloud and snack
>   Teacher leads prereading discussion.
>   During reading, teacher models fluent reading.

Math (students go to another teacher)

Lunch and recess

Sustained silent reading.

Students choose any reading material.

They may read alone or with two or three children together.

They may go anywhere in the room.

Reading Workshop

Independent activities reviewed.

Literature Circles.

Journal writing.

Thematic literacy activities.

Word study challenge activities.

Guided reading groups.

Discuss a book that has been read with a skill such as understanding a character's point of view.

Prepare for a new book with vocabulary development and background information about the story.

After previewing the book, have student read silently with a purpose presented by the teacher.

Teacher keeps records of students' progress as she asks different children to read aloud privately.

Writing Workshop

Mini-lesson.

Independent writing.

Conferences with the teacher.

Author's Chair.

Meeting at the end of the day

Important activities of the day reviewed.

Homework reminders.

Coming attractions for tomorrow.

When the students entered the room on this typical morning, there was a "Do Now" message written on the chalkboard. In this message, Nancy asked the students to use important vocabulary words in sentences in their journals. She also wrote "Guten Morgen!" to expose the children to world languages. While students were responding, some were also carrying out morning housekeeping items described by several charts posted around the room.

After about 15 minutes, students completed the "Do Now" task. Nancy then reviewed the sentences. One boy struggled with one of the sentences, and Nancy helped him complete the task. The class listened patiently as Nancy provided clues and supports to lead him to success. When he finally arrived at a correct response, she praised him sincerely.

Social studies (which Nancy teaches) was next. The class was nearing the end of a unit on the regions of the United States. Nancy found ample opportunities to gear her lesson toward literacy development. During the first part, she had the students listen to a new song called "Fifty Nifty United States" and follow along on song sheets that had several spelling mistakes on them. During the second part, she used a popular picture book—*Brown Bear, Brown Bear, What Do You See?* (Martin & Carle, 1967)—as the source for the format for a project. The students were asked to construct similar books of their own, using a particular state as the topic. Nancy showed a finished product to the class. She read from her book, "Ohio, Ohio, what do you see? I see Columbus shining at me." After going over the directions, with explicit information given regarding each aspect of the project, Nancy checked for understanding. Then the students went to work, either with partners or alone. At the conclusion of the time allotted for social studies, the work in progress was collected. The unfinished books were placed in a basket for the students to work on again at a later time.

Next on the agenda was a story to read aloud while students had a snack. Nancy had brought a book from home to share with the class. She announced the title, *Calico the Wonder Horse; or, the Saga of Stewy Stinker* (Burton, 1950/1996). Before beginning to read, Nancy led a brief discussion. She asked, "What's a saga? Why do you think it could be called 'Stewy Stinker'?"

The students discussed the title and made predictions based on the cover illustration. As the story was read, they stopped often to discuss issues prompted by the text. At the mention of the Badlands region as the setting for the story, Nancy asked the students whether they knew where that is. In this fashion, she tied the story to the content area of social studies, in which they had been learning about the regions of the United States. When the children were unable to provide the correct answer to the Badlands question, instead of giving the answer to them, Nancy replied, "I'll leave it as a challenge. See if you can get it."

During the course of the story, Nancy encouraged active engagement with the text. The questions she asked during the read-aloud provided a model for the questions she hoped children would ask themselves as they read independently. She asked them to predict, seek clarification of story elements, use context clues to understand vocabulary, and make connections between the text and their own prior knowledge. She read with expression, and used accents to portray the characters in the story. She made the reading an interactive experience, during which the modeling of effective comprehension strategies underscored the enjoyment one can derive from reading high-quality literature.

Next, the children collected their materials and proceeded to their assigned math classes. In this school, the children are grouped according to ability for mathematics. After math, the children returned to their regular classrooms and proceeded to lunch and recess.

After lunch, the remainder of the day was devoted to language arts instruction. When the students came back to their classroom, they began the independent reading activity. With the lights dimmed, a calm came over the classroom. Children, with reading materials in hand, made themselves comfortable. Some broke off into pairs and threes, while others remained alone. Some chose to read outside the room's doorway, since the weather was pleasant.

Reading materials included various genres. Two girls took turns reading from a picture book, *Martha Calling,* (Meddaugh, 1994). Another pair read a tall tale from another anthology. One boy read from a Spanish-language novel. A pair of boys shared the *Star Wars Trilogy Scrapbook* (Vaz, 1997). All around the room, children were engaged in reading various other works of children's literature, including *Mrs. Frisby and the*

Rats of NIMH (O'Brien, 1986), *The Encyclopedia of Dogs* (Fiorone, 1973), and *I Spy* (Marzolla, 1999).

After 15 minutes, Nancy switched on the lights and asked the children to put their books away. She then chose a student volunteer to write and administer the dictation—a weekly assessment for the skills of spelling, capitalization, punctuation, and listening. Each sentence, often referring to subject matter from the social studies or science curriculum, is read aloud three times. The sentences on this day were these:

1. We're living in the United States, so we're Americans.
2. "Trenton is our state capital," thought Sara.

When students finished writing, the class reviewed the correct formats for the sentences, which were recorded on the board.

The class then moved into the Reading Workshop segment of the LAB. Nancy met with guided reading groups for direct instruction. While she worked with these groups, the rest of the children met on this day for Literature Circles.

The five Literature Circle groups in Nancy's class consist of children who have all chosen the same books to read. As noted earlier, they use Post-its to question and comment about parts of a book they are having trouble with or wanted to discuss. The Literature Circle groups move together, with activities for independent work displayed in a pocket chart. The types of activities they participate in are reading books independently, discussion of the books led by a student, journal writing related to the book, or an art activity related to a book.

On this day, Nancy called five students in the class for the first guided reading lesson. They sat together at a round table. An easel was set up in front of them with a "Point of View" chart posted on it. First, they discussed this literary element in another book they had all read before. Then they directed their attention to the novel they were currently reading, *Shiloh* (Naylor, 1991) . This was a book for their guided reading selected by the teacher. Nancy modeled filling in the chart with one character, but eventually withdrew to allow the group to work on its own.

After the reading groups met, Nancy visited the Literature Circles' meetings. The first group she visited was reading *Mrs. Frisby and the Rats of NIMH* (O'Brien, 1986). Students were sharing their journal responses to the book. Afterward, they addressed discussion questions provided by the teacher about the book.

After about 45 minutes, Nancy asked the students to clean up their reading materials. She then began her Writing Workshop with a whole-class mini-lesson about the characteristics of nonfiction news articles. The students had been publishing this type of writing in a class newsletter. Together, they compiled a chart entitled "Amazing Articles." The children were then given the remaining time to work on their own newsletter articles.

SUMMARY

Nancy's classroom is a happy and productive place for fourth graders. The teacher has built a community for learning that includes cooperation, respect, and strong expectations for work and achievement.

The classroom is rich with materials for children to have choices, challenges, social interaction, and success. There is exposure to literature and commercially prepared reading instructional materials. The classroom has provisions for whole-group, small-group, and one-to-one instruction. The teacher provides varied experiences to develop skills and to motivate reading and writing. Children have routines and rules to follow. They are taught to be independent, self-directed learners. Teaching is explicit, direct, and systematic. It includes construction of meaning, problem solving, and taking advantage of spontaneous teachable moments.

Nancy is consistent in her management techniques; therefore, her children know what is expected of them. The affective quality in the room is exemplary; the teacher is warm and caring. Children are treated with respect, and consequently respect the teacher. The day flows smoothly from one activity to the next. The routines are consistent and therefore easy for the children to follow. The activities are varied to keep the children engaged. There is a lot to do, but it can be accomplished.

The children in this classroom experience literacy in many different forms: shared reading and writing, independent reading and writing, collaborative reading and writing with peers, and guided reading and writing for skill development. Children take part in oral and silent reading and writing, as well as mini-lessons modeled by the teacher. Content area themes are integrated into reading and writing experiences to bring meaning to skill development. Children have opportunities to perform or share reading and writing accomplishments.

Nancy is teaching in a school that supports and expects outstanding performance. The atmosphere in the building is professional, with frequent staff development sessions. Teachers often have grade-level meetings to share and plan, and the principal

The teacher reads a novel to the students in a whole-group setting.

plays an important role in supporting curriculum development. Teachers take the initiative to expand their knowledge by obtaining master's degrees in education, attending professional conferences, and reading professional materials.

It is apparent that Nancy is an excellent teacher. She has a great deal of knowledge about literacy development, as well as about organizing instruction. The instruction in literacy involves skill development taught explicitly, in the context of authentic literature, as a part of writing, and with content connections. This exemplary teacher uses both direct instruction and constructivism. Her explicit teaching of skills is a good start for constructivist activities, and the constructivist activities permit consolidation and elaboration of skills.

EIGHT

Third- and Fourth-Grade Activities and Plans

GETTING STARTED

Language Arts Block Time Schedules

The following schedules are presented as guidelines. And, as in Chapters 4 and 6, note that each one covers the LAB *only* and not the entire instructional day.) Your individual schedule may match one of them exactly or may vary greatly. Be flexible, be willing to try different models, and you will find one that works for you!

Schedule 1

8:30–8:50:   **Things to do when the students arrive**
Attendance sign-in
Lunch sign-in
Classroom assistants
Problem of the day

8:50–9:30:   **Morning meeting**
Overview of the day
Homework assignments
News
Status of the class
Book talks

9:30–10:25:   **Reading Workshop/independent activities**
Reading mini-lessons
Reading responses using buddy journals
Independent Reading
Journal Writing
Content-area-related activities
Reading assignments/guided work
Vocabulary search
Independent work at centers (or "stations," as they are often called in
    the upper grades)

10:25–11:20: Writing Workshop
Writing
Responding to writing
Writing mini-lessons
Author's Chair

11:20–12:00: Lunch/recess

12:00–12:15: Read-aloud
SQ3R reading strategy
Using content-area-related picture books

Schedule 2

8:30–8:50:   Things to do when the students arrive
Attendance sign-in
Lunch sign-in
Classroom assistants
Problem of the day

8:50–9:20:   Morning meeting
Overview of the day
Homework assignments
News
Status of the class
Book talks

9:20–9:30:   Independent activities
Independent reading
Journal writing
Content-area-related activities

9:30–10:15:   Reading workshop
Reading mini-lessons
Reading responses using buddy journals
Reading assignments/guided work
Vocabulary search
Independent work at centers

10:15–11:00: Writing Workshop
Writing
Responding to writing
Writing mini-lessons/independent work at centers
Author's Chair

11:00–12:00: Lunch/recess

12:00–12:15: Read-aloud
SQ3R reading strategy
Using content-area-related picture books

Schedule 3

8:30–9:00:   **Things to do when the students arrive/independent activities**
Attendance sign-in
Lunch sign-in
Classroom assistants
Problem of the day
Independent reading
Journal writing
Content-area-related activities

9:00–9:20:   **Morning meeting**
Overview of the day
Homework assignments
News
Status of the class
Book talks

9:20–10:00:   **Reading workshop**
Reading mini-lessons
Reading responses using buddy journals
Independent work at centers

10:00–10:50:   **Integrated arts special**

10:50–11:20:   **Writing Workshop**
Writing
Responding to writing
Writing mini-lessons/station work
Author's Chair

11:00–12:00:   **Lunch/recess**

12:00–12:15:   **Read-aloud**
SQ3R reading strategy
Using content-area-related picture books

Tools for Teaching Language Arts

Classrooms contain many materials—some supplied by the demands of the curriculum and the school district and some supplied by your own preference and personal ingenuity. You may have a fully stocked classroom, or you may have one with only a minimum of materials. Be creative with what you have. And be creative when your needs go beyond what is readily available to you. Don't be afraid to ask students to bring in anything from crayons to fabric to glitter and beyond! The following list is intended to help you get started. Then it's up to you!

- Individual chalkboards or white boards for each child.
- Chalk, a sock for an eraser, or dry-erase markers for each child.
- A large easel with paper for whole-class and small-group instruction.
- Sets of letter cards for each child to use in word-building activities.

- Crayons.
- Colored pencils.
- Markers of various shapes and for various surfaces.
- Colored paper (of various sizes and weights).
- Various sizes of writing paper, with age-appropriate spacing and margins.
- Rough-draft paper (newsprint).
- Colored writing paper for special projects.
- Rulers.
- Scissors (of various shapes and designs).
- Journals (of various shapes and sizes for buddy journals, word work, response work, etc.).
- Pocket folders for the students to store work (you may want one for reading and one for writing).
- Expandable folders to store student work or for distributing work at centers.
- Clear storage containers (shoe boxes) for supplies and organization.
- Baskets for storing class novels and other reading materials.
- An overhead projector, film, markers, and erasing materials.
- A cassette player for class-produced songs, and the like.
- For the Listening Center: tape recorder, headsets, audiotapes, and books.
- Staplers and staples.
- Glue.
- Tape (clear and heavy-duty for hanging student work).

Ideas for Classroom Organization and Management

Purposes:

- Use time efficiently and effectively.
- Provide structure to a classroom setting.

Methods for gathering attention:

- Put five fingers up and say, "Give me five." This is a signal for the following:
  1. Eyes on you.
  2. Lips sealed.
  3. Ears ready to listen.
  4. Hands free.
  5. Feet on the floor.
- Use clapping refrains.
- Turn the lights off.
- Give a two-finger "salute."

Methods for keeping track of students when you are working in small groups:

- An independent activity board (as shown in the first illustration that follows).
- A center/activity chart (as shown in the second illustration that follows).
- Class meetings (informal updates with students).
- Clipboards (hang clipboards conveniently around the room to record your informal observations of students).

Fostering independence:

- To open a new activity:
  - Use an attention-getting method.
  - Describe in three steps what you want the students to do.
  - Require that they listen while you give instructions.
  - Tell them how long they have to comply.
  - Tell them to proceed.
  - Expect them all to do as outlined.
  - Monitor the time it takes them to comply.
  - Praise them for their efforts.
  - Begin the new activity.

- To promote independence, generate several strategies for self-help:
  - "Ask three before me" (i.e., students ask three other classmates before going to you for help).
  - Have students check the day's activity board.
  - Have students use self-assessment checklists.
  - Assign buddies.

- To monitor student progress during work time:
  - Use an attention-getting method.
  - Ask students to assess their progress (are they doing what they're supposed to be doing?).
  - Ask them to make adjustments or realign their work, as needed.
  - Praise them for their efforts.
  - Tell them how much longer they have to complete their tasks.

- To close an activity:
  - Use an attention-getting method.
  - Tell the students how long they have to complete their activity.
  - Tell students what you expect them to be ready to do next (sitting in their seats ready to listen, lined up at the door, etc.).
  - Give them a time frame in which to complete their task.
  - Monitor their progress.
  - Praise them when they complete their assigned tasks in the allotted time.
  - Proceed to the next activity.

Station Work	Guided Reading
Independent Work	Silent Reading

Independent activity board

Station 1
Station 2
Station 3
Station 4
Station 5

Center/activity chart

THINGS TO DO WHEN THE STUDENTS ARRIVE

When you are planning the LAB, it is important to remember that virtually every activity performed during the day has a language component. Students use listening skills when they receive instructions from a teacher. They use speaking skills in class discussions, when they ask questions, and in formal presentations. Reading self-selected materials for pleasure and reading content-related materials both involve essential skills. Written responses to content area questions, Writing Workshop activities, and specific themed written work require the use of language arts skills.

The activities in this section (which should occupy about 20 minutes in all) will help you prepare for subsequent literacy activities as the students enter the classroom and begin their day.

Attendance Sign-In

Purposes:

- Encourage students to accept responsibility.
- Use literacy to take daily attendance.

Materials:

- Laminated poster board divided into two sections (one labeled "Present," the other "Absent") and decorated to match classroom themes, mounted in an accessible area in the class.
- Clothespins (or other markers) labeled with each student's name.

Activity:

1. As children enter, they move their clothespins from "Absent" to "Present."

Variations:

- → The sign-in board may take various guises, as developed through your (or the students') artistic eyes.
- → Instead of clothespins and tagboard, a magnetic board and self-decorated markers may be used.
- → Pictures of the students may be mounted on markers and used instead of, or along with, clothespins or name tags.
- → Pocket charts also work well for this purpose.

Management Tips:

- → Check the attendance sign-in board for accuracy before reporting attendance to the office.
- → Model for your children the proper way to move their clothespins from "Absent" to "Present."

Sample Attendance Sign-In Board

Attendance	
Present	Absent

Lunch Sign-In

Purpose:

- Build students' independence and responsibility.

Materials:

- Laminated poster board divided into two sections (one labeled "Buying," the other "Not Buying") and decorated to match classroom themes, mounted in an accessible area in the class. Note that if there are several lunch choice options, the poster board should be divided so that each choice is represented.
- Clothespins (or other markers) labeled with each student's name.

Activity:

1. Write the daily lunch choice (or choices) on the board.
2. As children enter, they move their clothespins or name markers to the appropriate area on the sign-in board.

Variations:

- ➜ A pocket chart may be used for this activity.
- ➜ Coffee cans labeled with the appropriate choices, and craft sticks marked with each student's name, are another means of tallying lunch choices (see Chapter Four).

Management Tips:

→ Model the correct way to move the clothespins to the appropriate area on the sign-in board.

→ One classroom assistant may be chosen to record the lunch choice and check the accuracy of the daily choices before reporting.

→ At the end of the day, have the student reporter remove names/markers so that the board is ready for the following day.

Sample Lunch Sign-In Board

Lunch	
Buying Today's lunch is: _____	Not Buying

Classroom Assistants

Purposes:

• Encourage students to accept responsibility and build essential skills by taking part in performing significant classroom jobs. (These will vary, of course, depending upon the age of the students and the needs of the classroom.)

Materials:

• Poster board and markers.
• Drapery hooks.
• Index cards.

Activity:

1. Organize a "Pocketful of Helpers" chart by drawing a pair of overalls on a piece of poster board.
2. Color and decorate it in a manner that complements the classroom themes. Then laminate it.

3. Cut pockets from additional poster board and label them with classroom jobs (assistants).
4. Mount the labeled pockets on the overalls.
5. Insert a drapery hook on each pocket. These will be used to hang cards with students' names, indicating who is responsible for each job during that week.
6. Provide index cards for each student in the class, which they can label with their names and/or decorate. These name cards are hung on the drapery hooks, identifying the classroom assistants.

Variation:

→ A "Tree Full of Helpers" is another theme that works well here. Tagboard apples, labeled with the students' names, can serve as the markers.

Management Tips:

→ Early in the school year, significant classroom jobs should be determined in a morning meeting. These may include a Class Librarian, Paper Passers, Attendance Monitor, Lunch Count Monitor, and so forth.
→ Each Monday morning, as part of the classroom meeting (or at an appropriate time as determined by you) the students select their jobs for the week.

- Name tags are shuffled and drawn one by one.
- As each child's name is called, that child selects the job he or she would like to hold during that week.
- Children not selected for a job one week should have their name tags held on an unused hook on the chart. Their names will be the first ones selected the following week.

Problem of the Day

Purposes:

- Encourage students to use reading for different purposes, such as learning and problem solving.
- Teach students to use reference materials effectively.

Materials:

- Posted problem relating to information studied in class.
- Locations for student answers (slips of paper in a shoebox, "Problem of the Day" logs for each student).
- Pen or pencil.

Activity:

1. Post the "Problem of the Day." It should be a problem students can answer based on what they already know, a contemporary issue discussed during instructional time, or a research-based question.

> **Sample problem:** Ms. Reynolds is a photographer. She is planning a trip to Arizona to take 200 photographs for a national magazine covering a story on deserts. Film costs $3.92 for one roll of 36 exposures. How many rolls of film must she purchase? About how much money must she take with her to the store?

2. Post the time the answers are due. The morning meeting or the end of the day is a good time to share answers.
3. Students submit their solutions with their name and the time of entry.
4. Students share their answers as a class. Students should also share how they solved the problem.

Variations:

→ Students work together to answer a "super-challenge."
→ Students submit possible problems of the day.

MORNING MEETING

The morning meeting (which should last from 20 to 40 minutes) helps you organize the instructional day through meaningful and authentic activities. The activities that take place during the morning meeting provide opportunities for literacy development. Although the first three activities should be done daily, the others may be done on a rotating basis.

Overview of the Day

Purposes:

- Sequence the instructional events of the day.
- Demonstrate the ability to gain information from a variety of media.
- Help students develop prediction and sequencing skills.

Materials

- "Daily agenda" (large erasable surface arranged by subject that students can easily view and have access to, or a large screen to project a computer presentation).
- Pointer.

Activity:

1. The class is seated on the carpet near the agenda.
2. After students complete their jobs and/or independent activities, they assemble in a designated area and read the daily agenda.
3. The "Organizer" for the day will read the agenda, using a pointer to help students follow along.
4. The agenda can be phrased as questions or open-ended statements, to give students the opportunity to predict what they will learn that day. (See the sample agenda that follows.)

Variations:

→ Students can record predictions for later comparisons. This is a way to track what they knew previously and what they have learned.

→ Predictions/responses can be shared to encourage speaking and listening development.

→ As children become more independent, they can take an active role in developing the agenda for each day.

→ This can be done as a *PowerPoint/Hyperstudio* presentation.

Thematic Tie:

→ It is ideal to have all of the activities centered on the current theme of study. For example, if the theme is "Friendship," the activities selected and some of the questions developed in the agenda can be connected to that theme (see the sample agenda).

Management Tip:

→ Post the agenda in the morning meeting area daily before the children arrive.

Sample Daily Agenda:

AGENDA

Language Arts

- What is new and exciting that you are reading? How does it connect to our "Friendship" theme?
- What does persuasion mean, and how will it help you be a better reader and writer? How do you try to persuade friends?
- What centers are you going to? What will you learn there today?

Physical Education

- What new activity will you try out today?
- How can you be a friend to someone in class?

Science

- What happens when you mix baking soda and water? Why?
- What do you think that looks and sounds like?
- What can you learn by conducting your experiments with a friend instead of alone?

Lunch

Social Studies

- How do people get elected?
- What do politicians do to make people listen and think about their message?
- What message would you give?
- How do we get our friends to listen to us and trust us?

Math

- How do you visually show who is winning an election?
- Where else could you use a visual aid?

Stay tuned for more tomorrow!

Homework Assignments

Purposes:

- Reinforce/extend skills and strategies introduced during the instructional day.
- Help students develop a sense of responsibility and independence.
- Encourage students to use viewing and note-taking skills.

Materials:

- Erasable surface easily viewed and accessible to the children (preferably one that matches the students' assignment books). See the sample display that follows.
- Assignment books (if possible, all of the students should have assignment books in the same style).

Activity:

1. The class is seated on the carpet near the assignments.
2. After reviewing the agenda as a class, review upcoming homework assignments with the students.
3. Model any necessary skills needed to complete the homework.
4. Assignments that are closely connected to activities taking place later in the day should be discussed in greater detail at the appropriate time.
5. The students will share progress and/or questions on long-range assignments.
6. Students will record assignments in their personal homework assignment book.
7. Monitor to ensure that the students are recording appropriate work.

Variations:

- → You may ask students to have parents/guardians sign their assignment books nightly.
- → If students are working on a long-range project, a "status of the class" on this project may be taken several times during the week to assess progress.

Thematic Tie:

- → When possible, connect homework assignments to the current theme of study. For example, if the theme is "Nature," develop assignments across the curriculum that are connected to this theme. *It is important that the assignments be meaningful; however, don't expect to connect every assignment at all times to the theme of study.*

Management Tips:

- → If you are purchasing a class set of assignment books from a publisher, look into purchasing a matching classroom poster-size page. If you assign long-term projects, more than one poster may be handy to post more than one day/week at a time.
- → Reinforce homework assignments at the end of the day.

Sample Assignment Display:

Homework for 9/15	
Reading Workshop	————————————
Writing Workshop	————————————
Other Language Arts	————————————
Social Studies	————————————
Science	————————————
Math	————————————
Other	————————————

News

Purposes:

- Integrate the literacy skills of reading, writing, listening, and speaking.

Materials:

- Large bulletin board located in the morning meeting area.
- Thumbtacks.
- Pens and markers.
- Construction paper.

Activity:

1. The students are seated in the morning meeting area.
2. The students bring in a news article they *read* or *wrote* to share. The article should fit into one of the following categories: "International," "National," "Community," or "School." For example, a student may bring in an article about the presidential election or a town election, or he or she may write an article about a school election.
3. Students will share their articles, and include the following in their presentations:

   - Summary.
   - Reaction.
   - Examples of interesting and/or confusing writing.

4. Students will then place the articles on the bulletin board underneath the appropriate category.
5. The class will ask questions of each student.

Variations:

→ This activity can be either contained in the morning meeting or, where appropriate, infused throughout the curriculum areas.

→ You may connect the news to the other content areas. For example, during November, you may choose to have an "issues session" and ask students to bring in articles about the issues being debated in local and national elections (a social studies connection).

→ A link can also be made to the Writing Workshop. Articles can be used as mini-lessons in the different types of writing—expository, narrative, descriptive, and persuasive.

→ Items brought in can also become the focus for a class. For example, if the town is having a debate about a garbage dump being placed nearby, debate teams can be established to research the different issues and opinions.

→ Every Friday, you may choose to ask the class to review the articles collected that week and see whether there are any patterns. For example, is one issue concentrated on more frequently than others? Are there a lot of community articles? This helps children develop the ability to compare texts and concepts.

Thematic Tie:

→ When possible, connect the news to the current theme of study. For example, if the theme is "Animals," ask the students to share articles that connect to animals in some way. This might include information about endangered species, information about a local zoo, or the like.

Management Tips:

→ News is introduced to the students at the beginning of the year and becomes part of their morning routine.

→ You will need to model the different types of news for students.

→ The student-written articles may be phased in after this type of writing is introduced in the Writing Workshop. (See "Variations" for suggestions for different modeling techniques.)

→ In the interests of time, it is best to assign students in advance for different days. Two a day is probably best, though this can be left to your discretion.

→ Possible sources children and/or you can draw news items from include the following:

   • Articles connected to students' lives (e.g., an article about a child's soccer team, dance competition, music recital, etc.).

   • News sources developed specifically for children (e.g., *Scholastic News, Weekly Reader, U.S. News and World Report for Kids, Time for Kids,* etc.).

   • Internet resources, such as the *Ask Jeeves* or *AOL Homework Help* Web sites.

Status of the Class

Purposes:

- Chart individual students' reading and writing progress.
- Encourage students to read and write a variety of materials and texts.

Materials:

- Large chart with students' names written alphabetically (see the form that follows).
- Markers.

Activity:

1. During the morning meeting, ask students what they are working on in their independent reading and writing. In addition, ask for specifics (such as page number, point in the writing process, etc.).
2. Students' responses will be posted on the chart for later work with you and for your analysis of student progress.

Variations:

- → As students become more independent, they can record the information themselves. This can also serve as a way of checking attendance.
- → Status may be assessed daily, every other day, or weekly, depending on time constraints and on your and the students' needs.
- → Status charts can be tailored to chart specific long-term projects or goals the class may be working on. (For example, if the class is working on a science report, this could become one of the columns you "check for" to see how the students are progressing.)
- → A computer database can also be used to check the status of the class, instead of a handwritten chart.

Thematic Ties:

- → When possible, students can include in the status chart how their work connects to the theme of study. For example, if the class is studying the theme of "Peace," students can share how their independent reading books connect to this theme.
- → Students can be encouraged to select books for independent reading that connect to the theme of study. You can use book talks to introduce titles that connect to the theme.

Management Tip:

- → The status chart should be clearly visible and posted in the same spot each day.

Status of the Class

Name	Reading Book, author, and page number	Writing Piece and step (ready to draft, conference, edit, final copy, etc.)	Other (Thematic ties, etc.)

Book Talks

Purposes:

- Encourage children to share books that other students may enjoy.
- Have children speak before a group to express thoughts and ideas, convey an opinion, present information, and tell a story.

Materials:

- Bulletin board.
- Copies of the Critic's Corner form (see the form that follows).
- Books to share.

Activity:

1. Upon completion of a book, students will sign up to share their critique.
2. Before critiquing, students will complete a Critic's Corner form, on which they will record a rating and a reaction to the text they read.
3. Students will present a lively reaction to a recently completed book, keeping the following guidelines in mind:

   - Use an animated and interested voice.
   - Share favorite sections of the book.
   - Don't give away the ending!
   - Limit your presentation to approximately 3 minutes.

4. Students will share what they liked or didn't like about the way the book was written. For example, if the students really enjoyed the author's character development, they will read passages that they feel reflect good character development.

Variations:

→ If a computer is available, reactions can be posted in the computer as a database. That way, if students are looking for a specific genre, author, rating, or the like, they can type their request into the computer. This also helps to connect literacy to technology in a meaningful way.
→ Presentations can be organized according to genre studies, author studies, and so on, to help students begin to identify and analyze patterns and themes in literature.
→ Videotapes of the PBS-TV show *Reading Rainbow* can be used to model kids' book talks for the students.
→ A Book Talk Activity Card can be used in lieu of the Critic's Corner form (see the blank card that follows this form).

Thematic Tie:

→ If possible, students can sign up for book talks based on the current theme of study. For example, if the theme is "Immigration," you can ask students to present talks about books that connect to this topic in some way.

Management Tips:

→ You should model this activity several times in the beginning of the year. When you are modeling, use texts that the entire class is familiar with (e.g., a picture book, a recently completed whole-class novel, etc.) After you feels the students have a strong understanding of the activity, then the talks should be turned over to them.

→ Post the filled-out Critic's Corner forms near the classroom library as a resource for other students who are looking for a book to read.

Critic's Corner

Critic's name: _____

Book title: _____

Author: _____

Genre: _____ Pages: _____

Theme: _____

Reading difficulty (circle one):

    Easy   Okay   A little tough   Pretty hard

Rating (1–10; 10 = highest, 1 = lowest): _____

Reaction to book (remember ... don't give away the ending!):

What I liked/didn't like about the way the book was written:

Book Talk Activity Card

Title:

Author:

Genre:

One- or two-sentence summary:

Recommendation (in a complete sentence):

Student's name:

INDEPENDENT ACTIVITIES FOR READING/WRITING WORKSHOPS OR OTHER TIMES

Independent activities are intended to reinforce good practices of literacy introduced during whole-class and small-group instruction. A variety of activities should be made available, to meet both the instructional needs of the children and their various learning styles.

The independent activities described in this section of the chapter are intended primarily for use when you are engaged in individual or small-group guided literacy instruction in the Reading and Writing Workshops (see later sections) and are "off limits" to other students. However, at your discretion, students may also engage in these activities at any time during the instructional day when they have completed required assignments; for example, Nancy Kimberly (see Chapter Seven) permits her students to write in their journals and read independently whenever they have free time. Within the context of the Reading and Writing Workshops, a rotating selection of these activities may be completed on a daily or weekly basis, or your choice of activities may be tailored to your changing schedule requirements and/or the students' differing needs. Two activities per day, with about 20 minutes per activity (though this may vary among individual students), is an appropriate beginning time frame.

Students should not be expected to know how to work on each of these activities independently or in a small group unless repetitive direct instruction with modeling and role-play opportunities are provided.

Organizing Independent Activities

Purposes:

- Provide structure and organization for multiple classroom activities.
- Record which activities students complete.
- Help students develop independent work habits.

Materials:

- Poster board, or portable magnetic chalkboard or whiteboard.
- Multiple sets of laminated color-coded name cards.
- Velcro for poster board, or magnetic tape for chalkboard or white board.
- Timer with a buzzer or bell.

Activity:

1. Follow the pattern shown in the following illustration to divide spaces for the independent activity board.
2. Make independent activity title cards for each option available (again, see the illustration).
3. Attach Velcro or magnetic tape to the backs of name cards, the backs of title cards, and the activity board for easy reuse and reorganization.
4. Furnish ways for students to provide written accountability for each activity. These may be organized with file folders for each student or one file folder per activity for students to file their papers.

Thematic Tie:

→ All content-area-related work and reading assignments/guided work should be tied to the current theme.

Management Tips:

→ The independent activity board should be centrally located and be at child level.

→ The name cards can be rotated to the right each day, so the children experience a variety of independent work.

→ If activity time allows for more than one activity, maintain the first time slot as the rotated activity and allow students to select their own second activity.

→ Content-related activities and reading assignments/guided work should be changed to include practice on newly introduced concepts.

→ Introduce new activities one at a time, allowing for student role play and practice before introducing another new activity.

→ If children don't finish an activity, they may complete it for homework or continue their work the next day as their second activity.

→ Establish an "off-limits" rule during independent activities, so that you have uninterrupted time for meeting with small groups or individual students (or for whatever else you are doing).

→ You need to have a system in place to check activity work. The children must know that you value the work.

Pattern for Independent Activity Board:

Independent Activities

Independent Reading	Journal Writing

Activity 1	Activity 2	Activity 1	Activity 2

Content-Area-Related Activities	Guided Work

Activity 1	Activity 2	Activity 1	Activity 2

Vocabulary Search	Other

Activity 1	Activity 2	Activity 1	Activity 2

Independent Reading

Purposes:

- Encourage students to select reading materials independently.
- Have students read independently and account for what is read.

Materials:

- A large variety of reading materials, including (but not limited to) novels, newspapers, magazines, pamphlets, content-area-related books (nonfiction or fiction), and student-made books.
- Reading area with pillows (optional).
- Timer.

Activity:

1. Students select reading materials.
2. Set the timer for the correct time period.
3. Model good reading habits by reading independently yourself, too.
4. When the time is up, students record in an independent reading log what they have read (see the form that follows).

Variations:

→ Allow students to read with a book on tape in a Listening Center.
→ Invite other adults to read with your class at this time (including other teachers, the principal, custodians, school secretaries, parents, etc.).

Management Tips:

→ To limit disruptions, children are not to select new material once they have settled down.
→ Students may read at their seats or any other predetermined location in the classroom.
→ To limit distractions, students should not place themselves too close to any other classmate.
→ Once independent reading time has started, there should be no sound or movement in the classroom.
→ Model the five-finger tip for picking out reading material. Students hold up one finger for each unfamiliar word. If five fingers are up by the end of the first page, the book is too hard and students should try another.

Independent Reading Progress

Name: _____ Week starting: _____

My independent reading goal for this week: _____

_____

_____

Record all reading below.

Date	Title	Page numbers read
_____	_____	_____ - _____
_____	_____	_____ - _____
_____	_____	_____ - _____
_____	_____	_____ - _____
_____	_____	_____ - _____
_____	_____	_____ - _____
_____	_____	_____ - _____

In a complete sentence, explain how you accomplished your goal this week. If you didn't meet your goal, explain why not, and tell what you would like to change for next week so that you may reach the new goal you set.

_____

_____

_____

_____

Journal Writing

Purposes:

- Have students follow written directions.
- Enable students to practice organizational and writing skills in a nonevaluating setting.

Materials:

- Journal. (Note: It is more efficient for students to keep prefabricated books, binders, spiral notebooks, or stapled sheets of paper than separate papers that are bound later.)
- Timer.
- Pens or pencils.
- Dictionaries and thesauruses (optional).

Activity:

1. Explain that a journal provides a place for daily thoughts and ideas.
2. Model a journal entry by creating one in a class mini-lesson.
3. Post the writing prompt on the board.
4. If all the students are in the classroom at the starting point, read the prompt aloud.
5. Students date the entry and write continuously through the set time.
6. Entries may be shared by reading aloud to the whole class, a small group, or a partner.
7. You or other students may respond to entries in writing.

Variations:

→ Use journal entries as prewriting for a finished piece. The students and/or you may select one piece to develop into a final draft.
→ Journals may be used as a form of one-to-one student–teacher communication, when you respond to students on selected entries.
→ Relate journal entries to fine art: Play a taped short classical piece of music or show a famous painting or sculpture. Students write what they think as they listen or view.
→ Journal entries may be written in letter form.
→ Prompts for journal entries may be student-selected from a list, calendar-oriented or taken from a book of journal prompts. Or students can write on a "free" topic.

Thematic Tie:

→ Relate prompts to a content area activity ("What did you think about . . . ," "Suppose you were Christopher Columbus . . . ," "In your own words explain . . .").

Management Tips:

→ Encourage students to pair up and share journal entries by responding to each other's entries.

→ Post the beginning and ending times for journal writing so that children may pace themselves.

→ Students are not to get up to sharpen pencils, check spelling of words, or the like.

→ You may want to give a 2-minute warning before the timer rings.

Content-Area-Related Activities

Purposes:

• Allow students to continue ongoing projects in a limited amount of time in various groupings.

• Have students read and use printed materials and technical manuals from other disciplines, such as science and social studies.

• Extend classroom learning through kinesthetic practice.

Materials:

• Will be determined by the activity.

Activities:

1. Students sign up for one option during the activity period. Possibilities include the following:

   • Science observations in long-term labs.
   • Games for facts or math skills.
   • Vocabulary games, such as crossword puzzles.
   • Spelling games, such as Mix and Fix.
   • Mad Libs for grammar practice.
   • Time line continuation.
   • Computer games.
   • Map skills.

2. Post an end time and cleanup time.
3. One laminated set of directions should be available at the activity site.
4. When activity time is completed and materials are stored properly, students should share the activity and tell how it relates to the content area they are studying.

Guidance/Direction Ideas:

→ If multiple choices are offered, prepare a sign-up system (chart, blackboard, paper, Popsicle sticks and cups, etc.).

→ Students should have training in each activity during class time or as a minilesson before it is offered as an independent option.

Reading Assignments/Guided Work

Purposes:

- Provide students with additional independent skill practice on a recently taught or reviewed concept.
- Have students read and respond to text, demonstrating comprehension in written form.
- Assess individual students.

Materials:

- Guided reading novel.
- Work materials (pencil, paper, diagrams, etc.).

Activity:

1. After meeting with guided reading group (see "Reading Workshop: Guided Reading," below), assign one activity for students to complete independently. (See the "After the reading" assignment following the sample guided reading lesson.)
2. Students use the current guided reading novel to complete their activity, in addition to any other necessary resources.
3. Students finish activity during independent activity time, or take home for homework. Assignment should not take more than 20 minutes to complete.
4. Guided work is handed to you in the same place every day for teacher evaluation.

Thematic Tie:

➜ Activity may have a tie to the current classroom theme.

Management Tips:

➜ Have students begin the activity in the guided reading group to ensure comprehension of directions.
➜ Assignment should be based on each guided reading group's needs.
➜ If possible, allow for discussion prior to requiring students to write answers.

Vocabulary Search

Purposes:

- Generate unfamiliar vocabulary from students.
- Encourage students to read carefully.
- Suggest meanings of unfamiliar words, using context clues.

Materials:

- Guided reading novel.
- Bookmark, reading log, or other formatted page.
- Pencil.

Activity:

1. Before meeting with a guided group to examine a new chapter, have students preread the next chapter of their novel.
2. Students record any unfamiliar words they encounter as they scan the page, noting page and paragraph number.
3. Have students try to guess and record the meaning of each unknown word by using the surrounding context.
4. Students then check a dictionary for accuracy. If a student did not correctly identify a word's meaning, record the new meaning in his or her own words.
5. Review work during guided reading group time.

Variation:

➜ Have students compile a group list to create puzzles, word searches, alphabetized and categorized lists, to complete and check.

Management Tips:

➜ Have students complete this activity on a regular basis, so that you can review context clue usage and ensure comprehension of the words they select.
➜ Allow each student to share one or two identified words. Check the remainder for accuracy at another time.
➜ Give a specific number of words for each student to locate in the assigned chapter (two or three is a good number). Assign fewer words to students with decoding and comprehension weaknesses, and more to speedy readers.

Technology

When you are implementing technology at these grade levels, allow students to work with partners or as a small group at a computer. This buddy system provides a second person to allow discussion of ideas and to remember cleanup rules. Whenever possible, a number of students should become experts with specific programs that you use regularly within the classroom. They can assist other students so that you can continue your instruction uninterrupted. Finally, vary the activities students complete on the computer, so that they have experience with a wide range of technology tools. Ask staff members, parents, or other students for support when using technology in center work or in content-related activities.

Assigning pairs of students approximately 20 minutes of computer time per week will easily accommodate a class of 25. Sometimes you may want each student to complete the same activity. To ensure wide exposure to many programs, have students keep a log of the activities they use technology to do. Over time, rotate students through programs related to the current unit of study, so that every few weeks all students have worked in each program you are teaching. For example, you may require that over a period of 3 weeks all students will complete a database project, word-process a short piece of writing, and complete a Venn diagram covering information in their current novel, or in the social studies or science curriculum.

Database Project: Vocabulary Picture Dictionaries

Purposes:

- Expand students' vocabularies.
- Have students work independently to compile a class book.
- Teach students to enter information on a computer database program.

Materials:

- Reading material with challenging vocabulary.
- Computer.
- Database software.
- Colored pencils.
- Printer.

Activity:

1. Ask students to keep track of unfamiliar vocabulary as they read either a textbook or a novel. Students should all be reading the same material.
2. Discuss with students methods to obtain accurate definitions (class discussion, using context clues, checking with a dictionary, using a thesaurus for synonyms, etc.).
3. Demonstrate to a few students how to enter information on a database program of your choice. Use the first column for the vocabulary term and a second column for the definition.
4. Have "expert" students practice by entering two of the terms from their individual lists of unfamiliar vocabulary.
5. Once the "experts" are proficient, give them time to teach the rest of the class one by one how to enter their vocabulary data into the program. This can be done either during center time or during other independent activities. Be sure they alphabetize each entry, using the Sort function.
6. Print out the dictionary. If there is time, allow students to illustrate one or two of their terms in colored pencil.
7. Bind and place in the classroom library. A second copy may be placed in the school library as well.

Variations:

- → Tie into grammar by including parts of speech.
- → Extend vocabulary by including synonyms where possible.
- → Incorporate spelling by having students include other word forms with suffixes at the end of each definition.

Drawing Tools and Text: Venn Diagrams

Purpose:

- Encourage students to compare and contrast information gained from text.
- Have students use to present information an organization tool.
- Teach students to enter information on a computer drawing program.

Materials:

- Texts to be compared.
- Computer.
- Drawing software.
- Printer.

Activity:

1. Allow students time in class to read given material to be compared.
2. Demonstrate to the class how each section of a Venn diagram works.
3. Have students work in partners to fill in their own diagrams.
4. During center time, cycle students through the Computer Center to create their own Venn diagrams, using the drawing functions. Students will type text in the correct location.
5. After each student has reviewed and spell-checked his or her piece, print it out.

Variations:

→ Students may use this information for expository writing.
→ Use thematic text such as social studies or science to compare the current unit to a prior unit of study.

PowerPoint Project: Presenting Research

Purposes:

- Teach students to prepare fact cards on *PowerPoint*, using appropriate clip art.
- Have students present information to the class orally, using *PowerPoint* as a visual aid.
- Encourage students to use writing, reading, and viewing to assist with speaking.

Materials:

- Researched information.
- Computer.
- *PowerPoint* software.
- Computer projector or large monitor.

Activity:

1. Have students complete paired research on note cards. Give them time during class to organize and arrange similar information.
2. Show the class a few examples of completed *PowerPoint* cards. Each one should be different in font, style, background, and illustration.
3. Demonstrate to the class on the large monitor how to create a new card and add it to the stack you have displayed.
4. Tell the class that each pair of students will be creating one five-card stack. The first will have the title of the project with the presenters' names. The next three will contain information they learned. The final card will contain the bibliography.

5. If you are in a computer lab, give students the rest of the time to create the first card on the stack. If they finish early, they can decide which graphics and backgrounds they will use for the remaining four cards. If you are not in a lab, allow the next 2 days during center work time for every pair to create their first card.

6. Cycle pairs through the Computer Center in 15- to 20-minute slots to work on their *PowerPoint* cards.

7. During the morning meeting or other sharing time, students present their topic to the class orally, using their *PowerPoint* stack as their visual aid and their guide.

Variations:

→ Students may give presentations to a larger audience of parents or other classes for practice.

→ Students may create a presentation in social studies or science.

Management Tips:

→ Have students work in pairs the first time they use *PowerPoint*, in order to accomplish more in a shorter time.

→ Prior to working on this project, it is a good idea to allow students to experiment with the program during a lab time or as a class project, with each student creating a card to retell one part of a familiar story.

→ Another good idea is to train student "experts" in using *PowerPoint*, then to pair the "experts" with less experienced students for the research project.

Word Processing: Weekly Classroom Bulletin

Purpose:

• Have students practice word processing.

• Help students write in clear, concise, organized language that varies in content and form for different audiences and purposes.

• Encourage students to publish information and share it with parents.

Materials:

• Computer.

• Word-processing software with newspaper-style template.

• Printer.

Activity:

1. Divide the class into groups of 7–10 students. Label each group with numbers, letters, or colors.

2. Assign students within each group to certain days of the week Monday through Friday. Assign each week to a different group.

3. During LAB wrap-up time, the students assigned to that week and day write a

brief article in a bulletin template about an activity they worked on. Articles may cover the entire day's activities, or may be limited to the LAB. The students are responsible for proofreading and spell-checking their work.

Variations:

→ Students can add clip art to articles.
→ Have students post the newest completed weekly bulletin on a classroom Web page.

Management Tips:

→ Each Friday before the end of the day, proofread the bulletin.
→ Friday's students are responsible for printing and distributing the bulletin to send home.
→ Keep a binder where each week's bulletin is saved, to remind the students of their favorite activities throughout the year.

Paint Drawings: Illustrating Stories

Purposes:

- Have students practice using the drawing tool on the computer.
- Teach students to insert drawings into a text program.
- Encourage students to publish writing.

Materials:

- Student-written work.
- Computer.
- Drawing software.
- Word-processing software.
- Color printer.

Activity:

1. Examine illustrations in picture books with the class. Discuss when and where illustrators place their illustrations in the text.
2. Instruct students to go back to a piece of completed work and locate two places where illustrations should be added.
3. During center work, allow students to word-process their selected piece. The first two time periods will be used for word processing.
4. Train a few student "experts" in how to open a new drawing document and how to operate each major tool. Let them draw their illustrations.
5. Show them how to cut and paste their illustrations into their completed text. Watch them practice this task.
6. During the next few center work times, have the student "experts" train small groups how to use the draw program.

7. Cycle students so that each student has two 15-minute slots to complete the illustrations and paste them into the text.

8. Have students print and publish the stories.

Variations:

→ Create one large class story or poem. Allow students to illustrate the work and to paste their illustrations on their individual copies.

→ Students may use the drawing program to illustrate historical events, math stories, science concepts, or foreign-language dictionaries.

READING WORKSHOP:
SCHEDULES, MINI-LESSONS, AND OTHER ACTIVITIES

The Reading Workshop is a block of time set aside for independent, whole-class, and small-group reading activities. Students work independently and in groups at their instructional levels, allowing you to meet each student's individual needs.

The Reading Workshop can begin with silent reading in self-selected materials or with a teacher read-aloud. Students may then move into more teacher-directed activities, either reading assigned portions of texts or applying skills taught previously. The Reading Workshop varies, depending upon the instructional purposes being addressed.

In a self-contained class, reading instruction usually takes place through direct teaching of procedures, skills, and strategies. Then students apply those procedures, skills, and strategies in appropriate texts. The highlight of the Reading Workshop is students' uninterrupted reading at their instructional level.

Reading Workshop Schedules

There are many ways that you may choose to schedule the Reading Workshop. Schedules depend upon matching the needs of the class with the instructional focus. Several suggested weekly Reading Workshop schedules are shown below:

- Option 1 is for use with whole-class instruction.
- Option 2 is for use with Literature Circles.
- Option 3 is for use with guided reading.
- Option 4 is for use with anthology or basal reading.

Option 1: Whole-Class Novels

Option 1 is for use with whole-class novels. It can also be used when you are instructing the class in the same skills and strategies while they are reading different materials based on their instructional needs. This option provides for student reading of assigned portions of texts (chapters, chunks, etc.); direct instruction and application of that instruction; discussion; written responses; and instruction in additional means and methods.

Time	Monday	Tuesday	Wednesday	Thursday	Friday
10 minutes	Silent reading or teacher read-aloud.	Silent reading or teacher read-aloud.	Silent reading or teacher read-aloud.	Silent reading or teacher read-aloud.	Silent reading or teacher read-aloud.
20–40 minutes	Mini-lesson; student application.	Review of Monday's mini-lesson and student application.	Student preparation for discussion.	Assign and discuss response for week's reading.	Sharing of student responses.
25–50 minutes	Student reading in assigned texts; application of mini-lesson.	Student reading in assigned texts; application of mini-lesson.	Student discussion.	Student preparation of response.	Instruction in guided reading; test preparation; content area work; or vocabulary work.

Option 2: Literature Circles

Option 2 works well when students are working in Literature Circles. In Literature Circles, student groups of four or five work together to prepare for discussion of reading materials. Each student has an assigned role that guides his or her reading and preparation for discussion. For example, a group may be composed of a Discussion Director, Word Wizard, Illustrator, Summarizer, and Passage Master. Because students have assigned roles, they work independently to read and prepare for discussion. However, there are times when students are working in Literature Circles that they need whole-class instruction. The following schedule allows for direct instruction; application of that instruction; independent reading; role sheet preparation; and discussion.

Time	Monday	Tuesday	Wednesday	Thursday	Friday
10 minutes	Silent reading or teacher read-aloud.	Silent reading or teacher read-aloud.	Silent reading or teacher read-aloud.	Silent reading or teacher read-aloud.	Silent reading or teacher read-aloud.
30–55 minutes	Students independently and in groups read their materials.	Students independently prepare for their roles in discussion.	15–20 minutes: Mini-lesson. 15–35 minutes: Student application of mini-lesson.	Student-led discussions and completion of self-evaluations.	15–20 minutes: Review of mini-lesson; discussion of mini-lesson. 15–35 minutes: Instruction in guided reading; test preparation; content area work; or vocabulary work.

Option 3: Guided Reading

Option 3 is designed to be used when reading instruction is provided via guided reading materials at students' instructional levels, and when direct instruction is delivered in a whole-class setting. Guided reading provides for the reading of multiple texts during the same time in which a class might read a whole novel. It also provides for students' reading in small groups at their instructional level, thus requiring that you spend time with multiple groups over the course of several days of the Reading Workshop. Thus planning for instruction must be approached differently.

Time	Monday	Tuesday	Wednesday	Thursday	Friday
10 minutes	Silent reading or teacher read-aloud.	Silent reading or teacher read-aloud.	Silent reading or teacher read-aloud.	Silent reading or teacher read-aloud.	Silent reading or teacher read-aloud.
30–55 minutes	Guided reading groups meet; teacher has conferences with individual students in these groups; other students work at centers or do other activities independently.	Guided reading groups meet; teacher has conferences with individual students in these groups; other students work at centers or do other activities independently.	15–20 minutes: Whole-class mini-lesson. 15–35 minutes: Whole-class application of mini-lesson.	Guided reading groups meet; Teacher has conferences with individual students in these groups; other students work at centers or do other activities independently.	15–20 minutes: Review of Wednesday's mini-lesson. 15–35 minutes: Instruction in guided reading; test preparation; content area work; or vocabulary work.

Option 4: Anthology or Basal Reading

Option 4 is for use with anthology or basal reading. Such reading may be done as a whole-class instructional component, or students may be broken into reading groups. The following schedule reflects the use of anthologies or basals when there are two reading groups in the class, each working on different materials and on different skills and strategies.

Time	Monday	Tuesday	Wednesday	Thursday	Friday
10 minutes	Silent reading or teacher read-aloud.	Silent reading or teacher read-aloud.	Silent reading or teacher read-aloud.	Silent reading or teacher read-aloud.	Silent reading or teacher read-aloud.
30-55 minutes	Meet with Group 1.	Meet with Group 2.	Vocabulary work.	Meet with Group 1.	Meet with Group 2.
30-55 minutes	Meet with Group 2.	Meet with Group 1.	Test preparation; content area work.	Meet with Group 2.	Meet with Group 1.

Reading Mini-Lessons

Many things help determine the sorts of mini-lessons that are done in a classroom. You will want to instruct students in the procedures for the various types of Reading Workshop groups and activities. You will want to provide direct instruction in the many skills that good readers use to comprehend text, genres, and vocabulary. And you will want to provide direct instruction in the broader strategies that competent readers use.

The procedures that may be addressed in mini-lessons include those to follow during independent reading, journal writing, Literature Circles, and so on. The first sample mini-lessons below provide the format of procedural mini-lessons. The needs of your class will dictate the other procedural lessons you will teach throughout the year.

There is a vast array of skills that students must acquire and use proficiently in order to become competent readers. These include predicting, summarizing, clarifying vocabulary, acquiring knowledge of story elements, and many others. The second and third provide the format of skill mini-lessons. The needs of your class will dictate the other skill lessons you will teach throughout the year.

There are also many broader strategies students must acquire as they become competent readers. They will need to learn to visualize, to make connections, and to question and reread. The fourth sample mini-lesson below provides the format of a strategy mini-lesson. The needs of your class will dictate the other strategy lessons you will teach throughout the year.

Sample Mini-Lesson in Procedures: Generating Discussion Behaviors

Purposes:

- Encourage students to listen actively in a variety of situations.
- Have students speak for a variety of real purposes and audiences.
- Establish a list of discussion behaviors that will be used for student self-evaluation and evaluation by you during class discussions.

Materials:

- Chart paper and markers, *or* white board/chalkboard and writing utensils.

Activity:

1. The students are seated, either around the easel and chart paper or at their seats.
2. Begin by announcing the topic for discussion: "Discussion Behaviors." This phrase should be placed either within a web or at the top of a list.
3. Elicit important discussion behaviors through questioning and encouraging students to reflect on their past experiences and knowledge of discussions.
4. A chart/list of student-generated discussion behaviors is created.
5. Then ask students to review the behaviors to determine which ones (five or six) are the most crucial for management of discussions.
6. These behaviors are highlighted.
7. The students are advised that these behaviors will become the basis for their self-evaluation and for evaluation by you during literature discussions.
8. Before the class's next discussion, prepare a discussion behavior form that is a checklist for student self-evaluation and comments and for your evaluation and comments. (Or use the form that follows.)
9. This evaluation form is shared with the students, and they complete one each time they have a discussion.

Variation:

- ➜ These can serve as the first of many self-evaluations the students do throughout the year.

Thematic Tie:

- ➜ When the class is practicing discussion behaviors in preparation for practice in a themed unit, have students take the roles of various characters who appear in their novels or in their nonfiction material.

Management Tips:

- ➜ Hang a chart in the classroom of the important discussion behaviors.
- ➜ Revisit the behaviors on a regular basis.
- ➜ Add new behaviors when necessary.

Discussion Evaluation Sheet

Name: _____

Discussion for: _____ Date: _____

Discussion behavior	Student	Teacher
Uses good manners		
Is prepared		
Stays on topic		
Listens carefully		

One thing I did well in discussion today is:

One thing I will work on next time we have discussion is:

Comments:

Remember to use polite interrupters:

    "I agree ... "

    "I'd like to add ... "

    "I disagree because ... "

    "Excuse me ... "

Sample Mini-Lesson in Skills: Completion of a Story Map and Written Retelling

Purposes:

- Teach students to use a story map to identify the elements of a story.
- Have students demonstrate comprehension through retelling.

Materials:

- Overhead projector and transparency with a blank story map.
- Copies of the blank story map for the students (see the form that follows).
- Chart paper and markers for generating a written retelling.

Activity:

1. The students are seated, either in the Story Corner (or Library Corner, Book Nook, or whatever this area is called) or at their seats.
2. Read aloud a picture book that has well-established characters, setting, problem, solution, obstacles, and events.
3. After the read-aloud, the class discusses the story.
4. Have the students return to their seats, and quickly generate a web on the chalkboard/white board that illustrates their knowledge of the story elements.
5. A blank story map is placed on the overhead projector.
6. The students are asked to help complete the story map for the read-aloud.
7. Once that is complete, model for the students how to use a story map to create a written retelling of the story.
8. The next day, read aloud another story with clear characters, setting, and so forth.
9. Then give the students copies of the blank story map and have them complete these in groups.
10. Each group works together to complete a group written retelling.
11. These are shared with the class.

This lesson will require 2 days to complete. At this point, depending upon the level of the class, written retellings may be added to the students' repertoires of responses to literature. If additional practice is required, the lesson should be repeated.

Variations:

→ Retellings may be used to assess comprehension.
→ Oral retellings may be generated instead of written ones.
→ The students may act out the story.

Thematic Tie:

→ Practice doing retellings using short stories with content that matches the area of study.

Story Map

Name: _____ Date: _____

Title: _____

Chapters: _____

Characters (and what you learned about them):

Setting(s) (time and place):

Opening event:

Other events (rising action):

Closing events:

Sample Mini-Lesson in Skills: Vocabulary

Purposes:

- Have students use context clues to determine the meaning of unfamiliar words.
- Teach students how and when to use a dictionary while reading.

Materials:

- A photocopied *short* story (no longer than three pages) for each student in the class. (The children will be writing directly on the story.)
- Highlighters.
- Dictionaries.
- Pens/pencils.
- Word-tracking sheet (see the form that follows).
- Enlarged computer screen or overhead projector.

Activity:

1. Using the computer screen or overhead, read aloud the first few paragraphs of a short story. (If every child is working with the same story, use that as a model; if not, select one that all the children can understand.)
2. While reading, highlight "challenge words."
3. Model how to use clues in the story to help identify the meaning of the challenge words. For example, if you read the sentence "The bobolink, holding an insect in its beak, flew toward the nest," highlight *bobolink* as a challenge word and then point to *beak, flew,* and *nest* as clues that a bobolink is a type of bird. Note that this is all the class needs to know for now, and the students can continue reading without knowing what a bobolink looks like. The students will be asked to look for further "clues" in the text that give additional information about the challenge word.
4. Now explain that sometimes a story doesn't offer enough clues to help us figure a word out. If the word is not necessary to understand the story, then a student should simply highlight the word and look it up later. If the word or words is interfering with comprehension, however, then the student must stop to "check it out" in the dictionary.
5. The students continue the activity on their own, highlighting as they are reading.
6. After completing the story, students complete the Challenge Words sheet to record which words were new to them and what clues they used to "figure it all out."
7. Students can check their "Assumed" definitions with the dictionary definitions to see how close they were.
8. After the independent work, pairs of students reading the same story meet and share experiences as well as the "new words" they learned.
9. As a culminating activity, the class meets as a whole and shares the new vocabulary the students have found individually and with their partners.

Variations:

→ The Challenge Words sheet should only be used when students are developing this skill. As students become increasingly proficient in identifying the "clues," they shouldn't need this form.

→ This activity can extend to content area texts. A social studies, science, or math article offers many challenge words. This activity can be used repeatedly to help children in these content areas.

→ Children can keep individual word boxes so that both you and they can monitor their vocabulary development.

→ Children should be encouraged to incorporate these words into their writing as further reinforcement.

→ A wall of "new and interesting words" can be kept in the classroom. Students should be encouraged to display interesting vocabulary along with its definition and sentence.

Thematic Tie:

→ When possible, use text that is connected to the current theme of study. For example, if the theme is "Conflict," select reading materials that have something to do with this theme for vocabulary activities.

Name: _____ Date: _____

Use your reading detective skills to "figure it all out." When all else fails, however, remember that the dictionary is your willing assistant through the mystery of reading!

Challenge word	My meaning	Clues that helped me "figure it all out"	Dictionary definition . . . is it a match?

Sample Mini-Lesson in Strategies: Visualizing

Purposes:

- Have students demonstrate comprehension through pictures.
- Teach students to apply visualizing techniques.

Materials:

- A passage or story to be read aloud that contains vivid descriptive sections.
- Chalkboard, white board, or easel and chart paper for recording student ideas.
- Art supplies.

Activity:

1. The students are seated, either around the easel and chart paper or at their seats.
2. Begin the lesson by writing the word *visualizing* on the board or chart paper.
3. Elicit student knowledge of visualizing and webs, or list the student responses.
4. Draw the students' attention to the root word, *visual.* Discuss its meaning and connects it to the meaning of *visualizing.*
5. Tell the students that they are to listen carefully to the read-aloud passage or story.
6. Read aloud.
7. The students return to their seats and illustrate their interpretation of the passage.
8. The students share their artwork.
9. A discussion of the similarities and differences in the class's interpretations is held.

Variations:

→ Students apply visualizing to material they are currently reading.
→ This lesson becomes the basis for the Illustrator or Artist Role in Literature Circles.
→ Visualizing becomes a response selection for literature throughout the year, and students are asked to add to their artwork the book's title, author, and specific written information about the passage that was illustrated (including the section of the text, why it was chosen, and why it is important to the story).

Thematic Tie:

→ When the class is practicing visualizing, select a short story or news article that connects to the theme of study. These practice pieces can become part of a classroom bulletin board based on the unit.

Management Tip:

→ The mini-lesson is repeated as needed.

Reading Responses Using Buddy Journals

Purposes:

- Encourage students to listen and respond to whole texts.
- Have students practice a variety of literary skills, including drawing conclusions, making inferences and predictions, sequencing, and following character development.
- Help students use prior knowledge to link text with personal experiences.

Materials:

- Two copies of the same reading selection per buddy pair.
- Pencils.
- Journal (constructed of stapled blank paper, composition or spiral notebook, loose-leaf paper and binder, etc.) for each pair of students.

Activity:

1. Students (and/or you; see "Variations") agree to read a certain number of pages, chapters, articles, or stories by a particular deadline.
2. After reading, one student records his or her personal reactions and reflections to the selection.
3. A second passage is agreed upon and read by both students.
4. In the journal, the second partner responds to the first student's comments and reacts to the second reading section.
5. Upon completion of the reading material, the partners work together on a culminating project or activity based on their written responses in the buddy journal.

Variation:

➜ Buddy journals may be kept as individual student journals that may be responded to by you or, on occasion, parents.

Thematic Tie:

➜ When possible, connect reading selections to themes of study. For example, if the class is studying the American Revolution, assign historical roles to the buddies. One can be a Tory, and the other can be a pro-American colonist.

Management Tip:

➜ You may want to guide the students to answer a broad, open-ended question about each selection.

Independent Work at Centers

In the third- and fourth-grade Reading Workshop, independent work at centers is used mainly to provide culminating practice for the skills and strategies students learn in mini-lessons. As Chapters 4 and 6 have described in much greater detail, this type of work is done by small clusters of students (three or four per center), working individually or as small groups on a rotating basis. Possible activities at centers for third- and fourth-grade students might include making puppets to represent literary characters, writing a letter to a character, listening to a story on tape, or creating part of a roll movie. When possible, activities at centers should unite one study theme, but (as noted above) their primary purpose should be skill/strategy reinforcement. The time allotted for center work in the Reading Workshop will vary, depending on the activities offered at the different centers, but ideally students should visit two centers per day. When a longer block of time is needed for more in-depth study or for the completion of detailed activities, some students may only be able to work at one center per day.

Purposes:

- Allow students to participate in individual or small-group literary activities.
- Enable students to complete one part of a whole activity and act as members of teams.
- Have students use reading and writing for a variety of purposes.

Materials:

- Materials will vary at each center.

Procedure:

1. In different areas of the classroom, set up materials and direction cards for each center (or activity within a center). See Chapters 4 and 6 for detailed instructions.
2. Decide which students will visit which centers each day, and set up a time guideline.
3. Assign students with varying abilities and interests to a starting center. Students will stay in these groups as they move through each center.
4. Set a time limit for completing each round of center work.
5. Once all students have worked at centers each day, bring students together for a wrap-up session. Students may perform a play, retell a story, or share their experiences.

Variation:

➜ Develop Learning Centers (i.e., content area centers where art, math, science, and social studies skills are reinforced; see Chapter One).

Thematic Ties:

➜ Tie center work in with the current theme of study.
➜ If you are reinforcing research skills, have students use nonfiction materials to make connections with the unit of study.

Management Tips:

→ If there are many children who need to cycle through a center or activity, create two of the same centers or activities to keep group numbers small.

→ If there is work to be handed in, place bins in the center areas or indicate spaces where students are to submit their work.

Scheduling Possibilities for Center Work and Other Independent Activities:

The diagram below illustrates how four different groups of students might be rotated among work at two different centers and two other types of independent activities (see "Independent Activities for Reading/Writing Workshops . . . ," above). Guided reading groups formed on the basis of students' abilities and needs would be periodically called out of these groups.

Group 1	Center 1	Center 2	Independent reading	Journal writing, etc.
Group 2	Journal writing, etc.	Center 1	Center 2	Independent reading
Group 3	Independent reading	Journal writing, etc.	Center 1	Center 2
Group 4	Center 2	Independent reading	Journal writing, etc.	Center 1

READING WORKSHOP: GUIDED READING

Guided reading is a time to instruct small groups of children in reading at their instructional level while focusing on one individual student at a time. A variety of texts may be used—from basals to novels to short stories. To organize guided reading, needs are assessed, groups are formed based on need, and appropriate materials are selected to address these needs. Each guided reading group should meet for about 20 minutes, for a total of about 60 minutes if you meet with three groups each day.

Grouping for Guided Reading

Purposes:

• Provide flexible grouping for children who are reading at a similar text level and who have similar instructional needs.

• Have students read and respond to a diversity of materials and texts in discussion and writing.

Materials:

• Running records. (See Chapter Six for a detailed description of these.)
• Observational notes.
• Recommendations from faculty members (reading specialists, students' earlier teachers).

Activity:

1. Guided reading is one of the only times children are homogeneously grouped. These need-based groups, however, are different from traditional reading groups. Children grouped for guided reading do not read a fixed sequence of books. Texts are chosen for their appropriateness for the group.

2. The number of guided reading groups in a particular classroom will vary, depending on the range of student ability. A typical reading classroom has between four and six groups. A guided reading group with no more than five or six children seems to be the most manageable. The lowest-ability groups should contain no more than four students.

3. Children are placed in guided reading groups based on the results of running records taken on leveled books and on your observational notations. If leveled books are not accessible at your students' ability level, evaluate the book based on length of story and chapters, size of print, number of words on a page, and difficulty of concepts and vocabulary presented. The groups are dynamic and are expected to change as the students' needs change.

4. You should aim to meet with three groups each day, depending on scheduling. The lowest-ability groups should be seen daily. A different child should sit next to you for each lesson; this will be the focus child on that day.

Assessing Students for Guided Reading

Purposes:

- Determine the appropriate group, materials, and instructional needs for each child.
- Measure children's progress throughout the year.
- Have children read and respond to a diversity of materials.

Materials:

Multiple assessment measures, including (but not restricted to) the following:

- Running records.
- Story-retelling test.
- Observational notes.
- Standardized tests.
- Independent reading selections.

Activity:

1. In the beginning of the school year, observe and evaluate each child, using some form of measure (running records, previous school year reports, reading habits, etc.). This will help you determine the appropriate group, materials, and instructional needs for each child.

2. Assess students during the school year on a regular basis. This can be accomplished during guided reading groups or independently. During each guided reading group, you can focus on one child while working with the whole group.

Thematic Tie:

→ Select a variety of reading material based on the same themes ("Friendship," "community," etc.), so that other areas of the LAB for all students have a common thread.

Management Tip:

→ Take a running record on one child from each reading group every day. (Use the running record form that follows: Or, if you prefer, use the more elaborate form provided in Chapter Six.)

Running Record Form

Name: _____   Date: _____

Book title: _____   Reading level: _____

Miscue record:

Comments/observations:

Fluency notes:

Score: _____

Selecting Materials for Small-Group Instruction

Purposes:

- Meet the instructional needs of every child.

Materials:

- Multiple copies of a variety of multileveled basals, novels, short stories, anthologies, and so on.

Activity:

1. Select the appropriate material for each guided reading group based on your assessment of students' needs.
2. The reading material must be carefully chosen to match the instructional level of the students. The children should be able to read the text with 90–95% accuracy. A cloze activity is helpful in determining this rate. When every fifth word is extracted from a 100-word passage, a student should be able to fill in 44–57% of the blanks exactly correctly without prior exposure to the material.

Guided Reading Instruction

Purposes:

- Have students use problem-solving strategies to figure out new words while reading for meaning.
- Help students use independent reading strategies.
- Have students demonstrate comprehension of text through discussion and writing.

Materials:

- Individual copies of texts, including one teacher's copy.
- Literature log or notebook for each student and one teacher's copy.
- Pencil.
- Teacher white board, chalkboard, or easel.
- Marker.
- Records for observational note taking.
- Assessment tool (running record).

Activity:

Before the reading:

1. Select an appropriately leveled book for the guided reading group. The selected book should match each reader's needs.
2. Before you introduce a new book, story, or chapter to the students in the group, they will read something familiar for fluency (a small section of a previously read page or a picture book used for instruction in writing, for example). Either

the students can read the familiar selection together, or one child can read the whole book aloud to the group.

3. Next, preview the new section of literature. The goal is to entice the students to read the next section or chapter and relate it to their own experiences. Discuss the chapter title and give a one-sentence synopsis of the chapter.

4. The group discusses predictions based on the chapter title, synopsis, and illustrations (if any) of the events in the story, and ask questions.

5. During the reading, focus on one child for assessment purposes, as suggested earlier. A different child will be chosen during each lesson. You can take a running record on a child during the rereading of the story.

During the reading:

1. Students read the passage silently to themselves. Use a silent signal to indicate which student will "whisper-read" so you can listen for processing and fluency. Take notes on the reading strategies the children are using. These strategies are highlighted as teaching points after the reading.

2. The students in the group should be able to read the story at about the same rate and level of success.

After the reading:

1. The group discusses the chapter. Encourage students to ask questions, to offer comments, and to give opinions. When the group discusses the story, you should be able to determine how well the students comprehended the passage.

2. Next, teach a lesson focusing on a skill difficult to this group of readers (sequencing, character analysis). The students may record information in their literature logs as notes for a related reading assignment/guided work.

3. Ask students to write a personal response to the chapter. The teacher should also write as a model for the students. If time permits, have students share responses with a partner or one at a time with the group.

4. Before the students leave the group, assign a short activity to be completed in less than 20 minutes relating to the lesson's reinforced skill.

Sample Guided Reading Lesson

Purposes:

- Help students use and develop reading strategies when reading unfamiliar text.
- Help students become successful independent readers.
- Have students practice fluent reading.

Materials:

- Multiple copies of *The Chalk Box Kid* (Bulla, 1987).
- Literature logs.
- Teacher white board.
- Running records.

Activity:

Before the reading:

1. Have the students reread a familiar section of the story that was identified during the previous lesson as one student's favorite part. It can be read aloud by that student or as a choral reading (with you joining in).
2. Fluency can be assessed with a running record on an individual student.
3. The students discuss new words discovered in the next chapter during a vocabulary search. Take notes while students share information.
4. Now introduce the next chapter of the book by reading aloud the chapter title. Take the students on a picture walk of the chapter, eliciting predictions of events occurring on these pages.

During the reading:

1. Take notes on strategies the students are using while "whisper reading," to be used as teaching points after the reading.

After the reading:

1. The group discusses the story. Students will talk about predictions they have made, ask questions, and form opinions.
2. Students will write responses to their reading in their literature logs.
3. Next, use the chapter to teach a skill. For example, focus on a comparison and contrast of character traits between the main character, Gregory, and a classmate, Ivy. Instruction will include usage of a Venn diagram as an organizational tool.
4. Students will start their Venn diagrams of Gregory and Ivy together as a group and finish them either as an independent activity or for homework.

Variation:

➜ After teaching this skill to all guided reading groups, use this concept as an independent activity—comparing and contrasting characters from different novels, classmates, or important people related to the classroom theme.

Guided Reading Evaluation

Purposes:

- Evaluate students' immediate reading needs.
- Observe students' skills and strategies while they read a variety of materials and texts.

Materials:

- A copy of the same written material (novels, short stories, etc.) for each student in the group.
- Teacher notebook.
- An evaluation form (see the form that follows).

Activity:

1. While the rest of the class is involved in independent work at centers or other independent activities, call one of the small guided reading groups as usual.
2. With shared literature, ask students to take turns practicing a previously taught focus skill or strategy.
3. Take notes on one or two specific students, selected prior to calling the guided reading group. Evaluate only those students selected, but allow all students to practice the given skill or strategy.
4. During each meeting time, repeat this process until each student has been observed and evaluated on the particular skill or strategy.

Management Tips:

→ Set up the teacher notebook with prenamed sticky notes, to save time while working with students. The sticky notes can then be rearranged alphabetically into the notebook on separate pages for each student.

→ Until you have established a comfort level in working with flexible guided reading groups, tape-record evaluation sessions to review your recorded observations.

Guided Reading Evaluation Form

Date: _____

Skill or strategy: _____

| Student | Evaluation/observations |

1.   1.

2.   2.

3.   3.

4.   4.

5.   5.

6.   6.

WRITING WORKSHOP

The Writing Workshop is a block of time (approximately 55 minutes) set aside for writing activities. Students work independently, in small groups, and as a whole class at appropriate instructional levels, allowing you to meet each student's individual needs.

Workshop time includes a writing mini-lesson, allowing opportunities for you to meet the specific needs of the students. Choosing to present a lesson individually, within a small group, or as a whole class depends upon the needs of the children.

Workshop time should be used for all the writing genres.

Writing Workshop: General Format

Purposes:

- Have students write in a variety of forms for different audiences and purposes.
- Use student work to develop writing procedures, skills, and strategies.
- Help students to connect *reading* to *writing*.

Materials:

- Folder for each student.
- Paper.
- Pencils.
- Markers, crayons, etc.
- Materials to bind work.
- Contest information board.

Activity:

1. Design a mini-lesson based on needs identified through student writing. The writing task may be connected to the mini-lesson introduced earlier that day or perhaps the day before (e.g., writing an individual description, an individual how-to paragraph, etc.). *Using texts students are working with during Reading Workshop time as a model helps students understand the connection between reading and writing. In addition, it provides a meaningful transition between the Reading and Writing Workshop.*
2. Model and review the assignment before students begin.
3. As students work, meet with individual students or small groups of students based on need. For example, if several students are having difficulty understanding topic sentences, bring them together and use the students' writing to model how to develop a topic sentence.
4. As students finish the writing task and revise their work, they may have conferences with other students.
5. Students may then work on independently developed pieces or contest submissions. Display information on current writing contests for students to see and

consider entering—newspaper contests, those sponsored by student magazines, school contests, Internet contests, and so forth.

6. Students may also work on previous "work in progress" pieces.
7. Students are encouraged to share excerpts from the writing they completed during the workshop session, reading from the Author's Chair.

Variations:

→ Some sessions may have students select their own topics. Each session does not have to be teacher-directed or teacher-initiated.
→ Providing editing sheets or rubrics for the teacher-initiated writing pieces can help students. (See the first and second forms that follow below.)
→ The different genres of writing should be explored in the Writing Workshop: descriptive, narrative, expository, and persuasive.
→ Writing skills can be reinforced during center work.
→ It is important to recognize that while Workshop time can be used for teacher-directed pieces, it also should be a time for student-generated writing.
→ When possible, students should write on the computer.
→ Workshop time can be used for content area writing. For example, students can be taught how to write an "observation" of a science lab.

Thematic Tie:

→ Use the theme of study to motivate writing topics. For example, if the class is studying emotions, children can be encouraged to include a description of an emotion in their writing. Or they can write narratives about a time they felt excited, unhappy, angry, or the like.

Management Tips:

→ Establish guidelines for the number of writing pieces that need to be brought to final copy. For example, you might require one piece a week to be brought to final copy; or you might require three a month (two that are teacher-initiated, one that is student-initiated).
→ Keep a class chart to record writing progress on specific pieces.
→ Students should be reminded of the steps in the writing process during the introduction of each assignment. (See the outline of these steps for students' use, provided later in this part of the chapter.)

Responding to Writing

Purposes:

• Establish and use criteria for self-evaluation and group evaluation of written products.
• Enable students to hold conferences with you.
• Have students speak to peers constructively to improve writing pieces.

Materials:

- Writing folder.
- At least one work in progress.
- Pens and pencils.
- Paper.
- An editing sheet or rubric (see the first and second forms that follow).
- Checklist of "things learned" (see the third form that follows).

Activity:

Responding to each other's writing improves children's oral communication skills and helps them edit their own writing. Reflection about works in progress during conferences with you also helps children learn to edit their own work.

1. After students have revised their pieces, they edit them with partners.
2. Partners use an editing sheet or a rubric to help them edit each other's papers.
3. The author and editor discuss their findings.
4. The author continues editing, keeping the editor's evaluation in mind.
5. After editing, the students meet with you. Each student should bring his or her own piece and the editing sheet or rubric completed by the partner.
6. Use this opportunity to help students edit these specific pieces, and to reinforce their strengths and to improve their weaknesses in general. Expectations will vary according to each child's ability.
7. A checklist, kept in each student's writing folder, is used to record procedures, skills, and strategies discussed during the conference. This serves as a reference for both the child and you of what is expected in the student's writing.
8. Students bring their pieces to final copy.

Thematic Tie:

➜ When writing is connected to the theme of study, peer editors should be asked to look for that theme in the writing and evaluate how successful their partners are in developing that theme.

Management Tips:

➜ Peer editing should be modeled extensively by you before you "turn it over" to the students.
➜ Take the students through the entire process, using overheads (or, if possible, modeling an actual conference with another teacher, or a student).

Editing Sheet

Name: _____ Partner's name: _____

Piece to be edited: _____

Ratings: 5 = highest possible rating; 1 = lowest possible rating

Questions	Rating	Comments
Is it interesting?	_____	_____
Is there one topic?	_____	_____
Is there enough detail?	_____	_____
Is there a beginning?	_____	_____
Is there a middle?	_____	_____
Is there an end?	_____	_____
Do the sentences make sense?	_____	_____

Optional:

Does it connect to the current class theme? _____ _____

Last words:

Rubric

Name: _____ Partner's name: _____

Piece to be edited: _____

Ratings: 5 = always; 4 = most of the time; 3 = sometimes;
2 = rarely; 1 = never.

Category	Rating	Comments
The writer stays on topic.	_____	_____
The writer uses supporting detail.	_____	_____
The writer is aware of his or her audience.	_____	_____
The opening clearly introduces the topic of the piece.	_____	_____
The middle clearly explains the topic of the piece.	_____	_____
The conclusion clearly summarizes the main points of the piece and offers the writer's thoughts about the topic.	_____	_____
The sentences are clear.	_____	_____
Correct capitalization, spelling, usage, and punctuation are used.	_____	_____
Total score/general comments	_____	_____

Individual Writer's Checklist

Name: _____

Date of conference	Lessons learned . . .

Writing Mini-Lessons

Sample Mini-Lesson in Procedures: The Writing Process

Purposes:

- Introduce students to the procedures in the writing process.
- Connect the procedures in writing to steps in mastering something that students enjoy.

Materials:

- Large chart paper.
- Journal paper.
- Writing process chart (a large version, plus smaller copies for students—see the form that follows).

Activity:

1. Ask students to write in their journals about something they do well that took a while to learn (competing in a sport, playing a musical instrument, etc.). Students should not only describe *what* they learned, but also *how* they learned it.
2. Discuss responses. Engage students in a discussion about making mistakes in the beginning, working with others to help correct difficulties, and so on.
3. Explain that this is very much like the writing process. As the discussion of the "steps" students experienced continues, take students through the "steps" of the writing process. Record connections on large chart paper.
4. Finally, describe the steps the students will take with most of their writing pieces, and distribute copies of a list of these steps (again, see the form that follows).
5. Students begin their first writing piece directly after this mini-lesson.

Variations:

- ➜ Connect the steps of the writing process to a science lab, so students can see that the content areas require thoughtful reasoning and procedures.
- ➜ An overhead transparency of the steps a student went through to reach final copy can be prepared to share.
- ➜ Additional procedural lessons can focus on each of the steps in the process more closely (modeling conferences, teaching various editing symbols, modeling how to submit work to a contest, etc.).
- ➜ Read-alouds about authors' writing experiences, as well as authors' autobiographies, are useful resources.
- ➜ When possible, invite authors to your class to speak about the craft of writing and the experience of being a writer.
- ➜ *PowerPoint/Hyperstudio* can be utilized for the presentation.

Thematic Tie:

→ The procedural mini-lesson should be connected to the current theme of study whenever possible. For example, if the class is studying "Growing Up," then the different stages in a person's life could be connected to the writing process.

Management Tips:

→ Introduce the writing process early in the year.
→ Display the large chart with the steps of the writing process in a prominent spot in the classroom.

Procedures of the Writing Process

BRAINSTORMING (PREWRITING)

- Begin listing ideas that you would like to write about.
- Or ... make a web of everything you can think of about a topic that you either want to write about or have been assigned.

DRAFTING

- Let's get going with the writing ... take one of your favorite brainstorming ideas and begin writing about it!
- Don't let your pen leave the paper! Don't ignore good writing, but don't focus on the mechanics too much. We will worry about the "fine-tuning" later.
- Write everything that comes to mind.

REVISING

- Once you have something written, read it to yourself.
- Decide what you want to keep, throw out, and add.

CONFERENCING

- Now that you know what you think about the piece, it is time to get someone else's opinion.
- Meet with either a friend or a teacher. Have him or her read your piece and tell you what is good, and what still can be made better.

EDITING

- Now that another pair of eyes has seen your piece, we can begin fine-tuning it.
- Make corrections, keeping your own revisions and conferencing session in mind.
- Read your piece aloud to help find missing words, punctuation errors, and so on.

FINAL COPY/PUBLISHING

- The end is in sight! Now it's time to present your polished piece.
- Neatly type or write your final piece to submit for publication.
- "Publication" can mean submitting your piece for a contest, for class sharing and display, and/or for teacher evaluation.

Sample Mini-Lesson in Skills: Sequencing

Purposes:

- Help students write in clear, concise, and organized language.
- Teach students to edit work for correct sequence of ideas.

Materials:

- Laminated comic strips, cut up, in envelopes.
- Overhead transparencies of writing that is "out of order" (see the two samples that follow).
- "Paragraph puzzles"—cut-up paragraphs that need to be put back together.

Activity:

1. Distribute "comic envelopes"—envelopes with comic strips cut up by frame —to students working in partners.
2. Partners work to put the pieces back together.
3. Discuss what students needed to do to figure out what went first, second, and so on. Discuss picture and text cues that helped organize the information.
4. Explain that this is "sequencing," keeping things in order—and it is something to pay careful attention to in writing.
5. Display an overhead transparency of an "out-of-order" piece of writing. As a class, with you modeling each step, discuss what to do to "fix" the piece (i.e., what sentences need to be moved, removed, words added, etc.).
6. Distribute "paragraph puzzles" for students to put back together.
7. Each student puts his or her "paragraph puzzle" in correct sequential order.
8. Share outcomes with the class. Note similarities/differences in putting the pieces back together.

Variations:

→ Students can be asked to write "how-to" pieces (a paragraph or so explaining how to complete something). These can then be shared with partners. Each partner tries to complete the task, using his or her partner's "how-to" paragraph.

→ Additional skill lessons can include focusing on frequent mechanical errors (e.g., when to use a comma), was to write a paragraph, grammar lessons based on errors found in students' writing, and so forth.

→ This is an opportunity to connect reading to writing—use students' reading as a resource for skill instruction.

Thematic Tie:

→ When possible, the sequencing mini-lesson should be connected to the theme of study. For example, if the current theme is "Favorites," strips about this topic should be used.

Sample "Out-of-Order" Paragraphs for Overhead Projection

OUT OF ORDER . . . HOW ARE WE GOING TO FIX IT?

I love the fall. It is my favorite season. I can't wait for summer. I like summer too. The four seasons are good and bad. When the leaves change, it's lots of fun to jump in them. Soon it is my birthday. We had lots of homework last night. The fall fair is soon, and I hope I will be outside working in one of the booths. I wonder what winter will be like. The pool feels good on a hot day.

OUT OF ORDER . . . HOW ARE WE GOING TO FIX IT?

I play the piano and violin. Collecting stickers is fun. I have lots of hobbies. My favorite subject is language arts. I like to read books. I ride bikes with my friends. I wish I didn't have so many chores at home. I think everyone should have hobbies. Math is hard for me. I also like to play computer games.

Sample Mini-Lesson in Strategies: Descriptive Writing and Revising

Purposes:

- Show students how to use figurative language and description to expand meaning.
- Connect the strategy of visualizing during reading to writing.
- Help students revise content, organization, and other aspects of writing.

Materials:

- Paper.
- Pencils.
- Cotton balls.
- Chart paper.

Activity:

1. Ask students to write a description of a cotton ball.
2. Discuss how people see the world. Talk about the five senses. List them on chart paper as questions.
3. Distribute cotton balls.
4. Individually or with a partner, students record all the sense words that come to mind.
5. Share words with the class.
6. Model how to turn these words into sentences.
7. Student partners continue writing descriptive sentences of the cotton balls.
8. Compare original sentences with newly authored ones.
9. Discuss differences. Note that the newer ones provide a clearer picture for the reader because of the descriptive words used.
10. Students revise earlier sentences, keeping this new strategy of adding description in mind.

Variations:

→ This activity can be extended to a "writing walk." Students go for a walk outside or around the building and select one thing to describe. They use a question sheet (see the form that follows) as a writing organizer. Students then write a description, and the rest of the class can "guess" what they are describing.

→ Students should be held responsible for this and other strategies in their Writing Workshop activities.

→ Other strategies to be introduced include using linking words in writing, writing to explain versus to persuade, writing speeches, and so forth.

→ Projecting the computer screen to a large area is a useful technique for students to see how quickly language becomes interesting when description is included.

You can type students' ideas directly onto the computer as a model for this approach to writing.

Thematic Tie:

→ As a follow-up, students can apply the strategy learned to a writing piece centered on the current theme of study. For example, if the theme is "nature," students can write a descriptive piece about some element of nature they have observed or studied.

What does it look like?

What does it sound like?

What does it smell like?

What does it taste like?

What does it feel like?

Author's Chair

Purposes:

- Develop pride in student writing.
- Generate ideas on writing topics.

Materials:

- Specially labeled chair in the classroom.
- Student writing volunteered to be read by the author.
- Student audience.

Activity:

1. Have students gather around the chair.
2. Ask for volunteers to share their writing pieces. A piece may have been completed through the writing process or may be in a draft stage.
3. One child reads from the Author's Chair at a time.
4. After each child has read, he or she calls upon two or three peers to comment on a positive aspect of the writing.
5. You should also periodically share your own writing in the Author's Chair.
6. End the sharing session by asking for volunteers for the following Author's Chair.

Management Tips:

➜ Select two or three students per Author's Chair session, depending on the length of the pieces and on scheduling.
➜ Model appropriate comments for the students to offer their peers:

- "I love the way you described . . . "
- "I wonder why the character . . . "
- "I think the story would be easier to understand if . . . "
- "Could you add some more description to . . . "

MAKING CONNECTIONS BETWEEN LANGUAGE ARTS AND CONTENT AREAS

All good things must come to an end. When the LAB is over, students may move on to other subject areas, break for lunch, or participate in a special area class. They may be regrouped to accommodate varying ability levels in the classroom. These groups may practice language arts skills and strategies even when beginning a content area subject. Possible activities may include vocabulary enrichment, journal writing pertinent to the content area, reading a schedule of activities and necessary materials, or working on a problem of the day. For additional ideas, see "Content-Area-Related Activities" under "Independent Activities for Reading/Writing Workshops . . . ," earlier in this chapter.

All subject areas have links to reading and writing. Regular connections to the content areas provide meaningful practice of reading and writing skills. Students should learn to use textbooks as a resource and a reference. They may need instruction on how to use and respond to these materials. This teaching may be done through the content area subjects or during the LAB as either Reading or Writing Workshop lessons. (In the LAB, such lessons should last about 15 minutes.) In addition, an abundance of science, social studies, and math read-aloud materials should be used to introduce new concepts and reinforce old ones.

SQ3R Reading Strategy

"SQ3R," or "Survey, Question, Read, Recite, Review," is one of many effective strategies for comprehending nonfiction text. Teaching students such strategies will give them a solid foundation on which to build year after year.

Purposes:

- Help students develop strategies for comprehending nonfiction reading material.
- Encourage students to make personal connections to information, aiding recall of facts.
- Have students practice reviewing small chunks of material at a time in a repetitive fashion.

Materials:

- Textbook.
- Paper.
- Pencil.

Activity:

1. Select a chapter or section of a textbook for the children to read.
2. *Survey*: Students take note of any illustrations, diagrams, chapter titles and headings, vocabulary, time lines, or the like within the passage.
3. *Question*: Students record a relevant question that will be answered after they have read the passage.
4. *Read*: One student reads the passage, aloud, or students read it silently.
5. *Recite*: Students discuss the factual information gained in the text.
6. *Review*: Students review the information read by answering their posed question in writing.

Variation:

→ Teach and practice other reading comprehension strategies, such as highlighting important information, using self-stick notes to indicate critical ideas, and turning headings of sections into questions as an oral review.

Using Content-Area-Related Reading Picture Books

There are many books that bring content area information to life. Picture books can be used to infuse subject area concepts into everyday reading. Listening to adults read stories increases oral comprehension and improves students' expression when they read aloud. Hearing content area topics addressed in published literature also increases the meaning of these topics for students.

Purposes:

- Connect reading and the content areas.
- Have students listen for a variety of purposes, such as enjoyment and obtaining information.

Materials:

- Fiction or nonfiction picture storybooks relating to the content area and the current theme of study.

Activity:

1. Regularly read storybooks to introduce or reinforce information or concepts.
2. Before reading, assess students' prior knowledge. One possible structure might be a "K-W-L" chart.
3. During reading, stop and ask comprehension questions for students to answer.
4. During reading, stop and use "think-alouds" to explain how you are connecting information in the storybook to the content area under study.
5. After reading, review important concepts or events in the story. Complete more of the K-W-L chart.

Variations:

- → Have students use a T-chart, Venn diagram, or other comparison tool to reflect on similarities and differences between the story and factual information from the appropriate content area textbook.
- → Have students search for content-related vocabulary in the story. Review meanings for these words.
- → Students may write a chronological bullet summary of important events in the story.

APPENDICES

APPENDIX A

Icons for a Center/Activity Chart

LITERACY CENTER

MATH CENTER

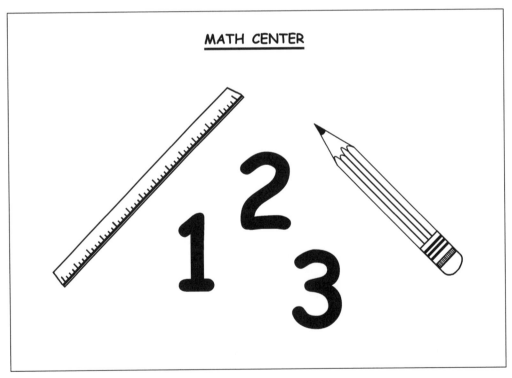

SOCIAL STUDIES CENTER

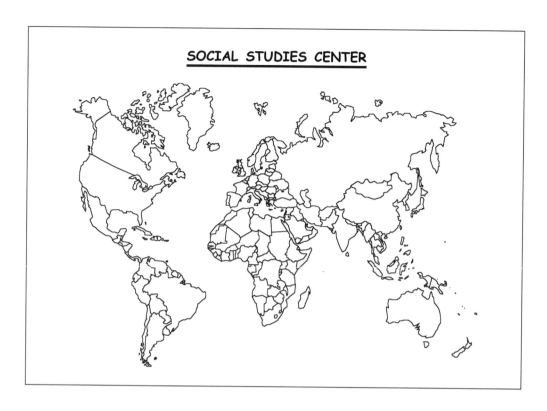

SCIENCE CENTER

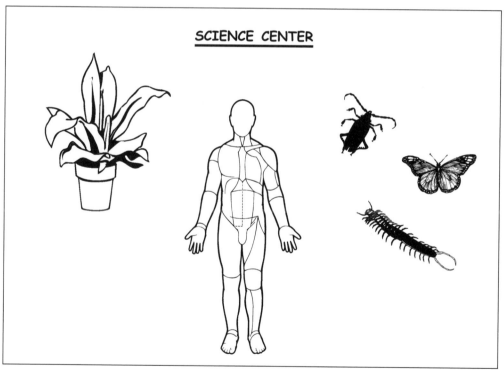

ART CENTER

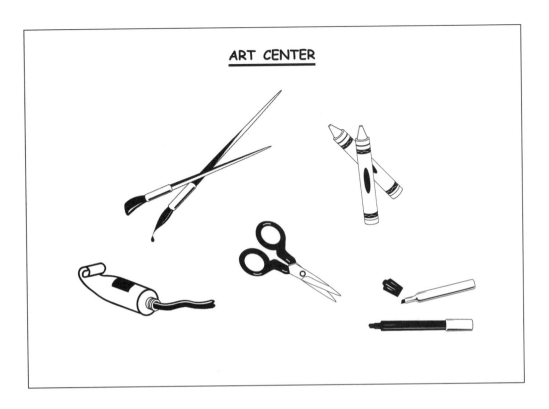

WRITING CENTER

COMPUTER CENTER

TECHNOLOGY CENTER

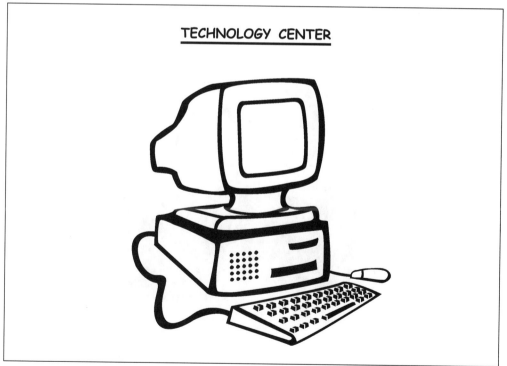

AUTHOR'S CORNER

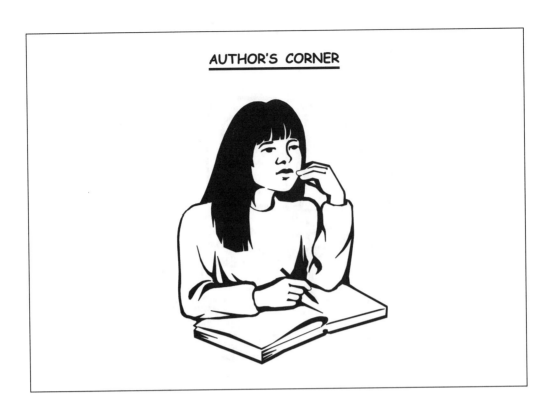

BUDDY READING

OVERHEAD PROJECTION CENTER

LISTENING STATION

LETTER STUDY CENTER

POCKET CHART

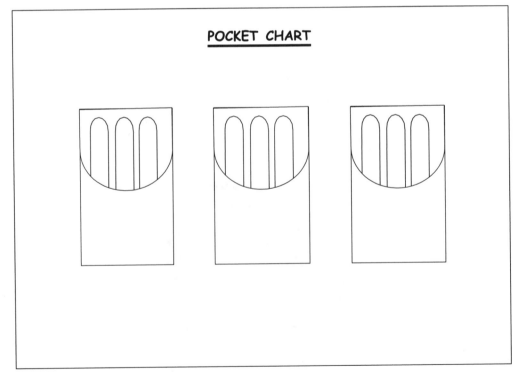

READING THE ROOM ACTIVITY

RHYMING CENTER

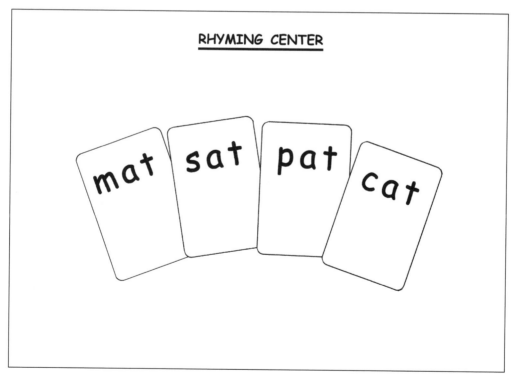

STORY PROPS CENTER

Felt Board Story

WORD STUDY CENTER

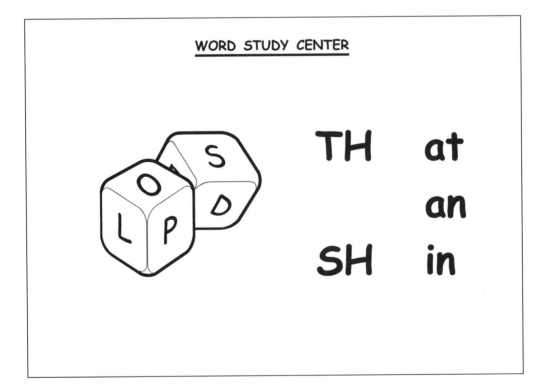

WORD WALL ACTIVITY

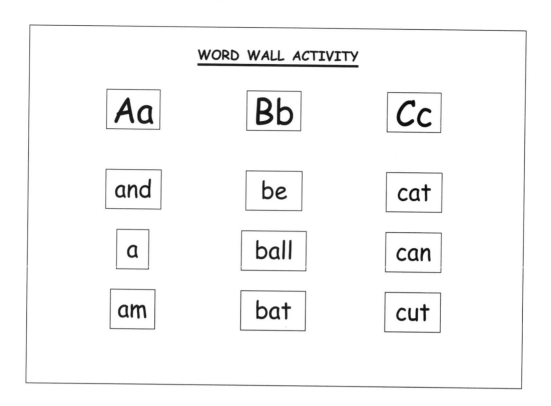

Aa	Bb	Cc
and	be	cat
a	ball	can
am	bat	cut

WORKING WITH WORDS CENTER

YOUR CHOICE

APPENDIX B

Word Study Games

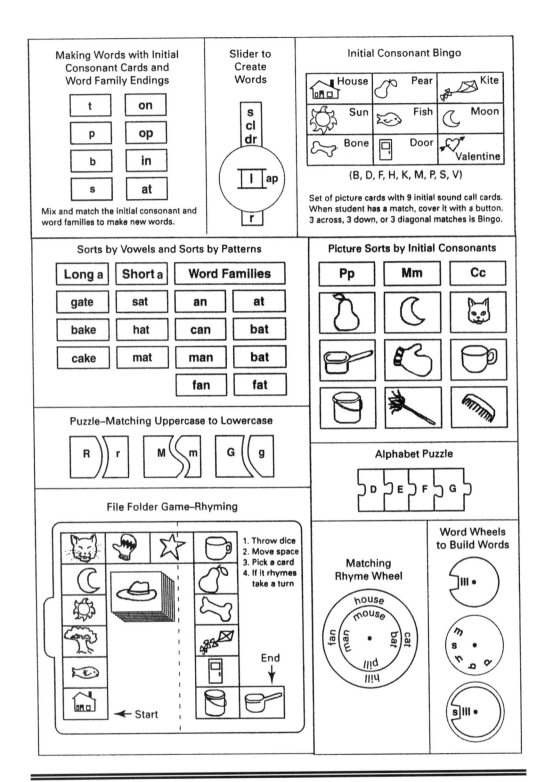

Making Words with Initial Consonant Cards and Word Family Endings

t	on
p	op
b	in
s	at

Mix and match the initial consonant and word families to make new words.

Slider to Create Words

s
cl
dr

l | ap

r

Initial Consonant Bingo

House	Pear	Kite
Sun	Fish	Moon
Bone	Door	Valentine

(B, D, F, H, K, M, P, S, V)

Set of picture cards with 9 initial sound call cards. When student has a match, cover it with a button. 3 across, 3 down, or 3 diagonal matches is Bingo.

Sorts by Vowels and Sorts by Patterns

Long a	Short a	Word Families	
gate	sat	an	at
bake	hat	can	bat
cake	mat	man	bat
		fan	fat

Picture Sorts by Initial Consonants

| Pp | Mm | Cc |

Puzzle–Matching Uppercase to Lowercase

R r   M m   G g

Alphabet Puzzle

D E F G

File Folder Game–Rhyming

1. Throw dice
2. Move space
3. Pick a card
4. If it rhymes take a turn

End

← Start

Matching Rhyme Wheel

house
mouse
fan
man
cat
bat
pail
nail

Word Wheels to Build Words

m
s
h
p

APPENDIX C

Assessment Forms

Directions: Tell the child that you would like to find out more about what kids like to do and how they feel about reading and writing. Ask each question in the interview and read the multiple-choice responses.

How often would you like your teacher to read to the class?
(2) Every day　　　　　(1) Almost every day　(0) Not often

Do you like to read books by yourself?
(2) Yes　　　　　　　(1) It's okay　　　　　(0) No

Which would you most like to have?
(2) A new book　　　　(1) A new game　　　(0) New clothes

Do you tell your friends about books and stories you read?
(2) A lot　　　　　　　(1) Sometimes　　　　(0) Never

How do you feel when you read out loud to someone?
(2) Good　　　　　　　(1) Okay　　　　　　(0) Bad

Do you like to read during your free time?
(2) Yes　　　　　　　(1) It's okay　　　　　(0) I don't read in my free time

If someone gave you a book for a present, how would you feel?
(2) Happy　　　　　　(1) Okay　　　　　　(0) Not very happy, disappointed

Do you take storybooks home from school to read?
(2) Almost every day　(1) Sometimes　　　　(0) Not often

Do you read books out loud to someone in your family?
(2) Almost every day　(1) Sometimes　　　　(0) Not often

What kind of reader are you?
(2) I'm a very good reader　(1) I'm okay　　　(0) I'm not very good

Learning to read is:
(2) Easy　　　　　　　(1) A little hard　　　(0) Really hard

Do you like to write?
(2) Yes　　　　　　　(1) It's okay　　　　　(0) I'd rather do something else

Do you write in your free time?
(2) A lot　　　　　　　(1) A little　　　　　　(0) Not at all

What do you like to read best?
(2) Books and magazines　(1) Schoolwork　　(0) Nothing

Emergent Reading Behaviors

1. Attending to pictures but not forming stories.

The child "reads" by labeling and commenting on the pictures in the book, but does not "weave a story" across the pages.

Yes _____   No _____

2. *Attending to pictures and forming oral stories.*

The child "reads" by following the pictures, but weaves a story across the pages through wording and intonation like those of someone telling a story. Often, however, the listener too must see the pictures in order to understand the story the child is "reading."

Yes _____   No _____

3. *Attending to a mix of pictures, reading, and storytelling.*

The child "reads" by looking at the pictures. The majority of the child's "reading" fluctuates between the oral intonation of a storyteller and that of a reader.

Yes _____   No _____

4. *Attending to pictures but forming stories (written-language-like).*

The child "reads" by looking at the pictures. The child's speech sounds like reading, both in wording and intonation. The listener rarely needs to see the pictures in order to understand the story. With his or her eyes closed, the listener would think the child was reading print. The "reading" is similar to the story in print and sometimes follows it verbatim. There is some attention to print.

Yes _____   No _____

5. *Attending to print.*

This category has two divisions:

   a. The child reads the story mostly by attending to print, but occasionally refers to pictures and reverts to storytelling.
   b. The child reads in a conventional manner.

   a. _____   b. _____

Phoneme Segmentation

Child's name _____ Date _____

Score (number correct): _____

Directions to give the child: Today we're going to play a word game. I'm going to say a word, and I want you to break the word apart. You are going to tell me each sound in the word in order. For example, if I say "old," you should say "o / - / l / - / d /." (Administrator: Be sure to say the sounds, not the letters, in the word.) Let's try a few together.

Practice items: *ride, go, man*. (Assist the child in segmenting these items as necessary.)

Test items: (Circle those items that the student correctly segments; incorrect responses may be recorded in the blank area following the item.)

1. *dog*	12. *lay*
2. *keep*	13. *race*
3. *fine*	14. *zoo*
4. *no*	15. *three*
5. *she*	16. *job*
6. *wave*	17. *in*
7. *grew*	18. *ice*
8. *that*	19. *at*
9. *red*	20. *top*
10. *me*	21. *by*
11. *sat*	22. *do*

Letter Recognition

Child's name: _____ Age: _____ Date: _____

Recorder: _____ Date of Birth: _____

Confusions:

Letters unknown:

Comments:

	A	IR		A	IR
A			a		
F			f		
K			k		
P			p		
W			w		
Z			z		
B			b		
H			h		
O			o		
J			j		
U			u		
C			c		
Y			y		
L			l		
Q			q		
M			m		
D			d		
N			n		
S			s		
X			x		
I			i		
E			e		
G			g		
R			r		
V			v		
T			t		

A = Alphabet response: (✓); IR = Incorrect response: record what the child says.

Test score: _____

Assessing Concepts about Print and Word Study

Child's name: _____ Date: _____

	Always	Sometimes	Never	Comments
Knows that print is read from left to right.				
Knows that oral language can be written and then read.				
Knows what a letter is and can point one out.				
Knows what a word is and can point one out on a printed page.				
Knows that there are spaces between words.				
Reads environmental print.				
Recognizes some words by sight and high-frequency sight words.				
Can name and identify rhyming words.				
Can blend phonemes in words.				
Associates consonants and their initial and final sounds (including hard and soft c and g).				
Associates consonant blends with their sounds (bl, cr, dr, fl, gl, pr, st).				
Associates vowels with their corresponding long and short sounds (a—acorn, apple; e—eagle, egg; i—ice, igloo; o—oats, octopus; u—unicorn, umbrella).				
Knows the consonant digraph sounds (ch, ph, sh, th, wh).				

(cont.)

Assessing Concepts *(cont.)*

	Always	Sometimes	Never	Comments
Uses context, syntax, and semantics to identify words.				
Can count syllables in words.				
Attempts reading by attending to picture clues and print.				
Guesses and predicts words based on knowledge of sound–symbol correspondence.				
Can identify structural elements of words such as prefixes and suffixes, and inflectional endings (-*ing*, -*ed*, and -*s* and contractions).				
Demonstrates knowledge of the following phonic generalizations:				
a. In a consonant–vowel–consonant pattern, the vowel sound is usually short.				
b. In a vowel–consonant–e pattern, the vowel is usually long.				
c. When two vowels come together in a word, the first is usually long and the second is silent (*train, receive, bean*).				
Uses word families often referred to as rimes and phonograms (such as *an*, *at*, *it*, and *ot*), and initial consonants to build words (e.g., *man, can, fan, ran*).				

Teacher comments:

Guiding Story Retelling

1. Ask the child to retell the story. "A little while ago, I read the story [name of story]. Would you retell the story as if you were telling it to a friend who has never heard it before?"

2. Use the following prompts only if needed:

   a. If the child has difficulty beginning the retelling, suggest beginning with "Once upon a time," or "Once there was a . . ."

   b. If the child stops retelling the story before the end of the story, encourage continuation by asking, "What comes next?" or "Then what happened?"

   c. If the child stops retelling and cannot continue with general prompts, ask a question that is relevant at the point in the story at which the child has paused. For example, "What was Jenny's problem in the story?"

3. When a child is unable to retell the story, or if the retelling lacks sequence and detail, prompt the retelling step by step. For example:

   a. "Once upon a time," or "Once there was a . . ."

   b. "Who was the story about?"

   c. "When did the story happen?" (day, night, summer, winter?)

   d. "Where did the story happen?"

   e. "What was [the main character's] problem in the story?"

   f. "How did [he or she] try to solve the problem? What did [he or she] do first [second, next]?"

   g. "How was the problem solved?"

   h. "How did the story end?"

Parsed Story: An Example

Setting

a. Once upon a time, there was a girl who liked to play pretend.

b. Characters: Jenny (main character), Nicholas, Sam, Mei Su, and Shags, the dog.

Theme

Every time Jenny played with her friends, she bossed them.

Plot Episodes

First episode: Jenny decided to pretend to be a queen. She called her friends. They came to play. Jenny told them all what to do and was bossy. The friends became angry and left.

Second episode: Jenny decided to play dancer. She called her friends and they came to play. Jenny told them all what to do. The friends became angry and left.

Third episode: Jenny decided to play pirate. She called her friends and they came to play. Jenny told them all what to do. The friends became angry and left.

Fourth episode: Jenny decided to play duchess. She called her friends and they came to play. Jenny told them all what to do. The friends became angry and left.

Fifth episode: Jenny's friends refused to play with her because she was so bossy. Jenny became lonely and apologized to them for being bossy.

Resolution

a. The friends all played together, and each person did what he or she wanted to do.

b. They all had a wonderful day and were so tired that they fell asleep.

Verbatim Transcript

(Beth, age 5) Once upon a time there's a girl named Jenny and she called her friends over and they played queen and went to the palace. They had to ... they had to do what she said and they didn't like it, so then they went home and said, "That was boring. It's not fun playing queen and doing what she says you have to." So they didn't play with her for 7 days and she had ... she had an idea that she was being selfish, so she went to find her friends and said, "I'm sorry I was so mean." And said, "Let's play pirate," and they played pirate and they went onto the ropes. Then they played that she was a fancy lady playing house. And they have tea. And they played what they wanted and they were happy. The end.

Story Retelling and Rewriting Evaluation Guide Sheet:
An Example of Quantitative Analysis

Child's name: __Beth__   Age: __5__

Title of story: __Jenny Learns a Lesson__   Date: _____

General directions: Give 1 point for each element included, as well as for "gist." Give 1 point for each character named as well as for such words as *boy*, *girl*, or *dog*. Credit plurals (friends, for instance) with 2 points under characters.

Sense of Story Structure

Setting		
a. Begins story with an introduction.		1
b. Names main character.		1
c. Number of other characters named.	2	
d. Actual number of other characters:	4	
e. Score for "other characters" (c/d):		0.5
f. Includes statement about time or place.		1
Theme		
Refers to main character's primary goal or problem to be solved.		1
Plot episodes		
a. Number of episodes recalled.		4
b. Number of episodes in story.		5
c. Score for "plot episodes" (a/b):		0.8
Resolution		
a. Names problem solution/goal attainment.		1
b. Ends story.		1
Sequence		
Retells story in structural order: setting, theme, plot episodes, resolution.(Score 2 for proper, 1 for partial, 0 for no sequence evident.)		1
Highest score possible: 10	**Child's score: 8.3**	

Reprinted from Morrow (2001). Copyright 2001 by Pearson Education. Reprinted by permission.

Story Retelling and Rewriting Evaluation Guide Sheet

Child's name: _____ Age: _____

Title of story: _____ Date: _____

General directions: Give 1 point for each element included, as well as for "gist." Give 1 point for each character named as well as for such words as *boy*, *girl*, or *dog*. Credit plurals (friends, for instance) with 2 points under characters.

Sense of Story Structure

Setting		
a. Begins story with an introduction.		
b. Names main character.		
c. Number of other characters named.		
d. Actual number of other characters:		
e. Score for "other characters" (c/d):		
f. Includes statement about time or place.		
Theme		
Refers to main character's primary goal or problem to be solved.		
Plot episodes		
a. Number of episodes recalled.		
b. Number of episodes in story.		
c. Score for "plot episodes" (a/b):		
Resolution		
a. Names problem solution/goal attainment.		
b. Ends story.		
Sequence		
Retells story in structural order: setting, theme, plot episodes, resolution. (Score 2 for proper, 1 for partial, 0 for no sequence evident.)		
Highest score possible: 10 **Child's score:** _____		

Checklist for Assessing Early Literacy Development

Child's name: _____   Date: _____

	Always	Some-times	Never	Comments
Concepts about books				
Knows that a book is for reading.				
Can identify the front, back, top, and bottom of a book.				
Can turn pages properly.				
Knows the difference between the print and the pictures.				
Knows that pictures on a page are related to what the print says.				
Knows where to begin reading.				
Knows what a title is.				
Knows what an author is.				
Knows what an illustrator is.				
Comprehension of text				
Attempts to read storybooks resulting in well-formed stories.				
Participates in story reading by narrating as the teacher reads.				
Retells stories.				
Includes story structure elements in story retellings:				
Settings				
Theme				
Plot elements				
Resolution				

(cont.)

	Always	Some-times	Never	Comments
Responds to text after reading or listening with literal comments or questions.				
Responds to text after reading or listening with interpretive comments or questions.				
Responds to text after reading or listening with critical comments or questions.				
Writing development				
Explores with writing materials.				
Dictates stories, sentences, or words he or she wants written down.				
Copies letters and words.				
Independently attempts writing to convey meaning, regardless of writing level.				
Can write his or her name.				
Collaborates with others in writing experience.				
Writes for functional purposes.				
Check (✓) the level or levels at which the child is writing:				
__ Uses drawing for writing and drawing.				
__ Differentiates between writing and drawing.				
__ Uses scribble writing for writing.				
__ Uses letter-like forms for writing.				
__ Uses learned letters in random fashion for writing.				
__ Uses invented spelling for writing.				
__ Writes conventionally with conventional spelling.				

(cont.)

Checklist *(cont.)*

	Always	Some-times	Never	Comments
Mechanics for writing				
Forms upper-case letters legibly.				
Forms lower-case letters legibly.				
Writes from left to right.				
Leaves spaces between words.				
Uses capital letters when necessary.				
Uses periods in appropriate places.				
Uses commas in appropriate places.				

BIBLIOGRAPHY

PROFESSIONAL LITERATURE

Anderson, R. C., Heibert, E. H., Scott, J. A., & Wilkinson, I. A. G. (1985). *Becoming a nation of readers: The report of the commission on reading.* Washington, DC: U.S. Department of Education, National Institute of Education.

Bear, D. R., Invernizzi, M., Templeton, S., & Johnston, D. (1996). *Words their way: Word study for phonics, vocabulary, and spelling.* Upper Saddle River, NJ: Merrill.

Clay, M. M. (1985). *The early detection of reading difficulties.* Portsmouth, NH: Heinemann.

Clay, M. M. (1993). *An observation survey of early literacy achievement.* Auckland, New Zealand: Heinemann.

Cunningham, P. M., & Allington, R. L. (1999). *Classrooms that work: They can all read and write.* New York: Longman.

Daniels, H. (1994). *Literature circles: Voice and choice in the student-centered classroom.* York, ME: Stenhouse.

Evertson, C. M., Emmer, E. T., Clements, B. S., & Worsham, M. E. (1994*). Classroom management for elementary teachers* (3rd ed.). Boston: Allyn & Bacon.

Feldman, J. (2000). *Sing to learn.* Atlanta, GA: Author.

Fountas, I. C., & Pinnell, A. C. (1996). *Guided reading: Good first teaching for all children.* Portsmouth, NH: Heinemann.

Froebel, F. (1974). *The education of man.* Clifton, NJ: Augustus M. Kelly.

Gambrell, L. (1993). Me and My Reading Scale. In *The impact of Running Start on the reading motivation of and behavior of first-grade children* (Research report). College Park: University of Maryland, National Reading Research Center.

Good, T. L., & Brophy, J. E. (1994). *Looking in classrooms* (6th ed.). New York: HarperCollins.

Grossman, H. (1995). *Classroom behavior management in a diverse society* (2nd ed.). Mountain View, CA: Mayfield.

Loughlin, C. E., & Martin, M. D. (1987). *Supporting literacy: Developing effective learning environments.* New York: Teachers College Press.

Montessori, M. (1965). *Spontaneous activity in education.* New York: Schocken.

Moore, G. (1986). Effects of the spatial definition of behavior settings on children's behavior: A quasi-experimental field study. *Journal of Environmental Psychology, 6*(3), 205–231.

Morrow, L. M. (1985). Retelling stories: A strategy for improving children's comprehension, concept of story structure and oral language complexity. *Elementary School Journal, 85,* 647–661.

Morrow, L. M. (1990). The impact of classroom environmental changes on the promotion of literacy during play. *Early Childhood Research Quarterly, 5,* 537–554.

Morrow, L. M. (1996). *Motivational reading and writing in diverse classrooms: Social and physical contexts* (Research Report No. 28). Urbana, IL: National Council of Teachers in English.

Morrow, L. M. (2001). *Literacy development in the early years: Helping children read and write* (4th ed.). Boston: Allyn & Bacon.

Morrow, L. M. (2002). *The literacy center: Contexts for reading and writing* (2nd ed.). Portland, ME: Stenhouse.

Morrow, L. M., & Asbury, E. B. (1999). Best practices for a balanced early literacy program. In L. B. Gambrell, L. M. Morrow, S. B. Neuman, & M. Pressley (Eds.), *Best practices in literacy instruction* (pp. 49–67). New York: Guilford Press.

Morrow, L. M., & Asbury, E. B. (2001). Case study of Patricia Lodu. In M. Pressley, R. L. Allington, R. Wharton-McDonald, C. C. Block, & L. M. Morrow, *Learning to read: Lessons from exemplary first-grade classrooms* (pp. 184–202). New York: Guilford Press.

Morrow, L. M., Tracey, D., Woo, D., & Presley, M. (1999). Characteristics of exemplary first grade instruction. *The Reading Teacher, 52,* 462–476.

National Reading Panel. (2000). *Report of the National Reading Panel: Teaching children to read.* Washington, DC: National Institutes of Health and National Institute of Child Health and Human Development.

Neuman, S., & Roskos, K. (1992). Literacy objects as cultural tools: Effects on children's literacy behaviors in play. *Reading Research Quarterly, 27,* 203–225.

Olds, A. B. (1987). *Designing settings for infants and toddlers.* In C. S. Weinstein & T. G. David (Eds.), *Spaces for children: The built environment and child development* (pp. 117–138). New York: Plenum Press.

Pressley, M., Rankin, J., & Yokoi, L. (1996). A survey of the instructional practices of outstanding primary-level literacy teachers. *Elementary School Journal, 96,* 363–384.

Rivlin, L., & Weinstein, C. (1984). Educational issues, school settings, and environmental psychology. *Journal of Environmental Psychology, 4,* 347–364.

Routman, R. (1994). *Invitations: Changing as teachers and learners K–12.* Portsmouth, NH: Heinemann.

Ruddell, R., & Ruddell, M. R. (1995). *Teaching children to read and write: Becoming an influential teacher.* Boston: Allyn & Bacon.

Rusk, R., & Scotland, J. (1979). *Doctrines of the great educators.* New York: St. Martin's Press.

Sanford, J., & Emmer, E. T. (1988). *Understanding classroom management: An observation guide.* Englewood Cliffs, NJ: Prentice-Hall.

Sulzby, E. (1985). Children's emergent reading of favorite storybooks: A developmental study. *Reading Research Quarterly, 20*(4), 458–481.

Weinstein, C., & Mignano, A., Jr. (1997). *Elementary classroom management* (2nd ed.). New York: McGraw-Hill.

Yopp, H. K. (1992, May). Developing phonemic awareness in young children. *The Reading Teacher, 45*(9), 696–703.

CHILDREN'S LITERATURE

Atwell, N. (1998). *In the middle.* Portsmouth, NH: Heinemann.

Barrett, J. (1982). *Cloudy with a chance of meatballs.* New York: Aladdin Books.

Blume, J. (1972). *Tales of a fourth-grade nothing.* New York: Dell.

Brown, M. T. (1985). *Arthur's tooth.* Boston: Little, Brown.

Brown, M. W. (1991). *Goodnight moon.* New York: HarperCollins. (Original work published 1947)

Buck, P. S. (1973). *The big wave.* New York: John Day. (Original work published 1948)

Bulla, C. R. (1987). *The chalk box kid.* New York: Random House.

Burton, V. L. (1996). *Calico the wonder horse; or, the saga of Stewy Stinker.* Boston: Houghton Mifflin. (Original work published 1950)

Cameron, A. (1989). *The stories Julian tells.* New York: Random House.

Cleary, B. (1982). *Ralph S. Mouse.* New York: Morrow.

Cole, J. (1986). *The magic school bus at the waterworks*. New York: Scholastic.

Cole, J. (1995). *The magic school bus inside a hurricane*. New York: Scholastic.

Corbitt, H. (1962). *Potluck*. Boston: Houghton Mifflin.

Coville, B. (1989). *My teacher is an alien*. New York: Pocket Books.

Cowley, J. (1999). *Mrs. Wishy-Washy*. New York: Philomel Books.

Dahl, R. (2001). *Charlie and the chocolate factory*. New York: Knopf. (Original work published 1964)

Dotlich, R. K. (2001). *When riddles come rumbling*. Honesdale, PA: Wordsong/Boyd Mills Press.

Ehlert, L. (1995). *Snowballs*. San Diego, CA: Harcourt Brace.

Fields, E. (1985). *Wynken, Blynken and Nod*. New York: Scholastic.

Fienberg, A. (2001). *Minton goes driving*. London: Unwin Hyman.

Fiorone, F. (1973). *The encyclopedia of dogs*. New York: Crowell.

Fleming, P. (1993). *Lunch*. New York: Henry Holt.

Gibbons, G. (1987). *Milk makers*. New York: Aladdin Books.

Henkes, K. (1996). *Lilly's purple plastic purse*. New York: Greenwillow Books.

Howe, J. (1987). *Nighty nightmare*. New York: Avon.

Kline, S. (1990). *Horrible Harry in room 2b*. New York: Puffin Books.

Lillegard, D. (1993). *Potatoes on Tuesday*. Glenview, IL: Scott, Foresman.

Lobel, A. (1970). *Frog and Toad are friends*. New York: Harper.

Lobel, A. (1977). *Mouse soup*. New York: Harper & Row.

Martin, B., & Archambault, J. (1989). *Chicka, chicka, boom, boom*. New York: Simon & Schuster.

Martin, B., & Carle, E. (1967). *Brown bear, brown bear, what do you see?* New York: Henry Holt.

Marzolla, J. (1999). *I spy*. New York: Scholastic.

Mathews, L. (1979). *Gator pie*. New York: Dodd, Mead.

McMillan, B. (1991). *Eating fractions*. New York: Scholastic.

Meadows, G. (1997). *After the rain*. Crystal Lake, IL: Rigby.

Meddaugh, S. (1994). *Martha calling*. Boston: Houghton Mifflin.

Meyer, L. (1993). *Grandma's helper*. Glenview, IL: Scott, Foresman.

Moss, M. (1997). *Amelia hits the road*. Berkeley, CA: Tricycle Press.

Munsch, R. (1999). *We share everything*. New York: Scholastic.

Naylor, P. R. (1991). *Shiloh*. New York: Atheneum.

O'Brien, R. C. (1986). *Mrs. Frisby and the rats of NIMH*. New York: Aladdin Books.

Palatini, M. (1997). *Piggie pie*. Boston: Houghton Mifflin.

Pappas, L. (1980). *Cookies*. Concord, CA: Nitty Gritty.

Paxton, T. (1993). *Engelbert's exercise*. Glenview, IL: Scott, Foresman.

Rees, M. (1988). *Ten in a bed*. Boston: Joy Street Books.

Rowling, J. K. (1998). *Harry Potter and the sorcerer's stone*. New York: Arthur A. Levine/Scholastic.

Rylant, C. (1982). *When I was young in the mountains*. New York: Dutton.

Schwartz, A. (1991). *Scary stories 3*. New York: Caedmon.

Scieszka, J. (1991a). *The frog prince, continued*. New York: Viking.

Scieszka, J. (1991b). *Knights of the kitchen table*. New York: Viking.

Scieszka, J. (1998). *Squids will be squids*. New York: Viking.

Seuss, Dr. (1990). *Oh, the places you'll go!* New York: Random House.

Silverstein, S. (1974). *Where the sidewalk ends*. New York: Harper & Row.

Simon, S. (1991). *Earthquakes*. New York: Murrow Junior Books.

Smith, K. B. (1991). *United States atlas for young people*. Mahwah, NJ: Troll.

Spang, B. (1997). *Grandma Jenny's trip*. Crystal Lake, IL: Rigby.

Stienecker, D. L. (1996). *First facts about the states*. Woodbridge, CT: Blackbirch Press.

Tolhurst, M. (1998). *Somebody and the three Blairs*. New York: Orchard Books.

Trussell-Cullen, A. (1995). *This is the plate*. Glenview, IL: Good Year Books.

Van der Meer, R. (1992). *The birthday cake*. New York: Random House.

Vaz, M. C. (1997). *Star Wars trilogy scrapbook*. New York: Scholastic.

Viorst, J. (1972). *Alexander and the terrible, horrible, no good, very bad day*. New York: Atheneum.

Weisner, D. (1991). *Tuesday*. Boston: Houghton Mifflin.

Westcott, N. (1980). *I know an old lady who swallowed a fly*. Boston: Little, Brown.

Williams, R. (1988). *The great big bug book*. Huntington Beach, CA: Creative Teaching Press.

Wood, A., & Wood, D. (1991). *Piggies*. San Diego, CA: Harcourt, Brace.

Wyndham, R. (1968). *Chinese Mother Goose rhymes*. Cleveland, OH: World.

INDEX